THE WIFE OF COBHAM

Stained glass from St Mary's Church, Burnham Deepdale, Norfolk

Joan, Lady Cobham and her children, from her memorial brass at St Mary Magdalene's Church, Cobham, Kent

The
Wife
of
Cobham

Susan Curran

Lasse
Press

First published 2016
by the Lasse Press
2 St Giles Terrace, Norwich NR2 1NS, UK
www.lassepress.com
lassepress@gmail.com

ISBN-13: 978-0-9933069-1-4

Typeset in Frutiger, Garamond and Stone Sans by
Curran Publishing Services Ltd, Norwich, UK

Manufactured in the UK by Cambrian Printers, Aberystwyth

Contents

Genealogies

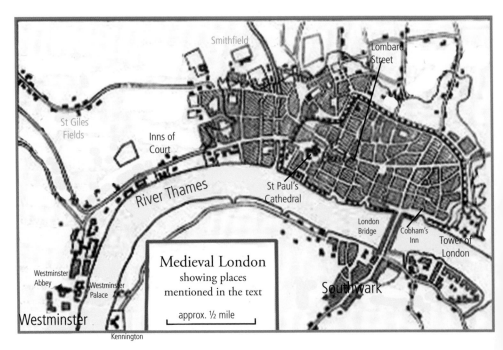

Base map adapted from http://legacy.fordham.edu/halsall/maps/London.jpg Adapted from *Muir's Historical Atlas (1911)*.

England and Wales in the 14th and 15th centuries, showing places mentioned in the book

Base map by Nilfanion (http://creativecommons.org/licenses/by-sa/3.0) via Wikimedia Commons.

Doulce chose est que mariage,
  Je le puis bien par moy prouver.
Voire a qui mary bon et sage
  A, comme Dieu m'a fait trouver.

[Marriage is a sweet device,
  And I for one can prove it.
Since I married a man both good and wise,
  And God helped me to do it.]

Christine de Pisan (rough translation by the author)

Introduction

In the year 1380, when she was perhaps ten years old, Joan de la Pole (who later became Lady Cobham) was married. That she should marry young was not surprising: she had expectations of sizeable inheritance through both her father and her mother, so she was a desirable property in the marriage market, and it was common then for heiresses to be married while still in childhood.

About eleven years later her husband died; and within a year Joan had married again. Then her next husband died, and she married again; and again, and again. The fifth of her husbands was to outlive her.

If it was rare good fortune in those days to live to a decent old age (as Joan was to do: she was around sixty-five when she died), it was singular bad luck to be widowed four times. But there was more than bad luck involved: it was not common for any woman to marry so frequently. Although almost all women who did not take the veil expected to make one marriage, it was not the case that widows were routinely pushed into marrying again shortly after their husband's death.

Joan's first marriage was of course arranged by her parents, and she probably had little say in it. It is just conceivable that her second was also arranged for her by her family or friends, but it is unlikely that anyone forced her to marry after that. Both her parents were dead by the time of her third marriage, all her grandparents before her fourth. And although Joan was consistent in always marrying men at arms, her choices became more eccentric after her second marriage. Her third husband seems to have been a foreign soldier of fortune, and her fourth was one of the most notorious men of the age.

Did she choose these marriages because it was how she preferred to live? Or did she perhaps feel that she had little choice? Was she a strong woman, striking her own path through life, or a nervous and retiring one, more comfortable to have a man strike it for her? Did society, or her friends and relatives, pressure her? Was her choice shaped by her lack of a male heir? (Although she had many children, only one, a daughter, lived into adulthood.) No information on these issues has passed down through the centuries, so to a large extent we can only guess.

All we have of Joan, bar a few legal documents that deal with those marriages and the financial deals that attended them, is the splendid brass that covers her grave.

But in an age when very few women's lives are known to us in any detail, there is something in the shape of those five marriages that gives us an image of the life of the woman who made them. Who was Joan? In this book I draw on the information we have about Joan's husbands, her family, the places where she lived and the events she lived through, to try to give a sense of the woman at the centre of this extraordinary skein of linked lives.

The first of these elements is Joan's ancestry, for the identity and character of our parents and grandparents shapes the lives of every individual: determining the place they call home, the kind of lifestyle they lead, the types of work they understand, their beliefs, and more. So let us begin by considering the de la Pole family in the generations that influenced Joan's life.

1 The king's beloved servant: the de la Pole inheritance

… considering in what manner our beloved merchant is worn out in our service and fatigued with labours and various troubles …[1]

Stained glass from St Peter's Church, Lowick, Northants

Although most paupers would doubtless swap places, it is not easy to be born the son of a man who has built up a vast business empire. Such men tend to cast a large dark shadow, and their sons inevitably fall under it.

Some sons manage to build on their inheritance. Some diverge from it, finding success in related fields. Some turn their backs on it, and look to build a life in an entirely different direction. And some sink under the weight of that shadow.

The de la Pole brothers – originally from Ravenser Odd, a now-lost small town on the Humber, and later based in Hull – were probably the most successful businessmen in England from around 1320 to 1340.[2] Or at least, Richard and William were: the third of the brothers, John, is a more elusive figure, and seems never to have rivalled his siblings, although at times he worked with and for them. Richard de la Pole was probably the eldest, although in fairness that counted for only a little when there was nothing significant to inherit.

The de la Poles seem to have come from nowhere. It has been speculated that they were the sons of a reasonably well-off family in Hull, but there is no proof of their ancestry. Their name might suggest that the family were Normans originally, and noble, but that is almost certainly not true. All we know is that their origins were obscure even in their own day. Certainly their parents had nothing like the renown or fortune of their sons. These were in every sense self-made men.

They were merchants, builders, shipowners, vintners and bankers – and as time passed, they became sizeable landowners too. They lent money most of all to King Edward III, who had lost his former Italian bankers simply because he had bankrupted them by failing to repay his huge debts. To replace the Bardis was clearly a high-risk enterprise, since everyone knew how, and why, they had fallen. But the de la Poles did so anyway, even to the extent of taking over the Bardis' former English banking headquarters, on Lombard Street in London. William obtained this building; in May 1328 Richard chose to buy a plot of land nearby on which to build his London base. It fronted onto Lombard Street, and stretched as far as the churchyard of St Michael Cornhill, a couple of streets away.[3]

By this point the brothers had outgrown Hull, although both maintained property there. And in 1331 they made a decisive move to separate their business affairs. We cannot be sure now whether it was a quarrel that had prompted this, although the fact that they employed lawyers to formalize the separation – and the deed that was drawn up includes an agreement to bury past differences – suggests that it was. Possibly the two had differed over business tactics, and it seems likely that William chose the more high-risk course. Their agreement was written in French and executed in London.[4]

Following this separation, Richard apparently moved the centre of his life to London, while William remained more Hull-based, and played an active role in its civic life. He was Hull's first lord mayor in the early 1330s, while at much the same time Richard was being elected an alderman of Bishopgate ward in London,[5] and building a grand new house on his London property. He worked closely with the king, and was described in documents as 'the King's beloved servant'.[6]

Rich merchants typically also owned country estates, and for a man as closely entangled in London affairs as Richard de la Pole, it made sense to acquire one that was nearer to London than Yorkshire. (Hull is about 200 miles from London. At this time that would have been several days' journey.) William de la Pole built his connections between Hull and

London in East Anglia, bolstering them with successive family marriages to women from that area, but Richard chose a more central route through the country. The estate that he acquired was in Northamptonshire, just south of the town of Northampton, and about 66 miles north-west of London.[7] So this man born and brought up by the great expanse of the Humber estuary chose to live almost as far from the sea as was possible in England.

The manor he bought in 1333 was then called Milton, although the village is now known as Milton Malsor.[8] It lay on the main Northampton to Towcester road, on rising ground just south of the Nene valley. This was good farming country, no hillier than a piece of rumpled linen writ large, and a convenient place from which to travel to London, Hull, or any of the other places where this extremely rich man had developed business interests. Richard also acquired other land in this area of Northamptonshire, so it became a major focus of his life and his financial interests.

Richard married, of course: his wife was called Johanna (possibly de Chaworth), although nothing more is known of her. They had a number of children, including a daughter who became a nun at the famous convent of Barking, much patronised by royalty. Their eldest son, named Roger, died during his father's lifetime, and it was the second son, William, who became his father's heir.

Few men who become immensely rich achieve that without treading on others and skimming the edge – at the least – of illegality. Both these things seem to have been true of the de la Pole brothers. As early as 1320 Richard was accused of manipulating the wine trade that he was supposed to be conducting on the king's behalf 'until he sees a profit for himself'.[9] While the brothers had power and influence, and above all while they were useful to the Crown, their more questionable dealings tended to be overlooked, but when it suited the king or others to be more curious, these activities left them open to attack. It was William who suffered the most during Richard's lifetime. In March 1340 Parliament petitioned King Edward to examine the dealings of those who had become involved in dealings over customs and loans to the crown. The king's foreign campaigns had contributed greatly to a financial crisis, so he colluded in these investigations (which were likely to bring him profit), and between 1341 and 1344 William de la Pole senior (that is, Richard's brother, not his son) suffered a period of imprisonment and a major attack on his property which saw him lose out and the king gain.

Relatively little seems to have been done against Richard, either because he was less exposed to these particular dubious dealings, or perhaps more likely because he was politically in a better position to avoid attack. But the assault on his fortune was only postponed;

Stained glass, left, from Canterbury Cathedral; right, from St Peter's Church, Ardwincle, Northants

it happened after his death in 1345. There were claims that he owed substantial sums to the Crown, and either because he felt there was no defence, or because he was unwilling to fight the king's agents and other claimants in this uncertain period for the family, the new heir seems to have accepted most of the demands. Other people too laid claim to some of the lands that Richard had bought, and in at least one case the claim was successful, or perhaps not even contested.[10]

There were claims for repayment of debts against William himself as well as against his father. It is difficult to judge now whether this was because he was financially incompetent, or was part of the general fall-out that followed his father's death.

In the reckoning that took place at that time, Richard's family had to give up the fine new building in Lombard Street, and some of their other properties as well. A part of Richard's great estate remained with his widow, who remarried after his death. Some went to his younger son John, some to his unmarried daughter (another married daughter got nothing, perhaps because she had been given her share on her marriage), and an annuity to his daughter the nun. William de la Pole junior kept the remainder, but that made him a far less rich man than his father had been. He does not seem to have continued his father's money-lending, trading and other business activities. Instead he settled for a lower-profile life as a country landowner.

The de la Pole family

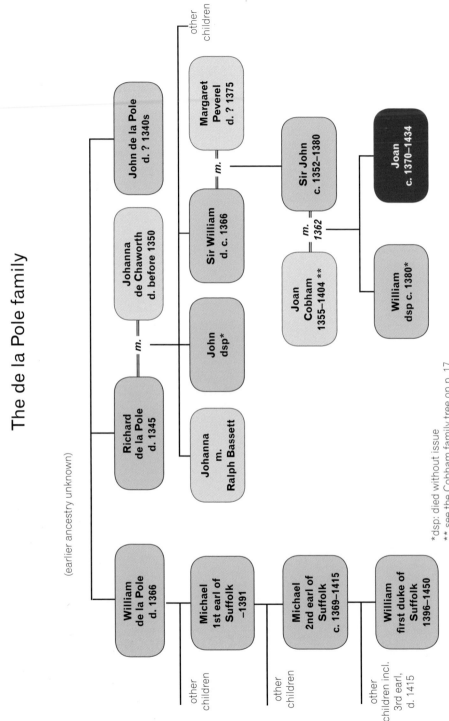

(earlier ancestry unknown)

Richard de la Pole d. 1345 — m. — Johanna de Chaworth d. before 1350

John de la Pole d. ? 1340s

other children

children of Richard and Johanna: Johanna m. Ralph Bassett; John dsp*; Sir William d. c. 1366

Sir William d. c. 1366 — m. — Margaret Peverel d. ? 1375

Joan Cobham 1355–1404** — m. 1362 — Sir John c. 1352–1380

Joan c. 1370–1434

William dsp c. 1380*

William de la Pole d. 1366

Michael 1st earl of Suffolk –1391

other children

Michael 2nd earl of Suffolk c. 1369–1415

other children

William first duke of Suffolk 1396–1450

other children incl. 3rd earl, d. 1415

*dsp: died without issue
** see the Cobham family tree on p. 17

2
The
dead goats

Nor for all their number were the
obsequies honoured by either tears
or lights or crowds of mourners; rather,
it was come to this, that a dead man was
then of no more account than a dead goat
would be today.

Giovanni Boccaccio[1]

Painting from St Thomas's Church, Salisbury (c. 1475)

The mid-fourteenth century was a time when the graveyards were full and the streets empty. It was a world where death lurked round every corner, unseen, unwatched, but ready to come and take people with little or no warning: a week, a day, even an hour.

A third, perhaps even half of the population of England (and Europe, and beyond) died between 1347 and 1349. The main cause of this, probably the worst catastrophe to strike humankind in recorded history, was the disease they called with brutal accuracy the black death – although accidents, other diseases, violence and starvation claimed their share. The black death (in its two main forms, bubonic and pneumonic plague) crawled its vile way across Europe, east to west, in those two years. By then it had taken all those vulnerable to infection. (It was not narrow in scope: it took the rich and poor, the young and fit as well as the old and exhausted, although a smaller proportion of the nobility seem to have died than of the peasants.[2]) It returned a few years later, and again, and again: killing first mostly the infants, then once a generation has passed, in mutated forms that also caught those grown up. It would recur with brutal frequency (though never quite predictable regularity) throughout the whole of Joan's life, and there were further outbreaks for centuries afterwards.

A disaster so great changed people, but it did not change them in any simple way. It certainly did not turn the survivors into saints. Rather, perhaps, it coarsened them. So many had been buried, and a fair proportion of them had died alone, probably believing the whole world was dying with them, with no one daring to tend them and ease their last moments on earth. They had been buried without the rites that people believed were essential for anyone to have a hope of salvation, so it had to be presumed that they had gone to hell. Not only were the graveyards bulging, and plague pits dug to take those who could not be found coffins and individually dug graves, in the minds of firm believers, as almost all people were, the depths of hell must have been uncommonly crowded too.

This brought about a time where people dwelled on death even more than they had done before, and dwelled on it in all its nastiness. The paintings done at this time in churches were full of crowded hellpits, of souls in torment everlasting. The monuments built, for those who had families surviving to build them, were stark in their depiction of ravaged bodies. Skeletons grinned their ghastly grins: as you are, so were we; and as we are now, so will you be.

It was not a world where the survivors shared generously the greater portions – of land, of food, of valuables – that were left to the fewer now living, but a world where they fought bitterly over each plot, each legacy. It was not a world where kings postponed war, and left their subjects to till their fields and mourn their dead. Instead it was a world where wars were as bitter and as frequent – and often as ill justified – as they had always been. It was not a world where people believed they had a right to happiness. The lesson of the church was that this was the vale of tears through which we must stumble before we come into the world hereafter. But for all that it was a world where people loved, where they gloried in beautiful things, where they savoured good food and fine wine; in short, a world where the lucky, at least, knew joy.

The de la Pole family were rich, so in that sense they were lucky. These were not people who would have known hunger, or toil so unremitting that it scoured their souls. But they all encountered plenty of bereavement and grief. That, they and their contemporaries believed, was the natural lot of humankind.

Stained glass from Canterbury Cathedral

3 Of murder, witchcraft and a bishop

The first stok, fader of gentilesse –
What man that claymeth gentil for to be,
Must folowe his trace, and alle his wittes dresse
Vertu to sewe, and vyces for to flee.
                    Geoffrey Chaucer[1]

William de la Pole (the son of Richard) must have married relatively late, since it has been estimated that he was over thirty when his father died in 1345, and his wedding did not take place till after that time.[2] It was not unusual to leave marriage until this age, but it seems a little strange when he was the main heir to his father's substantial possessions. Possibly he had not felt he was in a good position to marry when he was younger, a period when he appears to have acted as his father's agent in Hull. It could also have been because he was a second son. Efforts might have been made to arrange a grand match for his elder brother, and when that brother died, the family did not stir itself immediately to do the same for William.

Perhaps he had been betrothed before his father's death; perhaps he had not, and it was his married sister's husband, one Ralph Basset, who helped him find a bride.[3] The marriage that was agreed for him was a relatively modest one, which does not sound like his father's doing. Maybe he failed to make a better match because the Northamptonshire gentry felt uneasy about marrying an incomer like William, whose ancestry no one knew much about. (His cousin Michael seems to have had no such problems, though, and made a marriage which brought him extensive lands in Suffolk.) And probably it was already apparent that this son was one who would never surge out of his father's shadow and take his inheritance to a higher level.

William's wife was Margaret Peverell, the sister of a rich landowner. Although her brother had as yet no children, he was young, as was she, so it must have seemed unlikely that she would ever inherit his lands. She seems not to have been granted any of the family estates as her dower. It was common among her class at the time for a family to leave its lands together in one hand – that of the eldest son – and give cash dowries to daughters, so this was probably what was done for Margaret.

The family's main home was at Castle Ashby, only a dozen miles or so from the de la Pole house at Milton, and they owned a string of manors that spread from west to east across the land to the north of London. These included Ashley and Chadstone in Northamptonshire; Arlesey, Everton and Potton in Bedfordshire; Fulbrook and Westhall in Oxfordshire; Seething in Norfolk; Aspall, Debenham and Grimston in Suffolk; and Chrishall in Essex. The Peverells had acquired their estates not through trade, but from the Church. They had been put together by Walter Langton, who had been bishop of Coventry and Lichfield, and treasurer of England, in the early fourteenth century. Bishoprics at this time offered plenty of scope for moneymaking, not all of it legal, and Langton's career as a royal official did much the same. A controversial, indeed notorious (and deeply unpopular) man, he was accused at various times of murder, adultery, simony

Milton Malsor

(the corrupt sale of church appointments) and witchcraft.[4] He had left his fortune to his nephew (Margaret and John's father), as churchmen conventionally did. So the Peverells too were not a long-established family of landowners, they were just as newly come to their wealth as the de la Poles were to theirs.

The black death came after the marriage agreement had been drawn up, but before William and Margaret had actually married. (They probably did so in 1351.) They both survived it, as did William's siblings. But the wider Peverell family was not so fortunate. Margaret's grandmother died of the plague, and so did her brother John.[5]

Much as she might have mourned her brother, this was a financial stroke of luck for Margaret, and for her betrothed as well, for she was the natural heir to all the Peverell lands. However, it soon emerged that John Peverell had drawn up an agreement that put all his estate in the hands of a man called John Lisle of Rougemont.[6] It is not clear why this happened, and it did not necessarily mean either that Peverell had owed Lisle money which he was repaying in this way, or that he intended the man to become his heir. Such arrangements were often made as a way of avoiding inheritance laws and giving people more freedom in how they disposed of their estates, with the intention that the grantee would hand the estate back again.

Margaret was clearly anxious to retrieve the family's lands, and her new husband supported her. Not surprisingly, however, Lisle was not willing to surrender them without recompense. It took till the mid-1350s before the de la Poles agreed a settlement with Lisle that gave them firm title to much (though not all) of the Peverell lands. It cost them heavily: they paid Lisle £2,000, in an era when the average peasant earned just a few pence a day.

At this time William must still have been struggling to sort out his father's affairs. To obtain the funds to fight the case and pay Lisle off, he apparently turned to his uncle William, who had by this time recovered his liberty and rebuilt his business. William senior seems to have been the kind of man who could not resist making a hard bargain even with his own relatives. The debts that William junior had run up were only cleared by his handing over most of the land he had inherited in and around Hull.[7]

So it took ten years after his father's death before William de la Pole was clear of financial battles, and in a position to settle down. And he and his wife had clearly chosen to settle down in Northamptonshire. Bishop Langton had obtained a licence from the king to build a castle at Ashby, and it was here, not at Milton (which probably remained the home of William's mother), that the young couple chose to make their main home.

There is still a great house at Castle Ashby today, but that is an Elizabethan mansion: the castle that William and Margaret knew had become a ruin by early in the 16th century.[8] Although the Peverell estate included 160 acres of demesne land around the castle (that is, the quarter or so of the entire estate that was farmed directly on behalf of its lord, largely by those who owed him such service under the feudal system, and not let to tenants), it was reckoned to be worth no more than 40 shillings – a sum that puts the £2,000 in harsh perspective – because it had not all been farmed for some time. Of the twenty-four bondmen who had worked the land before the black death, only six had survived it.[9] When William and Margaret were finally in a position to move there it must have stood empty for some years, and was probably in disrepair. However grand the house was, it might have proved a bleak place to live, haunted by the ghost of the wicked old bishop, and in an area where those dead workers could not be replaced easily, if at all.

To step into the shoes of a man who died suddenly and young, and to be surrounded by decay and the aftermath of a multitude of deaths, is a situation that can easily make a man turn to religion. Or rather, it might make him do so even more than was usual in an era when people routinely went to church and believed in heaven and hell. The little that is known about this William de la Pole suggests that he became deeply, even obsessively religious. He handed over the one piece of land in Hull that he had not had to pass to his uncle, a great garden an acre and a half in size,

Stained glass from Tewkesbury Abbey. Photo courtesy of 'professor moriarty', http://professor-moriarty.com

to the Carmelites in 1352 'for the enlargement of their dwelling place'.[10] His uncle's family too had put a lot of resources into Hull's religious life, and perhaps William chose to renounce his last piece of property there as a way of responding on behalf of his side of the family.

He and Margaret had only one child who is known to have survived infancy: a son, whom they named John, and who was born presumably in the 1350s. None of his descendants took Richard de la Pole's first name, a fact that hints at how his family perceived their devious ancestor.

It was all but essential for a landowner such as William to become a man at arms, and he did so. He fought with the Black Prince at the battle of Crècy in 1346, a great English victory against the French, and accompanied the earl of March on Edward III's expedition to Reims in the winter of 1359–60.[11] At some time after this he decided to go on crusade. The great days when the princes of Europe had fought to uphold the Christian cause in the Middle East were well in the past, and the Christian presence there was largely gone. The 'crusades' that were available in this era were smaller affairs, that took men shorter distances. In the eyes of many, they were as corrupt in their planning and execution as was almost everything about the Church of the time. But the ideal of a crusade, a great endeavour that would both benefit the Christian world and help a man to save his soul, was one that must have lingered in many minds. Presumably this was how William saw it, as a kind of extended pilgrimage, rather than an endeavour he expected to bring him money.

He planned his expedition in partnership with another knight, Sir Thomas Ufford. It is not clear whether they joined one of the well-known crusades of this time, the Alexandrian crusade and the Savoyard crusade, or whether their venture was something more individualistic. They appear to have gone to Avignon and met up with the pope, and to have sailed east from Otranto in southern Italy, getting as far east as 'Romania' (a recent historian thinks this was more likely Greece), although not to the Holy Land.[12]

Clearly this was a major undertaking, and for much of his young son's first years William was abroad. If he was no businessman in the mould of his father and uncle, he did at least prove to be a careful planner. It was apparently as part of this planning that in 1362 he arranged a marriage for his son. Young John was betrothed to Joan, the daughter of Lord Cobham, a rich baron from Kent. Joan was an only child, so she was at the time her father's heir, but no girl could take it for granted that she would remain an heiress until her father was dead. His wife might bear a son, or if his wife was too old to do so, she might die before him, enabling him to marry again and sire a second family.

The de la Poles had been lucky (to a degree, at least) in acquiring the Peverell lands. They could not assume they would necessarily be lucky with the Cobham ones. The agreement that William de la Pole drew up with Joan Cobham's family included financial clauses designed to ensure that some of the Cobham estate would pass down to Joan when her father died whether he later had a son or not.[13]

Stained glass from St Mary's Church,
Saxlingham Nethergate, Norfolk

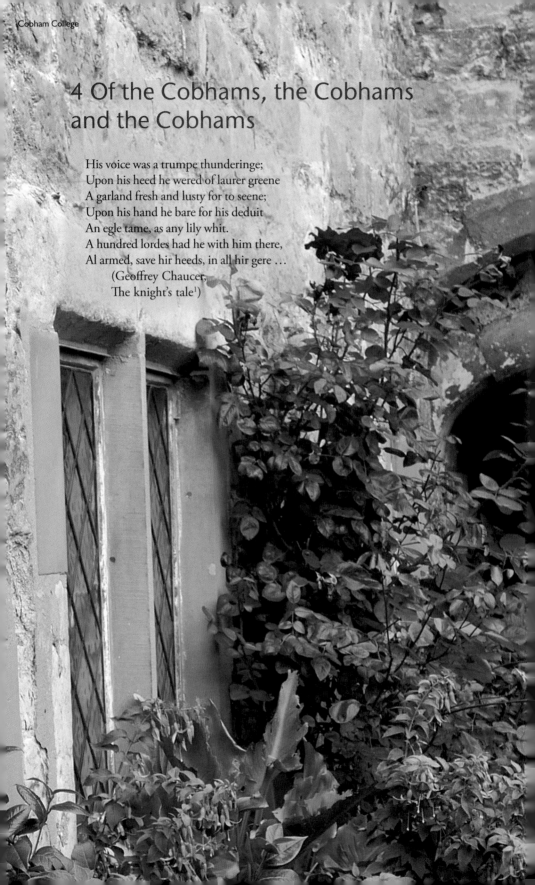

4 Of the Cobhams, the Cobhams and the Cobhams

His voice was a trumpe thunderinge;
Upon his heed he wered of laurer greene
A garland fresh and lusty for to seene;
Upon his hand he bare for his deduit
An egle tame, as any lily whit.
A hundred lordes had he with him there,
Al armed, save hir heeds, in all hir gere …
   (Geoffrey Chaucer,
   The knight's tale[1])

If the de la Pole family were classic nouveaux riches, their ancestors unknown more than three or four generations back, and the Peverell family too had come recently and dubiously by their fortune, the Cobham family were the opposite.[2] They can be traced reliably back to the twelfth century,[3] and for all of those 200 or so years before the birth of Joan de la Pole, they were associated with the small town of Cobham in Kent.[4] By the fourteenth century the family had grown and branched out, and confusingly, the heads of several of its branches held the title of Baron (or Lord) Cobham, at times doing so simultaneously.

In modern times the English system of nobility has become firmly hereditary, with titles generally passed down through the male line, and a small proportion being created in each generation to compensate for those lines that die out. It was not always so, however. In the early Middle Ages the titles of earl, lord, baron and knight (all of which seem to have been less formally bestowed and handed down than has become the norm since) were firmly linked with the ownership of land, and with control over the people who lived on that land. When the de la Poles and the Peverells invested their gains in property, slowly and carefully acquiring those estates that came onto the market, they were not doing so for financial gain. The income from land was comparatively modest, and those who made fortunes in their era did so mostly from trade and banking, or from acts of war. They did so because this was the route to political and social influence. A man who owned land could then be required to provide troops for the king, and this would effectively make him a knight or a lord.

The elder William de la Pole had done just this: he became a knight banneret, raised troops from his estate, and fought with them for Edward III. It is not clear that his brother Richard did so – in any case he died 20 years earlier than his brother, before the great campaigns that formed the centrepiece of Edward's long reign – but if his descendants were to be landowners, then they were also destined to be men at arms. His son William, and William's son in turn, did indeed become fighting men. Only those incapable of doing so (through ill health or mental deficiency) were excused from military service.

The old feudal systems were fast changing in this period, and a time was coming when fighting men of all ranks would be paid in coin, rather than providing their services as a form of payment in kind. To be a man at arms became much more of a consistent profession, rather than something that all men did on occasion, but not all of the time. This was an era of soldiers of fortune, of men paid to captain troops whom they in turn hired for pay, rather than bringing their tenants to war.

It was also a time when new ranks of nobility would be introduced. But in the mid-fourteenth century, the link between owning land, controlling men, and being a knight or a lord was still strong.

A nobleman was by definition a man summoned by the king to Parliament as one of his lords, rather than as a representative of the common people. This summons was something that could not be taken for granted. A man might be summoned at one time, but not at another, or he might be a regular attender, but his heir was not summoned. Or if his estates were handed down to an heiress, then her husband might acquire the title, since he was effectively the fighting man associated with those lands. Come to that, if the king wished a man to captain troops for him, then (provided he was of gentle birth; this was not a route open to peasants) he might grant that man lands, so that he would have the wealth and substance to equip himself as a fighting man and take on others to serve under him. Taking on the function and the associated title went hand in hand.

So if several branches of the Cobhams had thrived, and owned lands sufficient to enable them to raise troops from among their tenancy, it was logical that the head of each one should be regarded as a lord, or baron. (A baron was on the lowest rung of the English nobility, below a earl.)

The Joan Cobham who married John de la Pole was the daughter of John, third Baron Cobham of Cobham. The title that he had inherited was the oldest of the Cobham titles, but at times during his holding of it there was also another John de Cobham who was the second Baron Cobham (of another branch); there was a third John, succeeded by Thomas, who were the second and third Barons Cobham of Runham; and there was Reginald Cobham, the second Baron Cobham of Sterborough. Quite possibly their contemporaries found this just as confusing as it seems today.

The Lord Cobham (he could also be described as Sir John Cobham) in whom we are interested was, like most of his known ancestors, a well-respected man. The family had played a solid, if not quite outstanding, part in public life. The first and second barons had both been constables of Dover Castle and wardens of the Cinque Ports (the five historic ports strung like a small constellation along the southern Kent coast) and had attended the king's parliaments. The third lord inherited the title in 1355, at the time when William de la Pole was just emerging from his long battle to secure his wife's inheritance. So by the time he was negotiating his daughter's marriage with the de la Poles, he was comfortably established as a landowner as well as a man at arms.

Although they had been a prolific family in earlier generations, Lord Cobham was an only son, and his daughter too was then an only child. So although there was a huge clutch of other Cobhams among the English nobility, Joan had few very close relatives.

She was a very well-connected woman, however. Lord Cobham's mother and his wife, respectively a Beauchamp and a Courtenay, were related to a wide array of English nobility, and more distantly to royalty. That the de la Poles could make this marriage for their son was something new and impressive. Their branch of the family had not previously been linked with the aristocracy. It reflected, of course, the rise in their status that had come with the inheritance of the Peverell estates.

It was also to do something else: it was to weaken their ties with Northamptonshire, the county that Richard de la Pole and his son had both in turn chosen to make their main home. Kent was a long journey from Northampton. Whether she inherited all of her father's estates or not, Joan Cobham would continue to have ties with that county, and would never, it seems, really become a Northamptonshire woman.

Stained glass from the Church of St Peter Hungate, Norwich

The Cobhams of Cobham

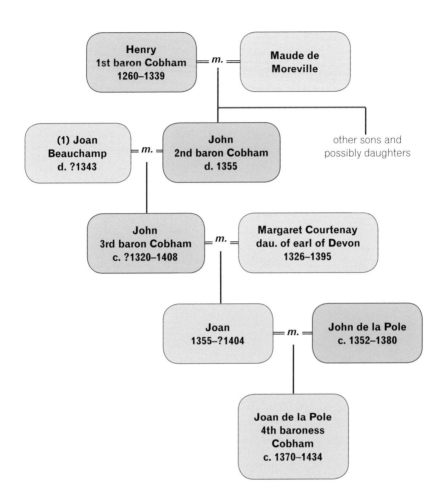

Henry
1st baron Cobham
1260–1339

m.

Maude de
Moreville

other sons and
possibly daughters

(1) Joan
Beauchamp
d. ?1343

m.

John
2nd baron Cobham
d. 1355

John
3rd baron Cobham
c. ?1320–1408

m.

Margaret Courtenay
dau. of earl of Devon
1326–1395

Joan
1355–?1404

m.

John de la Pole
c. 1352–1380

Joan de la Pole
4th baroness
Cobham
c. 1370–1434

5 Two bars wavy

Ne drede hem not, doth hem no reverence;
For though thine husband armed be in maile,
The arrwes of thy crabbed eloquence
Shall perce his brest and eek his aventail.
Geoffrey Chaucer[1]

John de la Pole and Joan Cobham were betrothed in 1362, when they must both
have been very young, although we cannot be sure how young, since their dates of
birth are not known. Quite likely they did not live together for some time after the
marriage, or at least not as an adult husband and wife might do, although Joan might
have come to join the de la Pole household. John, meanwhile, would probably have been
doing what young men of his class typically did. They attached themselves to other great
households, of the nobility or the higher gentry, where they acted as servants – of a higher
kind, they were not farm labourers, although some of their tasks might well be menial
– and learned both to oversee an estate and to wield the weapons used by men at arms.
These were the accepted roles for affluent young men; it was not usual for them to take
up any other profession, except possibly the law, unless they chose to take holy orders.

When the young couple did set up a household, it would not have been at Castle
Ashby, because this remained the home of John's parents, just as Milton probably remained
the home of his grandmother. (It is not certain when either woman died, although it
seems likely that his mother lived till around 1375.) Widows had power, in this era. They

Chrishall, Essex

typically retained many, even most of the family estates, which were not all passed down to the dead man's son until after their death. And they frequently continued to live in the family's main house, obliging their son to make his own household elsewhere.

The estate that John was granted by his parents on his marriage was Potton, one of the Bedfordshire manors, so it was in the middle of the chain of Peverell estates. But it is not clear if he ever lived there, and certainly before long he and his wife were living at Chrishall in Essex. This made a certain sense because it was the most easterly of the family's lands, so moving there put young John in a position to supervise the administration of estates that were too far-flung for his father – still primarily occupied with his crusade – or his mother to visit frequently.

At some point in the mid-1360s William de la Pole's health deteriorated, perhaps as a result of the stresses of his travels, and he died in 1366. That same year also saw the death of his uncle, William senior, by then a very old man, and some years past the height of his influence. This represented the end of an era for the de la Pole family. William senior had had a family much later than his brother Richard, so although it was Richard's grandson who now became head of his branch, it was William's son who inherited the other de la Pole fortune. Then in his forties or so, he had already had a very successful career as a man at arms, but he only married at about this time, and certainly did not yet have grown sons.

Joan and John did not move back to Northamptonshire when John's father died and he became head of the family. That seems a little strange. Northamptonshire had been the main home of John's family for a couple of generations, and it was the core of their land holdings. Even if the young couple chose to leave John's mother and grandmother in the two great houses there, at Milton and Ashby, they could have made a home elsewhere on the family estates in the county. But it seems they did not; not then, and not later.[2]

There are few known portraits of even the richest and most famous English men and women of their era, and those representations that survive are not necessarily portraits in the modern sense, reflecting what the individuals actually looked like. This is true of paintings, and even more so of effigies and brasses, which might have made by craftsmen who had never even met the people commemorated, following stock patterns that took only cursory notice of the realities of their lives. A knight, a merchant, a priest, a lady (peasants have no such memorials): brasses show us the person's station in life, but they are not reliable guides to their faces, their height, their idiosyncrasies. So it is a dangerous business to read too much into what a memorial shows us, but it would be perverse not to consider what it hints at, when we have nothing else to turn to.

In Chrishall Church there is still a great brass, not much short of life-size, which covered the tombs of Sir John and Lady de la Pole. (It has been moved in the church, so even if their bones are still buried there, it does not cover them now.) We know whom it commemorates, because it shows their arms. Two bars wavy at the top left is the arms of this branch of the de la Poles; the chevron with three lions (in a coloured version, a gold chevron on a red background) is the arms of Cobham; and the central shield above their heads shows the combination of the two. Sir John de la Pole wears full armour: modern armour, for this was a period in which chain mail was giving way to plate, and Sir John's is mostly plate, with a wide collar of chain mail almost burying his face, a jewelled belt and a very long sword. Most men at arms wore armour on their memorials, but not all;

it suggests he saw himself as a knight first and foremost, and not a merchant like his grandfather. The mournful moustache he sports was common, but not ubiquitous in his time. King Edward is shown in portraits with a forked beard, but Sir John does not have a beard, or at least none that can be seen.

Lady de la Pole wears a dress notable for the quantity of buttons, not just down the front, but down her narrow sleeves, with their very long trailing tippets. Though plain, this is not a workaday dress: it is quite low-cut, and it speaks of a maid to fasten all those buttons, and of a woman who never does work that would trail those tippets in the dust. Her hair is confined in a cylinder caul, a cage of fine metalwork. This was a fashion of the time for the upper classes, so it again emphasizes her rank.

They hold hands – bare hands. Not unique, but unusual, and a depiction they must have chosen. We can hope this means theirs was a close and loving marriage, their family a happy one.

The lion at Sir John's feet is a stock figure, found on dozens of similar brasses, and so is the merry little lapdog at Lady de la Pole's, but there is some life in this one. Quite likely he had a real-life counterpart.

A stone effigy survives too in the church, and the woman whom it shows is of the same period; her headdress is an echo of Lady Joan's (see page 70). There is no indication whose tomb this is, but it has been suggested it is that of Margaret Peverell, Sir John's mother. If Sir John and his lady had chosen to make their home at Chrishall, it might have made sense for them to establish this as the burial place of all the de la Pole family, even if Lady Margaret had lived most of her life in Northamptonshire. So this serene praying figure, not young but not old, might be the nearest we have to an image of her.

I t was some time before John and Joan had children, probably because they were very young when they married. The first born (or at least, the first to survive beyond infancy) was a son, whom they called William after his de la Pole grandfather. Both the de la Poles and the Cobhams must have been delighted that there was now a male heir who might grow up to carry forward both the de la Pole name and the Cobham title.

Their second child – their only other child, or at least the only one to live a significant time – was a daughter whom they called Joan after her mother. She was born probably around 1370.

So Joan – this Joan, the subject of this book – was not born an heiress. She was a younger daughter. None of the weight of expectation that falls on the eldest child landed on her. She was doubtless valued, loved, but not cherished as the embodiment of two families' hopes. She was the child of a rich family, and so her prospects were good, but they were not grand. As the second child, her parents would probably look to have her marry, rather than become a nun. They could be expected to find her a husband who was the heir to a moderately well-off gentry family, or a younger son of a titled family: a gentleman, but not a great lord. They might find this man in Northamptonshire, or in Kent, or now that her parents were settled there, perhaps he would come from East Anglia.

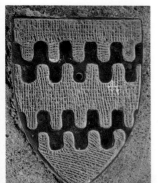

Both pictures: Holy Trinity Church, Chrishall, Essex

6
The highest hill
in Essex

'As my father did before me'.
A command regarding Chrishall
from Queen Matilda'

Chrishall, Essex

Joan was probably born at Chrishall, and it was almost certainly her main home during the first ten years or so of her life. That does not mean she lived there all the time, and indeed she might not have lived there much at all. Her young parents would not have been there all the time. They would have kept in close touch with John's relatives in Northamptonshire, and with Joan's relatives in Kent. Quite likely they spent some time (and saw these relations) in London too. The de la Poles might have kept a house there, and the Cobhams certainly did: they owned Cobham's Inn, a great mansion that stood on Tower Street, in the shadow of the Tower of London.

Joan's father was of course a man at arms. There had been ten years or so of respite from the long war against the French following the Treaty of Bretigny in 1360, but by the 1370s the treaty had broken down, and there was fighting to be done in France and elsewhere. Although never in the first rank of English captains, Sir John de la Pole had a respectable fighting career. He served in 1369 with the earl of Pembroke in an expedition the duke of Cambridge made to Aquitaine, then (after Edward III had died, and his grandson Richard II had succeeded him) he served with Thomas of Woodstock in a campaign to relieve English troops who had become blockaded at Brest. Finally in spring 1378 he joined in an (unsuccessful) assault on St Malo.[2] These were not ventures that would have enriched him greatly, but he probably valued his earnings from them, because this was a difficult time for a man who wished to make a living by managing his estates. Farm wages had gone up since the plague had first come, the price of food had come down, and landowners were not doing well financially as a result.

However frustrating they found these responsibilities, keeping oversight of their lands was something that families who owned several estates knew was essential. Even the best and most trusted servants could not be left unsupervised; every careful landowner made decisions of his own, and checked on those that were made for him. (Those who could not, or would not, do this had the option of leasing their lands to others, but the de la Poles do not seem to have done this to any great extent at this time.) So when he was not away at war, Sir John was obliged to travel around his lands. He needed to see for himself the state of the buildings, the sheep and cows, the crops; to administer justice, to hear what his tenants had to tell him. If he was not in England to do this himself, he would have looked to his wife to do it for him.

Kent, Northamptonshire, Bedfordshire, London, France: it added up to a lot of time spent away from Chrishall, even if the family regarded this as their main home. And even when the de la Poles were at Chrishall, it does not follow that Joan was with them. Many children were boarded out. As infants they might be tended by a wetnurse and then a nursemaid, and live in the household of that woman for convenience. As older children, they might stay in a convent or abbey, and learn their letters from the monks and nuns. And as they moved towards adulthood, they would be sent to other large houses, acting as servants and companions to the adults of other families, and learning from them how a household and an estate should be run. This was also convenient when their parents were travelling frequently; life was simpler if their children did not travel with them.

Husbands and wives too lived much more separate lives than they do in many modern families, at least in the upper classes, but it should not be concluded that married couples cared little about each other or their children. They loved, they grieved: but they had different expectations, and different ways of expressing their emotions – when, that is, they felt able to express them at all.

So we can make few assumptions about where Joan spent her time, but we can assume that the place she thought of as home was Chrishall. She probably realized, though, from a young age, that her family did not have the kind of deep-rooted commitment to Chrishall that guarantees to the young that it will be regarded as home always, whatever happens or wherever their life takes them. There were at the time of her birth no monuments to

the de la Poles or Cobhams in Chrishall Church, no families locally that could recall generations of service to the family. There was no web of relations close at hand. Although the other branch of the de la Poles was now based largely in East Anglia, their main home at Wingfield was not far off seventy miles away.

So hers might have seemed to her – as it seems to us, in long retrospect – a strangely rootless family, spread widely but thinly across southern and eastern England. Of course the de la Poles were not alone in having made a couple of major moves in as many generations. There were many reasons a man might go to a different part of the country, and marriage often caused a woman to do so, just as Joan's mother had done. But most people of Joan's time, it seems safe to say, lived where their parents had lived, in the shadow of the church where their ancestors were buried. That was never the pattern for her own family.

For the de la Poles, though, this had not been from necessity. They did not lack choice. If they stayed in Chrishall, it was because they wanted to.

The home they had chosen was in good farming territory, much like the Northamptonshire they had left behind. Essex is a low-lying county in the main, but Chrishall village is at its highest point, and the main house in that village, the one that was probably home to the de la Poles in those days, was set on the highest hill in this high-set village. The church too is set on a hill, but these are not hills that dwellers in mountainous regions would recognize: they are shallow rises, the greatest waves in an undulating landscape.

Although this was well populated countryside (as the number of moated sites, once those of medieval manors, in the surrounding villages and hamlets still attests), Chrishall was close to no large town. The nearest was Saffron Walden, and being in the north-west corner of the county, it was also not too far from Cambridge. But it was a village with good communications, because it lay on the Icknield Way, the ancient road that formed one of the great 'four highways' that linked the towns of medieval England. Although opinions differ about its route, it is generally thought to have run from Salisbury to Bury St Edmunds, and to have intersected with the other great roadways of the Middle Ages – the Fosse Way, Ermine Street and Watling Street – around Dunstable. There were linked roads to the south and west of Salisbury, and farther north, the Roman road we know as Icknield Street carried the route as far as Tynemouth. But in Essex the Icknield Way was

Stained glass from, above, St Peter's Church, Ketteringham, Norfolk, and right, St John the Baptist's Church, Thaxted, Essex

a track, not a Roman road, and it tended to use the high land because the valley bottoms could be boggy and difficult to navigate.

Chrishall's other main claim to fame was its owner three centuries or so before the de la Poles, Eustace of Boulogne, who had come over to England with the Conqueror. It was he who built the house the de la Poles probably lived in, which he called Flanders.[3] His daughter Matilda, who became wife to King Stephen, was brought up there, and mentioned the place in her correspondence. So the house the de la Poles moved to was already a very old one, but it must have been well built, for it was to survive for another couple of hundred years.

Since Flanders (the house, not the country after which Eustace named it) was destroyed many centuries ago, we can do no more than guess at its appearance. It seems never to have been called a castle, so it was probably a substantial wood-framed house, sturdily built, with a great hall as was the style in the eleventh century, in which much of the business of the household took place. There would have been some private apartments for the family to withdraw to, and a number of outbuildings, all set in a moat which both announced its grand status and provided its inhabitants with a degree of protection. It had a couple of large fishponds, and was set in isolation, about half a mile from the church and a little farther from the centre of the village. (The centre of Chrishall village is now some distance from its church, though perhaps it clustered more closely around it six or seven centuries ago.)

As the home of a great noble, this small village – it could never have been anything else – would have been better served with shops and facilities than many. It perhaps held an ancestor of the centuries-old inn, the Red Cow, that stands on the high street now, and the church – rebuilt after the Conquest, on the site of an earlier one – is a grand building, one fit to receive the tombs of a family such as the de la Poles. As well as the huge brass that covers the tomb of Joan's parents, there are a couple of other surviving brasses of local people from about the same era, which suggests that there were a number of quite affluent families in the parish.

What was life like day to day, for a girl of Joan's class? To some extent, we can only guess. Her family were rich, of course. This was a time when the incomes, and the lifestyles, of the rich and poor differed massively. Life for the peasant class had always been hard, and often short with it. Houses were basic and barely furnished, possessions few, work relentless, and food often hard to come by. When the black death had scythed its way through the population it had made a great difference: before there had been plenty of people to do the work on each landed estate, but

even in the mid-1370s, nearly thirty years since the first great outbreak, there was still a shortage. The recurrences of the plague had kept the population from recovering. Many working people hoped that the greater demand for their services would enable them to get more pay, but the government had passed statutes designed to ensure it benefited them not at all. (They failed to achieve this, and workers probably ate a little better and wore better clothes than their parents had done, but the improvement cannot have been great.[4]) And while the gains from the war tended to go to the rich, it was the poor on whom much of the burden fell of paying for it.

England might be a country where many still held servile status, and were not free to leave the estate on which they had been born, but it was not a land of slaves. There were many smallholders, leasing land from an overlord such as Sir John, who lived reasonably comfortable lives, ate meat pies for their supper and drank ale to wash them down. Nor was it a land that had been scoured by war; the English went to France and Scotland to do that. Even the poorest rarely starved, though their bellies would be empty after a poor harvest. But theirs had been difficult times to live through, and those who could look up to see the lord on his horse, watching to ensure they gave him a share of their crops, tilled and harvested his demesne land before they could turn to their own, knew that their lot was hard in comparison. So it was a world of sullen and resentful peasants, where many felt they had little to enjoy in this life. And it was a world where it was common to pass houses fallen into decay, strip fields untended, churches collapsing, whole villages deserted, because the repeated outbreaks of the plague meant that the damage of its first terrible occurrence had largely been left unrepaired.

Great magnates, and even lesser landowners like the de la Poles, lived in what by comparison was considerable luxury. They were upgrading the draughty castles and manor houses of their ancestors, and their homes typically had glass in the windows, hangings on the walls, and plentiful furnishings. As well as domestic servants (and labourers on their land), they kept retinues of liveried attendants, men hired not just to come to war with their lord, but to provide company and security in peacetime – and women too, to attend their wives. After a generation in which the English had plundered France, England was fat on its takings. Most women in rich families would have worn jewels which had once graced a Frenchwoman's outfit, and quite likely her clothes as well. The churches and the storecupboards of the rich groaned with gold and silver, much of which had been looted – in France, the Netherlands, and countries to the east as well.

The de la Poles were still perhaps not as rich as the first Richard de la Pole had been. Neither his son nor his grandson had a really distinguished career at arms. But the Cobhams had always been soldiers, and they had done well out of the wars. If not quite among the richest people in the country, still both families formed part of a small and very privileged minority.

So Joan's was an upbringing in which she would rarely if ever have felt hunger, and not even much cold in the winter.

How much teaching she had, it is hard to say. There were schools in her time, though many of these too had been affected by the plague, and the system had still not recovered to what it was beforehand. Girls were probably taught in them as well as boys, though not as many. It was probably more common for girls of well-off families to be taught

Stained glass from St John the Baptist's Church, Thaxted, Essex

their letters by their mother, a chaplain or another relative or servant of the family. Her family might well have owned books, as many affluent families did, and quite likely she was able to read them. Perhaps she could write too, although nothing she wrote down has survived.

A generation or two before, French was so firmly installed as the language of educated people that the de la Pole brothers, natives of Yorkshire, had had their business agreements drawn up in that language. But that was changing fast, and it was at this time that English started to become the standard language for the education of laypeople. Latin, of course, remained the language of the Church, and many legal documents were still written in it, but it was not spoken in daily life, where English had become the norm. Joan rarely if ever left Britain, and she might have spoken no French at all.

Perhaps more important to her than booklearning was to learn how to run a household. As well as the management of female servants that fell to a wife's lot, it was useful for any wife whose husband would be often absent (and her husband, whoever he might be, would certainly often be absent) to know how to deal with estate matters for him. With plenty of servants to hand, she would not have needed to learn to do menial tasks – spinning and weaving were jobs for the lower classes – but she would have learned to sew and embroider, and perhaps to sing and to play an instrument.

A family that had access to woods and forests would hunt in them, and invite its neighbours to do so too. Hunting to hounds for large prey was done by women as well as men, even if they stood back at the kill; and both men and women kept hawks and other birds of prey, and went out to hunt for smaller game with them. They ate a far wider variety of flesh than we eat today: wild birds, ducks and swans, rabbits and hare were all common parts of their diet. (Vegetables seem to have been eaten much less than today, particularly by those rich enough to afford plenty of meat.) So as she grew out of infancy, Joan probably learned how to train a hawk or falcon, and of course she would have learned to ride (side-saddle, in a modest ladylike way) and follow the hounds on the hunt.

She spent time in prayer, of course: in the family's chapel, if it had one (it probably did), and in the parish church too. The services, held in Latin, were incomprehensible to most people, but the ritual they represented was important. Priests and friars taught simple lessons about morality and the scriptures, so as a child her faith was doubtless as plain and uncynical as any child's faith must be. She believed that if she did not obey the Commandments and worship God in the ways she was taught, she would go to hell; if she did these things, she had at least a chance of salvation. She understood that the dead must be prayed for, as well as the living. Her parents, grandparents, great-grandparents had probably arranged for priests to say prayers for them (for a good payment), to help smooth their path through purgatory, but of course their descendants would pray as well.

She knew death; everyone in her time did. Dead animals, dead humans, were a frequent sight. And when Joan was ten or so, in 1380 the spectre of death crossed over the de la Poles' threshhold. That was a year in which her life changed totally. Her father died, and her brother died too. And she was married for the first time.

7 A marriage and two funerals

Do quetem fidibus:
vellem, ut et planctibus
sic possem et fletibus:
laesis pulsu manipus
raucis planctu vocibus
deficit et spiritus.

(Silence, my lyre.
If only I could also silence
my mourning and weeping.
My hands hurt from playing,
my voice is hoarse from crying
and my breathing is feeble.)

Peter Abelard,
1079–1142,
'David's lament
for Jonathan'[1]

Stained glass from St Mary's Church, Martham,
Norfolk

Two deaths close together, in a small family of four, removing both of its men and leaving only two women, can only be a disaster. But although this was tragic for the de la Poles, it was no more than commonplace to their neighbours. Their world was full of widows and widowers, full of orphans. Their relatives and friends would come to the funerals – huge funerals, especially for Sir John, but sizeable too for his heir – express their condolences and go back home. The brass makers would get to work, incising the memorial, or if the brass had been made in advance, setting it in place. The priests paid to do so would conduct many masses, held over many months, with each prayer and offering intended to take the dead man a tiny step nearer to heaven. The estate stewards would meet the funeral bills, and go on collecting the rents, selling the surplus produce from the farms. The lawyers would dust down the will, and set about implementing its provisions. Those who had served the dead men would move on, seeking some other position. And life would go on, little changed for everyone except Lady de la Pole and her daughter.

Losing a husband, a father, a brother and son, hurts no less because other people also experience it. It changes life no less. It does no less to bring home the cold reality of the death that lies in wait for us too. The grief, the loneliness, the upheaval of everything that had shaped their lives: these were the things that must have dominated Joan's and her mother's experience in the months that followed. There is always much to do in the time following the death of the head of a family, and there is no time when people feel less like doing it than when not just this, but another death too of another person much loved, much needed in the family, has torn up their roots and left them floundering.

It is not the best time to begin a marriage.

But for Joan to marry – or at least be unbreakably betrothed – before her father's death was all but essential. If he had had any time at all when he knew his death was approaching, her father would have made it a priority to ensure that she was firmly settled, and her mother and all their other relations would have been equally committed to assisting him. If a man or woman died leaving an under-age heir, that heir became a ward of the king. (The king might then pass on the wardship, as was often done in the system of reciprocal favours that made up this society, or simply for a fee.) The holder of the wardship then had the right to negotiate a single heir's marriage and to profit from doing so. Their surviving family had no say. No man wanted his daughter to be treated as a commodity, to be disposed of for someone else's profit. No man wanted the future of his own family to become a minor consideration in making its heir's marriage. This had to be avoided, even if matters were arranged in haste, and the match young Joan made was less advantageous than it might have been as a result.

It would have been even more of a priority for young William to be married, if he had been expected to inherit from his father. No information survives, but that he was not suggests either that he died before his father, or that he was already sick and not expected to recover. In those circumstances there would be no advantage in marrying him off, and having to contend afterwards with a young widow.

So it is likely that even before her father's death, Joan's position in the family had changed. A great void was opening up where her father and her brother had stood, and it was now for her to step into it, and fill it as best she might, or bring in a husband who would do so. And it is likely that her marriage was negotiated in the knowledge that she was, or expectation that she would soon become, her father's heir.

Joan was also in direct line to inherit the Cobham estates, but that was a much less certain expectation. Although Lord Cobham was now an elderly man with an elderly wife, it was not inconceivable that his wife would die before him, and he would remarry and get a son. Then Joan's mother would inherit only the lands specified in her marriage contract, and even those were not certain to pass to her daughter. It had been understood since the days of the Magna Carta that a widow should not be pressed into remarrying against her will, but it was quite likely that Lady de la Pole would wish to remarry, and then she would probably have further children with her next husband. If one was a son, he would elbow past Joan to become her main heir. Lady de la Pole was possibly still in her twenties, and certainly not past her thirties, so she might have had a long life ahead of her.

Even so: the second child had now become the only child, and she must have felt the weight of it. She had an importance now to the family as a whole that had not been hers before. The girl who would have been given only a modest dower if her brother had lived had become the heir to sizeable property. All those jostling in the marriage market, looking to find wives for their sons or their wards, would have known of that within days of her father's and her brother's deaths. There was no question now of matching her with a younger son: even if they had to rush negotiations, her family were able to secure for her a young man with considerable possessions of his own.

So we can imagine young Joan, shaken by the thunderstorm that had riven her family, unnerved by the responsibilities that pressed on her, and left breathless, perhaps, by the speed with which plans that would change her life for ever took shape, were made reality, and swept her away from Chrishall. Almost before the funeral candles had been extinguished in Chrishall Church, she was headed north as the wife of Robert Hemenhale.

Both pictures, stained glass from St Peter's Church, Lowick, Northants

8 Of oyster beds and salt pans

And know, dear sister, that all that I know you have done since we were wed until now and all that you shall do hereafter with good intent, was and is to my liking, pleaseth me, and has well pleased me, and will please me. For your youth excuses your unwisdom and will still excuse you in all things as long as all you do is with good intent and not displeasing to me. And know that I am pleased rather than displeased that you tend rose trees, and care for violets, and make chaplets, and dance, and sing ...

The Goodman of Paris to his wife, c. 1393

Stained glass from St Mary's Church, Burnham Deepdale, Norfolk

Robert Hemenhale's father had died when he was about three years old. When he was married to Joan he was about seventeen, so he had had fourteen years, all the life he could remember, under the yoke of the king's guardianship. His mother kept her dower lands, those that would be hers for the rest of her life, but the rest of the family's possessions were administered by his guardian, and not for the family's benefit.

And the boy's marriage was arranged the same way. He had no choice in it. It was the decision of other men that left him yoked for life to a ten-year-old child who was still staggering from her own father's death. He knew, of course, that this was how things were done, and it was by no means a grotesquely unsuitable marriage, or even a financially disadvantageous one. If no other heirs were born to the de la Pole and Cobham estates, it could carry him upwards in the world. It did not necessarily follow that he was grateful.

To own land worth, say, 40 shillings was not the same, in this era, as to have 40 shillings in your pocket. People understood that to a degree; but perhaps only to a degree, both because that is a hard lesson when the 40 shillings has gone from your pocket to purchase that land, and because the feudal system of land ownership and obligations had become so knitted with complexity over the centuries that it was full of knots and contradictions. For centuries lawyers had made a fat living from unravelling (or sometimes, in the eyes of ungrateful clients, ravelling further) those knots.

From one perspective, what is bought and paid for belongs to the purchaser. From the other perspective, all of England was the king's estate, and all titles to land were held of, and under, the king. (And under the lords who held it from the king, a great waterfall of lesser men held land on different terms, and leased it onwards to still smaller men.) This meant not only that ownership of land came with obligations and rights, but also that it

Burnham Overy Staithe, Norfol;k

was contingent on the king's favour. If a man was found guilty of treason, acting against the king, then his lands would be forfeit. If there was no adult heir to administer the lands and fulfil the obligations that came with them, then it was seen as reasonable for other men to do so (at the king's favour), and to take a profit.

These lessons were particularly hard learned by those who inherited as minors. A long minority could hollow out a rich estate, as its guardians veered between indifference to the long term, and greed to find profits over the short term. Two long minorities could leave only a shell for the adult heir to take over. But although all those who administered estates held in wardship expected to make a profit from the position, not all were cruel. Many were honest and decent by their own standards, and there is no reason to think the arrangements made for Robert Hemenhale were anything else. He did not reach his majority (then twenty-one for a man, fourteen for a married woman and sixteen for a single one) until 1384 or so, but it seems that not long after his marriage to Joan in 1381 he was granted use of the family's estate at Burnham Norton in Norfolk, presumably so that he could establish a household there and support his young wife.[2]

The Hemenhales owned a broad spread of lands – perhaps not far different in value from those that the de la Poles owned and controlled – from Burnham on the north coast of East Anglia, hard up against the North Sea, to Radwinter in Essex, only a dozen miles or so from Chrishall. It was hard on Joan, we might think, that the estate that was made available for the young couple was the farthest of them all from where her mother was living. But quite likely that was not intended cruelly either. Much of the land was probably leased out, and had been so for all those fourteen or fifteen years it had been under guardianship. Such arrangements had to be considered when the time came to take the manors back into the family's control. Although Robert came of age in 1384, he was

The Hemenhale family

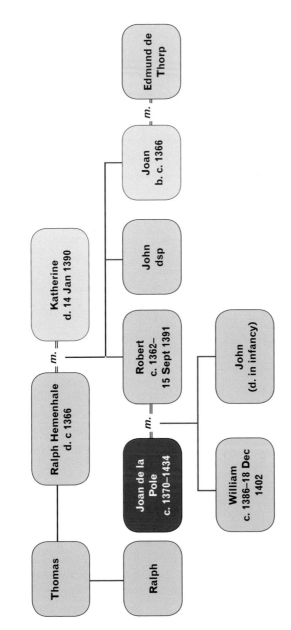

Thomas

Ralph Hemenhale
d. c 1366

=m.=

Katherine
d. 14 Jan 1390

Ralph

Robert
c. 1362–
15 Sept 1391

=m.=

Joan de la
Pole
c. 1370–1434

John
dsp

Joan
b. c. 1366

=m.=

Edmund de
Thorp

John
(d. in infancy)

William
c. 1386–18 Dec
1402

still involved in land transactions, probably concerned largely with taking back charge of his inheritance, for several years afterwards.

Joan too was a minor and a ward of the crown, something that did not change for either her or Robert on their marriage. So neither her husband nor her mother had full control of

the de la Pole and Peverell lands, and it was probably not an option for the couple to live on Joan's own estates. As the different estates came back into their hands, they would have travelled between them to some degree, but they probably spent much of their time at Burnham Norton. Robert was to be described as Sir Robert Hemenhale (of course he became a knight) of Polstead Hall in Burnham Norton, and it was at Burnham, in the church of its Carmelite friary, that he later asked to be buried.

His family most likely came originally from Hempnall, near Long Stratton in south Norfolk. (Hempnall is a variant of the name Hemenhale.) The family owned a manor called Sir Ralf's, or Curple's, Manor there, and perhaps his mother Katherine lived in the manor house. She survived until January 1490, so she was a widow for twenty-four years. She never remarried after her first husband's death.

Robert seems to have had a younger brother, John, and a sister, rather confusingly also called Joan. Once the young couple were fully adult, they probably did not live with these relations. But when she first became a child bride, young Joan de la Pole was most likely put in her mother-in-law's charge. So she probably moved initially from Chrishall to Hempnall.

Why did the de la Poles choose Sir Robert? There was not an endless supply of young men of the right class, more or less the right age, with the qualities to take on the Cobham inheritance should that happen, and enough possessions, and character, to shoulder the disappointment if it did not. The two families were not close neighbours, but the landed class of England was a relatively small one, and it was dense with cross-connections. There must have been people who knew both families, both in Essex and at the king's court, and who could act as intermediaries in the negotiations.

Stained glass from St John the Baptist's Church, Mileham, Norfolk, left, and St Mary's Church, Burnham Deepdale, Norfolk, right

One link between the two families rests on Dover Castle. Robert Hemenhale's father and grandfather had held – and Robert himself was to hold – the honour of Haughley, a title based on estates around the castle of Haughley, near Stowmarket in Suffolk. Haughley Castle itself was a ruin, no more than a few walls on a motte and some stretches of moat (which survive today). It had been burned down after a revolt in 1173, and never rebuilt, so the ruins must have been heavily overgrown by Joan's day. When the castle was standing, it had been the seat of

a baron, but the Hemenhales made no claim to noble status. However the title still brought a sizeable obligation with it, to provide guards for Dover Castle, or payment in their stead, something that both Robert and his father had to do.

The Cobhams had for a similar couple of generations furnished the constables of Dover Castle, so it was with them that the Hemenhales dealt over providing either men in person or money for hiring them. With her husband on his deathbed, Lady Joan probably turned to her father and mother for help and support in getting her daughter settled, so it might have been the Cobhams who first identified Robert Hemenhale as a good candidate. Then after the marriage, of course Lord Cobham would have patronised the young knight, trying to ensure that appointments came his way, and his fortune and reputation grew.

So we must judge Joan's life in her early teens from scant clues, but they are enough to give a rough sense of what it was like. The first ten years of her life were secure, affluent. Then came upheavals which must have shaken the easy self-confidence that is common to rich young girls. They were followed fast by the need to abandon her mother to the loneliness of a Chrishall where none of her immediate family now surrounded her, and to accustom herself to the ways of a new family. Joan had to learn from her mother in law how the Hemenhales ran their affairs. She perhaps saw little at first of her husband, but every meeting was imbued with the knowledge that these two near-strangers were now yoked together for their joint lifetimes. Her new brother and sister, the Hemenhales' servants, agents and friends: all these were people she had to learn to get along with.

If we cannot assume kindness, we have no reason to imagine cruelty. From time to time Joan must have returned to Chrishall, spent time with her mother, and joined in the masses for her father and brother. Her mother did not remarry quickly. Indeed, she never remarried at all. Perhaps Joan was glad that this element of her life remained unchanged, that her mother still lived in a Chrishall Manor little altered from when it had been her own home, and that she had no need to also get to know a stepfather.

She was a rich young girl, and although her husband and his family had authority over her, nevertheless that gave her a measure of power. Most likely at times she used it.

Then after a few years we can think of her moving to Burnham Norton, and taking control of her own household, guided probably by trusted servants she had come to know at Hempnall, and visited herself by her mother, her mother in law, her brother and sister in law. We can imagine her young husband spending time (although not all of his time) there with her, and the young couple slowly beginning their marriage in earnest.

Burnham Norton is one of a group of villages collectively known as the Burnhams. Although Polstead Hall was in the parish of Burham Norton, it seems to have been located in the area called Burnham Westgate, to the west of (and closer to) the largest of the villages, Burnham Market.

The name Burnham derives from the words for village and stream, so these were villages set around small streams that trickled into the North Sea. The suffix Norton indicates that this village was the northernmost of the group.

This was an area of salt marsh and scrub, frequently inundated by the sea, low-lying, and used for pasture, when it had any agricultural use at all. Salt pans and oyster beds provided a living for some of its inhabitants. There was a small harbour at Burnham Overy, so there was sea fishing and some trade, although it was never a major port. There was no great town less than a day's journey away. But the Hemenhales were an affluent family, and their household would have been quite a large one. Some of its members were in communication with their other estates, so news reached them relatively quickly.

This must have seemed strange and foreign territory to a girl brought up in the centre of England. The north Norfolk coast is a place of huge skies and wide coastlines, flat and marshy. And it could be frightening, with high seas and flooded expanses of sand, mud and marsh in the winter, and the

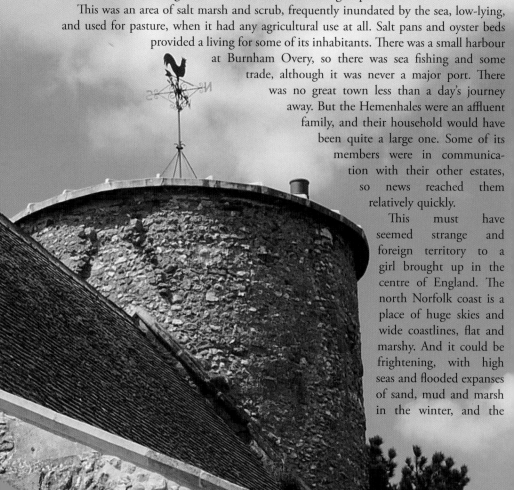

perennial threat of invasion by the Scots or the French, or pirates coming ashore to raid. But it was not empty countryside; this was a place where people lived, fished, farmed. It is a place that people come to love, and perhaps Joan was among them. Certainly she took some trouble to retain an association with Burnham for as long as she could.

Joan would have slowly got to know the house, the estate, the village, the shore; the merchants, the farmers, the labourers, the smiths, the pedlars: all those men and women who made up what was largely a self-contained and self-supporting community. She must have come to know Burnham Norton's church with its Saxon round tower, its thick flint walls and ancient font. In her time the village consisted of probably only a handful of houses clustered around the church. She would have visited the friary, with its great gatehouse that still survives today, the small church in the walled precinct behind it, the friars, their servants, the travellers who lodged with them. The friary was then about a hundred years old, and for most if not all of those years it had been supported by the Hemenhale family as lords of the manor.

Polstead Hall is long gone. There is no stone suited for building in north Norfolk. The churches are made of flint, either rough pebbles, or knapped and polished into cubes. Perhaps the house too was of flint, or perhaps it was mostly of wood. Because of the dangers of living near the coast, it was probably well fortified, with a good wall around the house and yard.

Joan was to become a woman who liked to be married. That much is evident, or she would not have chosen to marry so frequently. True, she had little or no choice about this first marriage, but if she had chafed at the life of a married woman she might well have opted afterwards to do as her mother had done, and settle for a long widowhood. That was not the path she chose.

Or perhaps she was a woman who was afraid of not being married. It takes courage to face life alone. Mind, a woman of her time could not expect day-to-day company from her husband. Women and men moved largely in separate circles, had separate friends and companions. Men at arms were away from home when fighting, often abroad, and necessarily absent for months or even years. Men who took part in public life were called to London or another city to play that part. Men who had lands to administer needed to visit them, preside over local courts, meet with lawyers and merchants. Peasants might never travel far beyond the boundaries of their home village, but that was not true of the higher classes. Travelling was arduous and difficult – and at times expensive – but men travelled nevertheless, frequently far and often.

Women travelled far less. It was a rare woman who followed her husband abroad; many did not even follow him around his lands, especially if they were expecting a child, or recovering from the birth of one. So a married woman could not expect to sleep every night at her husband's side, dine every day with him at her table. More often a woman would remain at home, carrying out her husband's instructions – given before he departed, or in letters since – and liaising with servants and neighbours, acting as a powerful partner to him, even if in theory her rights were strictly limited.

As Joan came to her majority, grew from girl to woman, she also came to the age when she must fulfil her first duty as a wife, and bear children to her husband. That would have been a major focus of her life in the years that followed.

Burnham Deepdale, Norfolk

Stained glass from Canterbury Cathedral

9 The new king, the old king

... the king of England, on the Feast of the Nativity of Our Lord in the year 1376, held a solemn assembly in his Palace of Westminster, which he ordered all the bishops, dukes, earls, barons and knights of England to attend. There Prince Richard was brought before the king and ... declared to be the heir to the lands and crown of England .... [The] king set him beside his throne and caused all the bishops, earls, barons, knights, mayors of the cities and chief ports and harbours of England to swear to acknowledge him as their lord and sovereign.

From the chronicles of
Jean Froissart[1]

If a woman's life in this era was always more circumscribed than a man's – if she travelled less, met fewer people, played much less of a part in public life – this did not mean that a woman knew nothing, or failed to think for herself. As Joan grew into adulthood – and an adulthood that was clearly going to carry large responsibilities, with a big household dependent on her to run it, and a wide spread of land for herself and her husband to administer – she would have learned more of the world in which she lived, and the events that had shaped it.

She had been born in the reign of one of the longest-lived English kings. Edward III ruled the country for fifty years, more than many people's entire lifetimes. He had made a hesitant start as a young man, struggling to wrest control from his mother and her notorious lover, Roger Mortimer. Later, after coming to maturity and a successful war with Scotland, he laid claim to the throne of France as well, and started a long war with that country. At first it had gone remarkably well, with outstanding victories for the English at Crècy in 1346 and Poitiers (under his eldest son, the Black Prince) in 1356.

But it is one thing to win a battle, even a great battle, and another to conquer a country. The English had never had enough men to take control of France, a much larger country with a population perhaps five times as great, and the French had never shown an inclination to offer Edward their throne, if he had not imposed himself on it. In the treaty that Edward signed at Bretigny after the battle of Poitiers, he renounced his claim to that throne, although he was granted clear possession of a vast sweep of land in western and southern France. This was land that had belonged to his ancestors for many generations, although the English hold on it had ebbed and flowed.

The truce made at Bretigny had crumbled slowly over the years that followed, as Edward worked to hold his territory, the French king and his nobles made efforts to take back parts of it, and the army that had been assembled to fight the earlier campaigns struggled to find employment. Many of them resorted to chevauchées, sorties in which bands of knights would make long rides through the country, living off the land, laying waste to farms, sacking towns, stealing everything movable, and killing or capturing for ransom those who had failed to flee.

These years had made the English hated in France, and rightly so. There is a vast gulf between the fiction of a noble and gentle knight, and the reality of plundering churches, raping women and indiscriminate butchery. If the men who took part in these expeditions knew that all too well, the women and children back home did not; no sane man comes home and boasts of such exploits, and no circumspect woman asks twice where his new-found riches have come from. Still, anyone who followed events knew that during Joan's childhood the war had not gone well, but had become enmired in ventures that might have brought short-term gain to some, but had done nothing to make England safe or to deliver France to the man the English believed to be its rightful king.

Then Edward had descended gracelessly into a miserable and corrupt old age, at the same time as his heir had sunk into a long illness and headed for death. By the time of the king's death, his son was already in his grave, most of his French possessions were beyond his control, and his other country, England, was exhausted by the war. Those raiding knights had some of them made fortunes, but the smaller men who had been taxed to pay for their expeditions were as broke as the treasury.

The king's death in 1377 had brought a child to the throne: his grandson, Richard of Bordeaux (he was known after the place of his birth), who was to rule as Richard II. And because this was a world in which the character and actions of the king shaped his entire country, it had brought a waiting period, when the councillors who advised and governed for the king could do little more than tread water until he reached his majority and set a direction for them to follow. So Joan's first years of adulthood were not years of dynamic government, but years when the country knew frustration and indeterminacy. They were years too when the king's relatives and his barons, who had none of them known another royal minority, struggled to determine how they might best see the country governed until the king was old enough to govern it for himself.

As well as knowing something of this, Joan knew, of course, something of the religious events of her time. The Church – the Roman Catholic Church, there was as yet no organized other – had been soused in corruption for generations. The bishop who had amassed the lands that passed down to Joan's parents from the Peverell family was not unusual: it was common for bishops to enrich themselves through their positions, even while parish priests scraped a poor living. Nor was he the only senior cleric to have killed another man, or to have gone to war.

At the time Joan had been born, the popes were based not in Rome but in Avignon, and for generations they had been Frenchman – and as such, the enemies of the English. When Joan was about seven, there was a great schism, when the Romans demanded that an Italian pope be elected on the death of the French pope Gregory XI. They got their Italian pope, who became Urban VI, but as it began to be apparent that he had been a disastrous choice, dissenting cardinals elected a rival, who returned to Avignon as Clement VII, while the Italian pope remained in Rome. For political reasons the English acknowledged the Italian rather than the French claimant, but both were deeply flawed men, incapable of uniting the church and disposing of their rival. The schism was to persist throughout much of Joan's life, and even the most conventional and credulous of Christians would have known it discredited a Church that claimed in theory to be united and to be headed by a single pope who was infallible.

Almost everyone in England was a Christian believer; turning one's back on the Church was not seen as an option. But there were men, increasingly, who believed that it must be reformed – and not just superficially, but changed wholeheartedly and completely. Perhaps the most influential reformer in Britain was John Wycliffe, an Oxford academic who had argued powerfully about the problems of the papacy and the extravagance and corruption of the Church the pope led, who claimed that individuals should look to live according to the bible, and not as the clergy ordered them, and who was pressing for the bible to be made widely available in English, so that men and women might read its teachings for themselves.

Wycliffe had powerful supporters and protectors, not the least of them being John of Gaunt, the greatest of the surviving sons of Edward III. His arguments were much discussed, albeit there was intense opposition to them from those with a vested interest in keeping the Church much as it was.

What Joan thought of these developments, and what her husband thought, are things we shall never know. But her later life gives us reason to think that she must have considered them, although perhaps not until she was some years older. True, her life was luxurious and sheltered – and she might well have been the kind of arrogant, self-centred young woman that heiresses, paid too much attention too young, can often become – but she is unlikely to have been so coddled and blind as to be convinced that all was well with England and the Church.

And if she was so blind up till her marriage, she would have been knocked clean out of her complacency by the events that shook the country to its core in 1381.

Stained glass from St John the Baptist's Church, Mileham, Norfolk, left, and Canterbury Cathedral, above

10 The bishop wields a two-edged sword

The noble lord and commons assembled in this parliament fully appreciate the great charges and almost insupportable expenditure to be met by our lord king ... to maintain the war and the defence of the realm as well as for other purposes. Therefore they ... have granted to our lord the king four pence to be taken from the goods of each person of the kingdom, both male and female, over the age of fourteen years.

From the records of the parliament of 1377

Families such as Joan's were part in this era of a system of liveried retainers. Great men made formal contracts of service with lesser men, and provided them with uniforms that announced their status as part of the household. A man such as Sir Robert Hemenhale typically became a retainer of a greater lord, spending time not just as a young man, but also as an older one with his own household, attached to that grand household, attending on the lord and wearing the lord's livery. But at the same time he and his wife would take on retainers of their own. These were not quite servants, more in the line of companions, although they provided services of an appropriate kind. These did not only consist of fighting in the lord's retinue (with their own retained men under them) at times of war; they also involved providing security in times of relative peace.

It was a system the king and his council regarded with ambivalence, because it was easy for men who built up what were effectively private armies to become over-powerful. But it persisted, in spite of attempts at regulation, because men and women thought it necessary. As well as the threat from invaders and pirates, there were plenty of threats on land from native-born Englishmen. The system of law enforcement, never much more than rough and ready, had suffered from the recurrent plague epidemics, and violence was not just a remote risk, it was common. Just as everyone must have known of people who had died of the plague, everyone knew of people who had been set upon by thieves, or by men who regarded them as enemies, and robbed, beaten, not infrequently killed.

No man or woman of substance ventured from their home unattended. They travelled always in company with others – armed others, who could be trusted to draw their swords and provide support if the group were to be attacked.

Young Joan might have lived in a remote part of the country, but she was not someone who knew solitude; there would always have been people around her. Inside the house, no one was private; no one slept without others in the room for company, no one spent their day without others around them, mirroring their activities. And when she ventured out, it would always have been with men and women to protect her.

She must have been grateful for this in the year after her marriage.

A shiver in the air, becoming a breeze, then a light wind, then growing into a storm. Not smoothly, but punctuated by pauses, gusts, flashes of lightning; checked sometimes by obstacles, funnelled at other moments into fury. That is how a hurricane begins, and it is how a revolution typically begins too. At first only those out in the open, and sensitive to currents, are aware of what is happening. But if the storm mounts unchecked, every last hermit in distant bogs and moors learns of it.

Stained glass from All Saints Church, Bale, Norfolk. Photo Mike Dixon

And so do rich young ladies cosseted by their own households. What did Joan notice first? Perhaps a familiar servant no longer around, and scandalised whispers that he had gone to join the rebels. Perhaps a warning sermon in the priory church, of men's (and women's) duty of obedience. Did she pay attention, or did she half-listen and carry on with her daily life, as so many must have done? Since she was to become heavily involved in revolutionary activity in her later life, we can speculate that perhaps she did notice, did ask questions. Many of those around her would have told her it was nothing to bother with, and changed the subject, but perhaps one or two – a chaplain, a steward, a trusted maidservant, maybe with relatives who had joined the rebellion – gave her answers that made her think.

Many adults as well as children never query their own privileges, or the greater poverty of others. But others do so, and if what came to be known as the Peasants' Revolt was primarily a revolt of the poor against the rich, it had plenty of well-off sympathizers. Perhaps there were those among Robert's friends who thought out loud that the government had pressed the poor too hard when it imposed the poll tax that had triggered the rebellion. It was a charge that would scarcely be noticed by the well-off, but for many peasants it was an insupportable burden. Thoughtful masters of those peasants were perhaps not so very surprised when the families on their lands refused to, or could not, pay up.

Where was Joan, at the time? Probably in Norfolk, in Burnham Norton or Hempnall, or perhaps Essex. The revolt began in Essex, not so far from where her mother lived. It raged in London, and men must have brought tales of the happenings there to places across the country – the archbishop of Canterbury attacked and killed! The duke of Lancaster's great palace burned to the ground! Men threatening to do away with kings! And it came to Norfolk too.

Over a hot June, the crisis rumbled for weeks. The Hemenhales must have kept their gates locked and barred, their goods and their servants shut up inside them, pikes and daggers at the ready in case rioters came their way. Normal life came to a pause, the fields untended, the animals penned, the harbour at Burnham Overy and the market down the street at Burnham Market deserted. Boredom and prayer were probably her main experiences.

And an appalled fascination, perhaps, as the storm blew out, and people emerged to view the devastation; as visitors came to the house once more; as the field hands and stable hands who had slunk off to Norwich slunk back again, to be tactfully ignored or brutally punished as their master chose.

Polstead Hall had not been attacked, as far as we know, but Sir Michael de la Pole, the knight who headed the other great branch of Joan's father's family, had his house invaded, his family records destroyed and his goods despoiled. All Norfolk must have heard of the dyer who led his men to Norwich Castle and set up the rebel headquarters there. They heard too of the bishop of Norwich who had armed himself and ridden to North Walsham (some way to the east of the Burnhams, north east of Norwich), where he had fought a battle, a real and bloody battle, against rebels who had dug themselves into position. 'A wild boar, gnashing his teeth', the chronicler Thomas Walsingham called him.[2]

Hurrah for King Richard! Even those who might have wished for a more positive outcome must have cheered the news that the young king had bravely ridden out and confronted the rebels – although the cynics would sense the trouble he had banked by making them promises he had no intention of keeping. Men the Hemenhales knew (though not Robert, he was too young) would have presided at the trials in Norwich, North Walsham, and perhaps a hundred other places across the east and south of England. Thousands watched the hanging, drawing and quartering of convicted men like the one they called the 'king of Norfolk'. Most likely Joan was not among them, but perhaps she and her servants rode out to the road from Walsham to Lynn, and watched a portion of the corpse being paraded past on a pike by the bishop's men.

And for months afterwards the surly depression must have been apparent of the men and women in the fields around Burnham, manning its boats, toiling in the stables, the laundry, the forge, whose relations and friends had risked their all, and been given nothing but brutality in return.

11 Knoweth your friend from your foe

This rhyme was given as evidence against John Ball, claimed to be one of the ringleaders of the Peasants' Revolt, at his trial for treason. It was said to have been part of a letter he sent to men in Essex, found in the tunic of a man who was hanged for his role in the disturbances:

> John the Miller hath ground small, small, small
> The King's son of Heaven shall pay for all.
> Be ware or ye be woe;
> Knoweth your friend from your foe;
> Haveth enough, and saith 'Hoo'.
> And do well and better, and fleeth sin,
> And seketh peace, and hold you therein;
> And so biddeth John Trueman and all his fellows.[1]

Ball was found guilty. He was hanged, drawn and quartered at St Albans, and the four quarters of his corpse sent to four cities, to be a warning to others.

Above, St Margaret's Church, Burnham Norton, Norfolk;
right, stained glass from St Mary's Church, Burnham Deepdale, Norfolk

12 The natural

Champains in Cotton is held of John Knevet by knight service, annual value 20
marks. Of whom and by what service the others are held is unknown; annual values,
Gipswich in Cotton 20 marks, Campines in Cotton 20 marks, Boles in Yaxley £10
and Wickham Skeith £10. He also held in his demesne as of fee 2 messuages, 1 mill,
200 a. arable, 5 a. meadow, 15 a. pasture, 10 a. wood and 35s. rent called 'Gernouns'
in Thornham Magna, Stoke, Gislingham, Wyverstone, Braiseworth and Yaxley, of
whom and by what service is unknown, annual value 25 marks; and 1 messuage,
40 a. arable and 40s. rent in Old Newton and Dagworth of the king in chief by the
service of a tenth part of a knight's fee, annual value 5 marks.

Part of the Calendar of Inquisition Post Mortem into
Robert Hemenhale: lands held in Suffolk

A major role of any married woman in Joan's time was to produce children. That was even more true when the hopes of three families rested in her. Of course she knew that, as did her young husband. As soon as she was old enough – perhaps no more than fourteen or fifteen – it was his duty to consummate the marriage. Then they, and all those close to them, prayed that she would conceive. First an heir (a boy for preference), then a spare, then a few more: a good large family of strong healthy children, so that at least one or two would survive even the most disastrous epidemic.

We shall never know much of what Robert Hemenhale did in the early years of their marriage, or indeed in its later years, just as we shall never know whether he and Joan warmed to each other, or merely did their duty. At any rate, they did what was required of them: Joan first became pregnant around 1385 or 1386, when she was probably fifteen or sixteen. This was a time for a woman to take care; for her mother in law, and probably her mother too, to spend time with her in the quiet months while her child quickened and grew in the womb.

Those must have been days of joy and hope. Then there was the trauma of the birth – rarely easy, especially for the first child of a young girl. And then – horror, dismay, shame, disaster.

The child was a boy. And he lived. But perhaps all those around them thought, even if they dared not say it out loud, that it would have been better if he had not. For this child was a 'natural'. By this, they did not mean a person with wonderful innate gifts – even if perhaps in his own way the boy had them – but someone who was mentally handicapped, a simpleton.[1] Whether he had grown awry, or been injured during his birth, the child was damaged beyond repair.

This – this simpleton, this shameful failure, this born idiot – this was their heir.

The practically minded, the brutally realistic, have ways of dealing with such disasters. Some achieve acceptance. Handicaps and deformities were not, after all, unusual in their times. Crude medicine, simplistic management of birth, and everyday violence in both war and peace, meant that the crippled, the damaged, the witless, were common sights. Everybody had scars mental, physical or both, albeit some had them worse than others. People lived their lives in spite of their deficiencies, as best they could. The blind king of Bohemia had even fought in battle, and men with their wits deranged had remained as kings of England and France.

Some opt for a more ruthless solution. It was common for children to be born dead, or to die within days, even moments of birth. An accident, or even a degree of inattention, a bribe to the midwife, and who would know better? Or if that smelled of too much danger to their immortal souls, well, a child could be bundled off to the nuns or to a wise woman, payment made to ensure forgetfulness, and attention turned swiftly to producing another son.

And some are not practically minded at all, in circumstances such as this. Instead they are overwhelmed by a tide of despair. Of grief for lost hopes and expectations. Even, perhaps, of a sudden compassionate love for the poor battered scrap that was newly come into the world.

Whatever their thoughts and motives, the Hemenhales clearly ensured their son was looked after, because he survived his infancy, and lived on well after it. They christened him William. To say that Joan was blamed for the disaster is to say only what was taken for granted in their time. To give birth to a girl and not a boy, or a damaged boy and not a whole and healthy one, or come to that, to fail to conceive at all: all were assumed to be the woman's fault and not her husband's. But if she blamed herself, and was blamed by Robert, this cannot have led to an irrevocable breach between the couple, because they evidently tried again, and conceived another child.

Joan gave birth to another son. This one they called John.

And he died as an infant.

Even in an era when people typically endured much, that must have been enough to destroy her bright young confidence. Perhaps it broke something in her marriage too. Theirs was a harsh God, who presided over a world where many terrible things occurred, and this God was evidently punishing them, even if they were not clear why. These births had not left Joan incapable of conceiving again: she was to do so later, with her

other husbands. But there was no other child born to the couple, or at least none that lived, and perhaps this is an indication that one or both of them could not find in themselves the willingness to try a third time. Or perhaps it was no more than chance. By no means all families were large in their times. Many noble women had only one or two children, not least because their husbands were absent so much of the time.

Little William seems to have thrived. And in time it must have bred in his parents a kind of acceptance, at the least, that this child was destined to live, and to remain as their heir.

Stained glass from St Peter and St Paul's Church, Bardwell, Suffolk

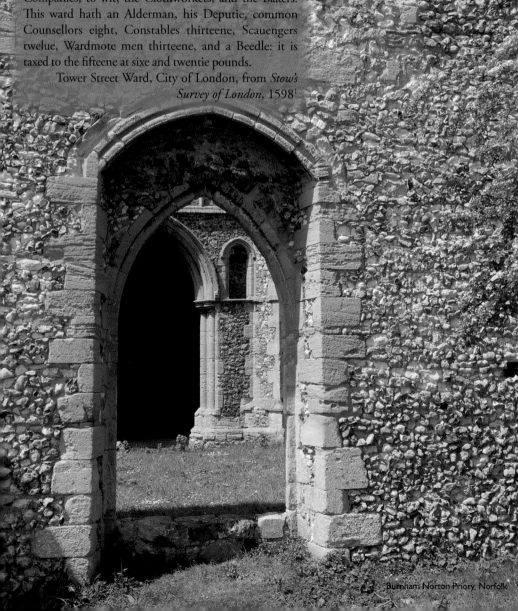

13 Of patience and piety

I reade in 44. of Edward the third, that an Hospitall in the Parish of Barking Church was founded by Robert Denton Chaplen, for the sustentation of poore Priests, and other both men and women, that were sicke of the Phrenzie, there to remaine till they were perfectly whole, and restored to good memorie. Also I reade that in the 6. of Henrie the fift, there was in the Tower ward, a Messuage or great house, called Cobhams Inne … Thus much for the boundes and antiquities of this warde, wherein is noted the Tower of London, three Parish Churches, the Custome house, and two Hals of Companies, to wit, the Clothworkers, and the Bakers. This ward hath an Alderman, his Deputie, common Counsellors eight, Constables thirteene, Scauengers twelue, Wardmote men thirteene, and a Beedle: it is taxed to the fifteene at sixe and twentie pounds.

Tower Street Ward, City of London, from *Stow's Survey of London*, 1598[1]

Burnham Norton Priory, Norfolk

Her pregnancies – these two for certain, and perhaps there were others, that never went to full term, or resulted in babies born dead, or dying within days – would have limited the scope of Joan's life. A woman to whom childbearing came easily might only withdraw from public life in the later months of pregnancy, but a young girl expecting a much-wanted child for the first time, and that young girl conceiving again with the heavy knowledge of all that could go wrong, could be forgiven for keeping to her house when she was with child.

But there were times when she was not so limited, both before and after her sons were born, and in these times Joan probably joined her husband in his travels. She would have gone, with him or indeed without him, when he was otherwise occupied, to visit her mother in Essex; to stay with her mother-in-law and the other members of the Hemenhale family; to London, and to the King's court.

She probably went less, if at all, to Northamptonshire. And there is no indication that she ever went to Yorkshire, to pray at the Carthusian monastery in Hull where her great-grandfather had chosen to be buried, to see the great houses that he and her great-great uncle had built, the ships on the Humber that they had financed, the old harbour at Ravenser Odd that was slithering under the cold waters of the estuary.

Richard de la Pole's sons were all dead, his grandson dead, his great-grandson dead, his only living great-great grandson a simpleton child. And it seems that not only were his descendants almost all gone to dust, much of his fortune had evaporated too.

It was barely fifty years since Richard had bought his first lands in Northamptonshire, and he had done so as one of the richest men in England. He had been a valued associate of a king, a man whose business interests stretched from north to south of the country, and across into Gascony as well. The banking, the trade in wine, the ship-building, the ferries the de la Poles ran across the Humber: all this was now no more than a memory, and fading fast from recollection. This vast trading empire, so quick in emerging, seems to have disappeared almost as speedily.

Of course Joan was not poor; indeed by most people's standards she was rich. But she was not living with her husband in the great house Richard de la Pole had built at Milton, and nor did she ever apparently do so during the rest of her life. If she had a fortune, it was in essence what had been kept of the Peverell fortune. The lands she lived on were her husband's lands. The future expectations she had were from her mother's Cobham ancestors. Was anything left to her of what her de la Pole forebears had built up? If there was, there is very little sign of it.

Small fortunes tend to be stable, on the whole. Some families die out, and some others suffer from a foolish or profligate heir, but many continue in a modestly affluent way, their finances and their lives largely unchanged for century after century. Perhaps there is something inherently less stable, too thinly set in the earth, about the kind of great fortune that grows over everything like a virulent weed, then dies with the first frost.

It seems almost incredible that all the de la Pole money might have gone, almost all the estates have been lost. Richard de la Pole had been so rich, his interests so extensive. But none of his descendants seem to have pursued the kinds of money-making venture that had built up his assets, and nor had any of them made a fortune at war. Perhaps all of them had carried on living the kind of grandly extravagant life that the family founder had brought them to expect, without ever bringing in the funds to pay for it. And two

heirs running, Joan's father and then Joan herself, had come into the estates as minors.
That was a situation which could devastate the richest estate, taking into account all the
years when there was no owner to provide military service, and it was thought acceptable
for the king or his assignees to extract plenty of money from the lands in compensation.

So even taking the Hemenhale lands, the Peverell lands, the Cobham expectations as
well as the lees of the de la Pole lands, Sir Robert Hemenhale and his lady were probably
not among the richest people in the country, or at least not so at this point in their lives.
This is apparent, arguably, in the little that is known of Sir Robert's early career. He seems
to have been an enterprising young knight, but nothing more grand than that.

An enterprising young knight needed work – not just the work of overseeing his
estates, now that he had come of age and reclaimed them all, but work that would help
him build his career. Given commissions to do, appointments to fill, he could hope to
grow in power and influence. And in time, when Joan came of age and the pair took
control of her inheritance from her father, and then (as seemed increasingly likely) her
inheritance from her Cobham ancestors, he would have a fine fortune to go with these
lands, and he could look to rise further.

This was reason for both Sir Robert and his young wife, when they were able, to go to
London, and make themselves known at the king's court. They needed contacts to help
them do this. And thin as their families might have seemed, they had good contacts at
Westminster: not least, in the form of two powerful relations of Joan's. Both were elderly
men, more than a generation older than the young couple, and than the young king as
well. But both played a prominent role in the first years of that king's reign.

One was of course Joan's grandfather, Lord Cobham. His fighting days were behind
him, and he was devoting much of his time to spending the money he had made at war.
He spent it in Kent, in building up a college of monks attached to Cobham church, and
in building a great castle a few miles away from Cobham, at Cooling. But he must also
have spent time in London, because he was one of the council of nobles that initially
ruled the country, when the king was too young to do so himself, and then, as Richard
took more of a part, provided him with advice and liaised with his subjects, in parliament

and beyond. There were other Cobham lords too, as we have seen, and the branches of the family seem to have worked closely together at times, so this was a web in which the Hemenhales could enmesh themselves. But John, Lord Cobham was perhaps the richest and most influential of them all.

The poet John Gower knew Cobham well; indeed Lord Cobham was an executor of Gower's will. And Gower paid homage to his friend and (probably) patron in his verses on him:

Unus erat dignus, patiens,
pius atque benignus
Providens, et Justus,
morum virtuti robustus
Non erat obliquus, regni
sed vevus amicus
Hunc rex odivit, in quo bona talia scivit
Ut dieunt mille, dorninus Cobham fuit Hie.

(He was worthy, patient, pious, and liberal, provident and just, strong in the virtue of manners; he was not an indirect, but a true friend of the kingdom.)[2]

Poor poets have always flattered their rich patrons, and other men too have hesitated to be any less than fulsome in praise of those with power and influence. But from what is known of Lord Cobham's life, Gower's words seem to be accurate. Cobham was blessed with competence, though apparently not with brilliance. He was the kind of man who would pad out a king's council, and provide sensible support to its leaders, but not the kind of man who would forge its direction. Patient and pious: that summarizes well what his career suggests of him.

The other man to whom Joan and Robert would have turned was somewhat different; a man, most likely, for whom nobody would have chosen that description. Sir Michael de la Pole was even richer than Lord Cobham, and even more powerful. The de la Pole fortune that had come down to Joan might have melted to a sliver of the empire that had been built up in Hull fifty years or so before, but the other half of that fortune, the half that had stayed with the first William de la Pole, was in much better shape. William de la Pole had lived twenty years longer than his brother Richard, years in which to recover

left, Westminster; above, stained glass from St Mary's Church, Saxlingham Nethergate, Norfolk from the attacks on him, and consolidate his interests. And while Richard's son and grandson were both dead, William's sons were very much living. Sir Michael had done as Lord Cobham had done – as indeed many men of their class did – and first made his reputation as a man at arms. Then he had returned to England, and established himself in the king's court. In 1383 he was rewarded by being granted one of the great offices of state. He became the chancellor of England. In this role he effectively headed the king's government, taking the lead in the King's council, and setting policy under the direction of the king itself.

This was no easy task in the aftermath of the Peasants' Revolt. And it was a task that by no means all men felt should have fallen to Sir Michael – or as he was made in 1385, after two years as chancellor, the earl of Suffolk. His had been the only family of merchants in this era to rise to the nobility. That too was not popular with other men. Many believed the lead in the young king's government should have been taken by the king's uncles, and not least the richest and most influential of them, John of Gaunt, who had become (through his wife) the duke of Lancaster. That it was not was probably because too many men did not trust Gaunt, who seems always to have been a man concerned more with his own interests than with those of his country.

The precariousness of Suffolk's position did not stop him from exercising patronage, and some of it must have come the way of young Hemenhale. By today's standards we might think that this cousin of Joan's, not much younger than her grandfather, was too distant a relative to look the way of the Hemenhales, but the standards of the time were different. This was a society in which men knew both their own lineage, and that of others. Joan's father had shared the chancellor's name, and of course he acknowledged the relationship to her, just as she was aware of hers to him.

The Hemenhales must have been very conscious, though, that their branch of the family was now a junior branch, and that when the name de la Pole was mentioned, it referred not to Joan's late father, but to his cousin.

Although Sir Robert evidently began to establish himself at court, if he wished to make a reputation as a man of arms he would have found it harder. King Richard showed

Stained glass from St Mary's Church, Saxlingham Nethergate, Norfolk

no inclination to become a fighting man, and – to the relief of some, and the despair of others – he had made no real move to recover the lands in France that his grandfather had lost. The battling bishop of Norwich led an expedition to Flanders which he described as a crusade, although it was even more debased an effort – and if anything even less successful – than the crusades of Joan's grandfather's time. And there was an expedition the king led to Scotland, but little fighting took place, and even less glory was earned. There were no great and glorious victories of English armies in Sir Robert's time, so it is no wonder that he is not known for having taken part in any.

So what exactly did Sir Robert do? On that, the record is alas silent. But it is clear that he did come to know the king – know him personally, and be known by him. It seems evident that he did not just carry out run of the mill duties, but performed some service, or services, that were sufficient to earn him the king's exceptional gratitude. Perhaps these were personal services; perhaps they comprised little more than good friendship, or perhaps they added up to rather more.

Richard II as a king attracted much criticism, and some of it was because men disapproved of those to whom he gave his favours, but no one seems to have claimed that these favoured individuals were the King's lovers. More of them seem to have been father figures, and this was perhaps Suffolk's appeal, as a man more than a generation older, and from a very different background. (The king's tutor, Sir Simon Burley, became another.) There is no evidence that Richard had lovers; he was said to be devoted and faithful to his wife. He needed friends, though, as all men and women do, and Sir Robert Hemenhale might well have been one of them: discreet, reliable, not attracting the attention of the chroniclers, but indispensable nonetheless.

One other possibility is worth considering. He might have become a spy. As well as the public business of warfare, the long tussles with England's continental enemies, and their sometime friends as well, gave plenty of opportunity for clandestine work. Some estimates are that as much as a third of the country's budget for war went on spying and diplomatic activities. A young man like Sir Robert might well have found a role in this field.

So much must be conjecture, but we can be confident that Sir Robert, and his young wife too, came to know the court, and to play a role in it. We can think of them staying in Cobham's Inn, attaching themselves to Lord Cobham's retinue, sleeping in the shadow of the Tower of London, and joining his household knights in the barges that sailed down the river to Westminster, to make their appearance at the king's court.

Although much is known of the events of Richard II's life, he is in many ways an enigma to us today. He was described by his contemporaries as tall, good-looking and intelligent. He was the son of a prince who had been universally admired and respected. He had shown exceptional bravery in confronting the men of London, Kent and Essex during the Peasants' Revolt. He was not dissolute, not cruel (by the standards of his time), not lacking in wits. And yet he was to become so unpopular that he would be driven from his throne. The seeds of that failure lay buried in the early days of his personal rule – and he began to take charge of the country early, when he was still only in his mid-teens – but at the time Joan and her husband first came to court, it was still in the future. Those who paid personal attendance on him might be learning that the King was capricious, headstrong, difficult to deal with, but they surely hoped that he would develop into a great king, such as his grandfather had been judged to be, at least for much of his reign.

Richard was a cultured man, and reasonably well educated, although he never became a great patron of the arts. His wife, Anne of Bohemia, is an even more shadowy figure, not least because she died young, before she had had an opportunity to set much of a mark on her adopted country.

Bohemia is a long way from England. Anne's native language was not only not English, it was not the French that had been widely spoken at court for generations either. No English person could fail to be conscious of her foreignness, and there were some who despised her for it, and resented the retinue of fellow Bohemians who formed a part of the court. Although there have survived no portraits of Anne – or indeed of Richard – that we can be sure are accurate representations of their appearance, there are illustrations that represent the royal couple in a more generic way. Some of these suggest that Anne looked like a typical Saxon woman, fair, with her hair fastened in long plaits.

Each king's court is different, and Richard's was shaped by his youth, his happy marriage, his lack of martial instincts. It was a court where a young couple might hear the best music in the country, listen to the most intelligent men and women, watch masques and entertainments, attend tournaments and displays. At times, this would surely have been the experience of the Hemenhales.

The queen had not conceived a child, and must have agonized over her failure. A woman whose only living child was one who could not be brought to the court, not paraded in pride in front of her neighbours, whose adulthood could not be looked forward to, could surely sympathize with that.

The chancellor was the father of a huge family, including several strong young men. That must have aroused in Joan Hemenhale rather less sympathy.

Stained glass from the church of St Mary Magdalen, Mulbarton, Norfolk

14 The forest of masts and the wooden fort

touz ensemble, ou .vi. des prelatz et seigneurs avantditz au meins; appellez a eux chanceller, tresorer, seneschalle et chamberleyn, et auxint les sergeantz le roy quant il busoignera. Et tendront lour place en la chaumbre de chaumberleyn, pres de la chaumbre depeint.

to act all together, or at least six of the aforesaid prelates and lords; consulting with the chancellor, treasurer, steward and chamberlain, and also the king's serjeants when necessary. And they will hold their session in the chamberlain's room, near the Painted Chamber.

Guidance for the triers of petitions in
the 'Wonderful Parliament' of 1386[1]

Stained glass from Canterbury Cathedral

It would have been about the time when Joan was pregnant with her first child, that unhappy natural, that news came that a fleet had been sighted off the coast of North Norfolk. Polstead Hall was a few miles inland, so perhaps she did not see it, but she must have heard about it. She would have known this was no English fleet. It was a fleet of French ships, good sized for all the English had done to try to hamper its departure (from Sluys, in the Netherlands), sailing to join the Scots and attack England from the north.

If people could read the banners and know this for an enemy fleet, still they had little idea where it was headed, or what would happen next. Fear sprouted in that uncertainty. Men would have polished their swords and restrung their longbows, repaired holes in the boundary walls, strengthened the bolts on the doors that had, many of them, been battered by the rebellious peasants only four years earlier.

If she was at Polsted, Joan and her household might have thought of heading inland to Hempnall, or even down to Chrishall. But before there was time to do much the fleet was gone, sailing on west along the coast. Its wake washed over the coast and rippled inland, though.

It was followed by a muster of troops, so men from Burnham, perhaps under Sir Robert, joined the army that headed north with the king at its head. King Richard was eighteen years old now, so his people must have expected that he would show his mettle as a fighting man, and unite the country behind him. And high time too, they probably muttered. This had never happened in the old king's time. It was the result of a king and council that had not taken the war back to France, but left the French unharried enough to take the initiative, and bring it to them.

The Burnham men came back, and less than triumphant at that. They had not won a battle, although they had not lost one either. There had been little more than some aimless to-ing and fro-ing, hardly worth missing the harvest for. Some damage had been done in northern parts, but there was none in East Anglia.

This expedition had not made them safer. Word came the following year, 1386, that the French were assembling a much bigger fleet. It created a forest of masts, according to the chronicler Jean Froissart. The aim was to bring to England the greatest army that Western Europe had known, with anything up to 30,000 men. The vast supplies that

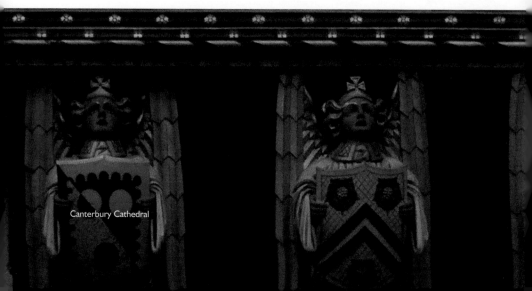

Canterbury Cathedral

were being assembled to support them included a prefabricated wooden fort 3,000 paces long, with walls 20 feet high.[2] With this, the French intended to create a bulwark on the shore, from which they might ride out to ravage the countryside, much as the English had been doing for decades in France.

This was an even more scary prospect. What was more, Sir Robert probably realized, as did his friends, that the king and his council had no viable plan – indeed, no plan at all – to ensure the safety of places like Burnham. They would make efforts to protect London, but that was about all. People on the coasts would have to fend for themselves.

Quite likely he sent his family to London, as hundreds of other men did at the time. So Joan – now pregnant perhaps with her second child – might have headed down to the capital that summer with her mother or mother in law, or both, and joined the crowded household at Cobham's Inn. Possibly she did as Froissart claimed most of the southern English did, and went on a spending spree, looking to enjoy her wealth before the French came and stole everything from her.[3]

A sweaty summer in the city, waiting every day for news of the French invasion, and every day hearing nothing. On 13 September all London households were ordered to lay in three months' food supplies. Cobham's Inn was probably already well provisioned, but this must have provoked a flurry among the servants. The streets would have been crowded, and labourers at work everywhere strengthening shutters and rolling crates and barrels into cellars.

And those with contacts at court, like the Hemenhales, would have known the chaos there was if anything even greater. John of Gaunt, the duke of Lancaster, had sailed to Portugal and Spain, to pursue his attempt to claim the throne of Castile. He had taken a good fighting force with him. No wonder the French were planning on invading, his critics must have been grumbling. And why had the king permitted it? Because his administration was in turmoil, that was why.

That was the administration that had the newly ennobled earl of Suffolk, Joan's relative, at its helm. It was coming under criticism from a party which included Lord Cobham, also Joan's relative. There was a battle brewing here which was in its way as dangerous to families like hers as the French invasion might prove to be.

Perhaps she understood the issues, because they must have been debated round the

table at Cobham's Inn, or perhaps, wrapped up in her pregnancy and her own concerns, she let them pass her by. Finance was at the heart of them, as usual. The English kings of this era invariably had serious financial problems. Their resources were rarely if ever great enough to fund such activity as wars – or at least, they chose to spend them in such a way as to not leave enough money to fund their wars – so at times such as this they had to seek funding from their subjects. There was no continuing agreement on taxation, so every time this occurred the chancellor had to go to parliament and ask it to agree to levy a tax. Parliaments in these days had limited powers, but those powers they did have were closely tied to their ability to refuse a request for taxation, or to make demands in return for granting it.

With the tales of the French forest of masts to back him up, the earl of Suffolk asked that parliament grant a larger tax than had ever been demanded before. It was doubtless true that without the money even London could not have been defended adequately, and the rest of the country certainly would not have been. But Suffolk by this point in his career had acquired plenty of enemies, and this request provided an opportunity for them to attack him. Rather than grant the money, they chose to do so.

To some degree, in attacking Suffolk men were doing what they were far less willing to do directly, and attacking the king himself. It was becoming apparent to men at court that the king was one who took far more interest in what England could give to him, than in what he could give to England. He was proving a disappointment to those who had hoped for greatness, but men must still have hoped that with different guidance, his governance might improve. Why was he not guided by John of Gaunt, or his other uncle the duke of York? Why had he instead elevated a merchant's son to be his chancellor? To those used to a country being governed by men from its long-established noble families, this in itself was a sign of major error.

Most likely Suffolk was not a popular man. Many perhaps thought – and perhaps they were right – that this son of a businessman who had been regarded as ruthless and unscrupulous was little better than his father. And there was resentment too, among men such as Lord Cobham, who felt themselves sidelined from a government in which they would have preferred to play a greater role.

The 'Wonderful Parliament' – as it must have seemed to some, though clearly not to the earl of Suffolk – demanded that Suffolk be dismissed from office, which they made clear would be a prelude to impeaching him – that is, calling him to account for his perceived misdeeds. This was a drastic procedure which had first been used only a few years earlier, and all the more drastic for being invoked in the shadow of the threats from the French. The king resisted vigorously, but Suffolk's opponents persisted, and eventually the king was obliged to dismiss him. The Commons – with many of the Lords supporting them – then went on to draw up a series of charges against him, claiming that

Stained glass from Canterbury Cathedral

he had acquired property while in office far in excess of what he should have received, and that he had failed in his duty to ensure the safety of the country.

Suffolk opposed the charges vigorously, and the Lords agreed that he could not be held guilty for failings of policies that were not determined by him alone. But they did find him guilty of peculation, or the dishonest use of public funds, and he was imprisoned pending his payment of a fine. (It was a large fine, of 20,000 marks, or more than £13,000,[4] which must have done lasting damage to his family's finances.)

Within months Suffolk was free again, and in the company of the king again – and in even less time England was freed of the threat of invasion, since strong winds and heavy rain that autumn prevented the French fleet from setting sail, and as winter drew in, the planned invasion was called off. The message must have trickled through from spies and informers that this abortive venture had all but bankrupted the French king, and he was unlikely to try another invasion for several years.

The same was not true of the threat to Suffolk. Although he was free, his opponents ensured that a new council was appointed, with a brief to reform the government. Lord Cobham was among its members. Suffolk never regained office, and two years later, in what became known as the Merciless Parliament, he was accused with a group of other lords of treason. He was found guilty, but he fled abroad before the sentence was pronounced, and died in exile.

It was a dramatic end to the power of the de la Poles. Now instead of an influential relative, Joan carried the name of a traitor. In the fluctuating politics of the next century the family was to come to prominence again, and the earldom that had been stripped from Michael de la Pole was eventually restored to his son. But no other de la Pole played a major role in the affairs of England until Joan was an old woman.

Meanwhile Lord Cobham had benefited – or had he? Joan must always have been closer to her grandfather than she had ever been to Suffolk, and her grandfather now was in a faction that had more power. But since Suffolk's chief supporter was the king himself, those who had opposed him had also opposed the king, and that was always a dangerous thing to do.

The courteous, pious knight of whom Gower wrote must have given great thought to the line he should take, and how forceful he should be in taking it. He probably sincerely believed that the king and his previous councillors had been misguided. He also had a more personal motive. It must have rankled with him that one of the king's favourites and core counsellors, his former tutor Sir Simon Burley, had been granted extensive lands in Kent, and was grabbing influence in the county, positions for his supporters, that Lord Cobham felt should have remained under his control. Together, these factors had prompted him to support the reformers.

He was not exposed and alone in taking action, he was securely located among the majority of lords who joined the Commons in seeing Suffolk, Burley and other men removed from their positions. (Burley was not as fortunate as Suffolk: he was executed for treason in 1388.) But he must have known there was some risk. King Richard was not a fool, and he had a good memory. He would never forget those who had opted to stand up against his chosen advisers.

Over the next decade the English lords and royalty would be divided, with King Richard fighting to retain authority and power, and the majority of his nobles fighting to keep that power for themselves. And it would steadily become apparent that this was a struggle that could only end with the downfall of one party or the other.

It was perhaps lucky for the Hemenhales that Sir Robert was still a young man, and not in a position that forced him to support one side in the same way. He had no part in the parliaments that saw Suffolk and his faction crash to the ground; he was neither a baron to be summoned in his own right, nor chosen as a knight of the shire. No Gower described his personality, but he must have had a degree of charm and judgement, because in spite of his family's close association with the Cobhams, and his need to keep the regard of his wife's grandfather, he came through this crisis still in possession of the friendship and respect of his king.

Westminster

15 Leading the knights on silver chains

the king had for a long time been of tender age, and had now come to such age, thanks be to God, that he possessed greater knowledge and discretion than ever before: and although he had always had the good will to govern his people in quiet, peace, and tranquillity, right and justice, he now had a greater and better intent and firm purpose to govern his said people and his land well, as best he could.

The bishop of Winchester's opening address to Parliament, January 1390[1]

Stained glass from St Mary's Church,
Mendlesham, Suffolk

Meister des Codex Manesse (Grundstockmaler), early 14th century, via Wikimedia Commons

If there were times of stress, and times of grief, in Joan's life, there must have been times of gaiety and of joy as well. Quite likely one was in 1390, when if she had been remotely capable, she would surely have come to London – as did thousands of others – to watch and participate in the great festivities that the king and queen were putting on.

King Richard was a lover of tournaments, and the one he planned for after Michaelmas (that is, early in October) that year was designed to outdo the stories that had come to England of the great festivities to celebrate the entry of Queen Isabella of France into Paris shortly before.[2] The details were publicized not just across England, but all across Europe, and the preparations must have taken many months. Every knight in England would have pressed to take part, and a great many of them did, so it is probable that Sir Robert played a role.

Among the foreign nobles who responded to the call for challengers to the knights of England was the count of Ostrevant, son of the count of Hainault in the Low Countries. He came with a large retinue, and travelled with them via Canterbury (where he spent a full day, and made offerings at the shrine of Thomas Becket) to Rochester, which was firmly in Lord Cobham's sphere of influence. Lord Cobham and another wealthy knight, Sir Robert Knolles, were building a stone bridge across the Medway at Rochester, to replace an old ruined Roman bridge. It was not finished until a year later, but construction had been going on for three years when the count d'Ostrevant and his party arrived in the town, so perhaps they were among the first to cross it. If not, they could at least have admired the works from the ferry that took them across the broad river.

Maybe Lord Cobham was there in person to greet these illustrious guests, and perhaps his granddaughter and her husband were also among the party who made their slow way on to London. They stopped again at Dartford, then came to the city, where they lodged overnight. Lord Cobham's party would of course have stayed at Cobham's Inn, which could not have been more convenient for the next morning, when the procession that would inaugurate the festivities set off from the Tower of London.

So we can hope that Joan was among the sixty rich and well-born ladies who came to the Tower that morning in their finest gowns. (If she was not, the tales of the tournament spread all across England, and have echoed down across the centuries, so she heard tell of whatever she did not see for herself.) It would have taken some time to line up the procession: first the trumpeters and other musicians, then sixty great coursers, warhorses strong enough to support a knight in full armour. The knights did not mount yet: a finely dressed esquire mounted each horse. Then the ladies mounted – sidesaddle – their palfreys, lighter horses, the kind they normally rode, and each one was equipped with a silver chain. Out came the sixty knights in full armour, each wearing a surcoat that showed his coat of arms (so that the audience could identify him during the melee), and the emblem the king had newly decided to adopt as his own, a white hart with a gold crown around its neck. The horses too carried this emblem on their trappings.

There must have been much laughter and joking as the ladies claimed one knight each – not their husband, naturally, they would choose some other man for the honour – and the knights submitted to being fastened to their chains. Then the procession set off, at a slow walking pace, to Smithfield, the great open space on the outskirts of the city, with the ladies riding and the knights walking alongside them. All the way through the streets of the city, the people lined up to watch the great sight and cheer the knights on their way.

The king and queen were already at Smithfield, settled in their 'chambers' – more than a bench, comfortable accommodation must have been arranged for these grand spectators – and when the procession arrived there, the ladies were helped to dismount by their servants, liberated their temporary captives, and went to join the royal party in the stands. The esquires dismounted too, and each went to help his knight fasten on his helmet and mount his courser.

Smithfield must have been thick with the crowds that had followed the procession in – and those who had settled in the day before, to be sure of a good place – and among them would have been entertainers, sellers of drink and food, pickpockets, preachers, rich merchants and poor beggars. Most of London would have been there, to watch the

Stained glass from Canterbury Cathedral

equally impressive arrival of the count d'Ostrevant and all the foreign knights he had assembled.

It must have been mid-afternoon by then, since they had not set off until three o'clock, but the tilting continued till it was too dark for more. These were probably individual bouts, with two chosen knights riding at each other, lances held horizontal before them, from opposite ends of the long lists. As the knights prepared for each charge there would have been plenty of time for giggling and gossip, for glancing over at the king and queen. Then when it was growing dark, torches must have been lit to take people to where they had arranged to dine.

Perhaps Joan and Sir Robert – and her grandparents – were among those lucky enough to receive an invitation to the bishop of London's residence, where the king and queen were staying, and where a great banquet was being held.[3] They might have been there to watch the entry of the count d'Ostrevant, changed into his court clothes, and to see the king graciously present the prize for the best of the challengers to one of his supporters, the count of St Pol. The prize for the English went to the earl of Huntingdon. There was music; there was dancing before supper, and afterwards too, and a great meal, doubtless punctuated with many toasts, before those not staying at the palace were collected by their servants and taken back home.

This was not all. The next day the squires and servants were busy readying the armour and horses of every man who had not been favoured with a slot in the individual bouts, since this was the day for a general melee to which all the knights were invited. If he had not taken part as one of the chosen sixty the previous day, Sir Robert Hemenhale would certainly have found an opportunity to show off his prowess that day. The fighting was lusty, according to the chronicler Froissart. Quite a few men were unhorsed, and many more lost their helmets.

Another great feast, another presentation of prizes – this time the foreigners' prize went to the count d'Ostrevant, a diplomatic choice if ever there was one – and in the morning yet another tournament, for the squires. The dancing that night lasted till daybreak. Then there was still another day's jousting, for any and all who chose to take part – and even if they were weary of watching the charges and clashes by then, the lords and ladies of the court all turned out again with the king and queen.

On the Thursday the ladies (both foreign and English) went to dine with the queen, while the knights dined separately with the king. The next day it was the turn of the duke of Lancaster; and after that, the king and his courtiers and their foreign guests all headed off for Windsor, the great royal castle a day's journey away. Here there was more feasting, more prizes and honours – including the order of the Garter for the count d'Ostrevant – and handsome presents were handed out all round before the exhausted visitors made their way home.

Perhaps Sir Robert and Lady Hemenhale had opted out before this grand finale. The common people of London certainly had: a day, or two for those who could afford it, of time off work to watch the knights and listen to the minstrels, then it was back to their usual grind. Fighting in the lists was not for them, it was only for those with the money to buy armour, horses and trappings, the leisure to practise the moves of the joust, the clout to claim a place from the heralds. But it must have been exhilarating for those rich participants.

16 Of fraud, collusion and an abbey

'Noon oother lyf,' seyde he, 'is worth a bene!
For wedlok is so esy and so clene,
That in this world it is paradys.'
Thus seyde this olde knyght, that was so wise.

…

For who can be so buxom as a wyf?
Who is so trewe, and eek so ententyf
To kepe hym, syk and hool, as is his make?
For wele or wo she wole hym nat forsake;
She nys nat wery hym to love and serve,
Thogh that he lye bedrede, til he sterve.
Geoffrey Chaucer, The merchant's

Effigy possibly of Joan's grandmother from Chrishall Church

tale[1]

Opinion varies among historians over whether Richard II can be regarded as a great patron of literature, but it is certainly true that during his reign, English literature thrived. And the greatest of those who caused it to do so was Geoffrey Chaucer, brother-in-law to John of Gaunt (they had married sisters), and sometime servant to the king himself. Joan and her husband must have known him.

Chaucer was a clever and subtle writer, and when he put in the mouth of an old knight who was thinking of marrying this airy acclamation of the state of wedlock, he was firmly tongue in cheek, as the rest of the merchant's tale makes clear. In the real world marriage rarely represents a state of bliss, and sometimes it degenerates into a state of war.

How was it for Joan and Sir Robert Hemenhale? There are only a few faint clues to tell us, and only a few pieces of evidence of the events that shaped their marriage from the inside.

Joan's mother died probably in 1388. For a woman with a bare handful of close relations, this must have been a serious blow. Her mother was not old: she was only in her mid-thirties or so. There is no record of the cause of her death, so perhaps it was the plague or another infection. The elder Joan had not remarried after Joan's father's death, so her daughter inherited Chrishall and her other estates, and also became the direct heir to her grandfather. Perhaps her grandparents were able to comfort her at this difficult time: she seems to have been close to them later in their lives, and this closeness might well have been strengthened during the mourning period.

Did her husband offer her sympathy and support? Did his mother, brother, sister? We can only guess. But we do know some of what he did in the year or so following Lady Joan's death – and in particular, about a series of land transactions.

The meaning of the transactions that are noted in surviving legal records is not always easy to comprehend. Francis Blomefield, the great early Norfolk historian, reported that 'In 1389, Sir Robert Hemenhale, Knt. of Hemenhale (where this family always resided) released to Sir George Felbrigge, Knt. and other trustees, his manors in Hemenhale and Pulham in Norfolk, Cotton and Wickham Skeyth, Boleshall and Yaxley in Suffolk, and all the possessions of his father Sir Ralf.'[2] This was done by means of a deed called a 'quitclaim with warranty', which was a method of ensuring that no hidden claims would later affect a land transaction. According to a legal inquisition that was held after Sir Robert's death, 'The enfeoffment was made on condition that they enfeoffed William his son and heir when he reached full age, as clearly appears in Robert's will; so by fraud and collusion excluding and barring the king from the wardship and marriage of his heir.'[3]

Sir Robert was still a young man, but he was obviously taking steps already to try to ensure that if he were to die, his family would not be affected by wardship proceedings. He did not want his estates to suffer the blow of another minority, in which an outsider would cream off all the profit and more. Even if young William was never going to be capable of running the estates without help, he wanted to ensure that his family as a whole would maintain control.

Doubtless he did not think of what he was planning as 'fraud and collusion': those are strong words, and the arrangements he was making were probably little if any different from those made by many other men. But he must have known that they were plans that would attract some disapproval if they became widely known; and they were also plans that would have involved legal (and perhaps other) expenses. He surely would not have taken these steps unless he felt it was really necessary.

Did he anticipate that he would die young? Was he in poor health? Or perhaps more likely, was he planning to embark on some hazardous venture from which he knew he might not return?

Perhaps these legal transactions were connected in some way with another set of transactions which followed. In 1390 the Hemenhales sold the greatest of the Peverell family estates. Joan and her husband 'levied a fine' of the manors of Castle Ashby and Chadstone in Northamptonshire, and Chesterton in Huntingdonshire – that is, they carried out a formal sale transaction – to members of the Braybrooke family.[4] They obtained for them the very sizeable sum of £2,000.[5]

Why did they do it? For the money, presumably. The estates cannot have been improved by the long years of Joan's minority, and they perhaps did not have the funds to do the work necessary to get them back into good order, or had decided that those funds they did have should be spent on the Norfolk and Suffolk lands. Also, Joan had probably never lived at Castle Ashby, and it was a good long way from Hemenhale's homes in Norfolk, or indeed the rest of his family's possessions across East Anglia. But this was the jewel among the lands that Joan had so far inherited, a great manor that had been the home of her ancestors. Did she mind that it had been lost to her and her descendants? Subsequent events were to suggest that she did.

If Sir Robert had been making all these legal preparations to ensure that his affairs were in good order should the worst happen, he was right to do so. He died in September 1391, when he was about 28 years old. Whether his death followed an illness or an act of violence, we cannot know. But there must have been something remarkable about the circumstances of his death, because following it, the king overruled Sir Robert's own request that he should be buried in the choir of the Carmelite friary at Burnham Norton, and instead ruled that he should be interred in Westminster Abbey.

This was – as indeed it still is – a rare honour, which lays the deceased alongside generations of kings and queens of England, and it is still more rare for it to be conferred on someone sufficiently obscure that it is not known why he deserved it. Sir Robert was no great magate, no famous soldier, not known to history as a friend of the king's so close as to attract attention or scandal. He must have done something extraordinary to justify it, and frustratingly, we cannot know what.

So this knight who had meant to be laid to rest under the broad North Norfolk sky had his body taken instead to the great royal abbey at the centre of Westminster. Would he have been glad, had he known of the honour? Perhaps, but perhaps not. Was his widow glad? That too seems doubtful. There is something slightly bleak about so great an honour, one that takes a man's bones from those of his ancestors, and from those of his successors too, since Westminster Abbey would never have become the traditional resting place of the Hemenhales. There must have been a cold edge, too, to carrying out all the long mourning ceremonies – the masses held daily, then weekly, then monthly, going on ahead as far as could be imagined – not in the familiar surroundings of Burnham Norton church, but under the unforgiving vault of the vast abbey.

It would have fallen largely to Joan to organize a grand funeral for him, with perhaps some help from his brother and her elderly grandfather. Even country funerals were often

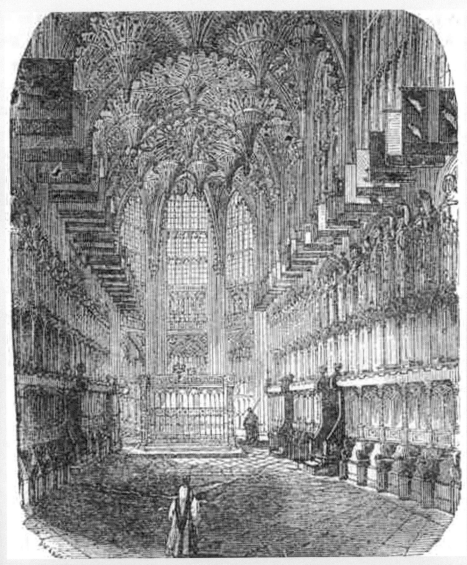

The chapel of Edward the Confessor, Westminster Abbey, from *Collins Guide to London* (1911), via Wiimedia Commons

grand occasions in her day, and for Westminster Abbey, a major effort had to be made. She perhaps went to stay at Cobham's Inn for the week or two that would have passed between Sir Robert's death and the ceremony, and supervised the staff who ensured that all those necessary – their tenants, their staff, their friends and colleagues – were brought from across East Anglia and beyond. This might well have involved paying some of them to attend – it was quite normal to make a donation to priests and nuns who came to funerals, which amounted in effect to payment – and providing mourning garments for them, as well as organizing their travel.

We do not know where Sir Robert died, but if it was not in London, arrangements would have had to be made to bring his body there, and for a funeral procession to travel perhaps by barge from Cobham's Inn to Westminster. The family's London friends would have joined with those who came from out of town. The abbey church is a very large one, so it would not have done to provide a tiny congregation for the funeral mass.

Although the abbey church remains – as do some of the other buildings – Westminster has not been an abbey, home to a community of monks, since the Reformation. But in the fourteenth century it was a Benedictine monastery, and the black-clad monks would have met the funeral party, and handled the arrangements at the abbey. The king himself might well not have attended, but surely some representatives of his court would have done so.

Sir Robert was laid to rest in St John the Evangelist's chapel, one of the nine chapels that curve around the east end of the church, and perhaps his bones still remain there,

although any monument to him was long ago lost. But Joan would have arranged for one to be erected, no doubt; whatever her feelings about her dead husband, it would have been unthinkable not to.

Nor was it done with when the guests dispersed after the funeral meats had been consumed. Although there would be no burial at Burnham, there needed to be some form of commemoration there – perhaps a physical memorial, certainly arrangements for masses to be said. Masses might have been said too at Hempnall and other of the Hemenhale estates, and perhaps by the college of priests that Lord Cobham had established in Kent.

And then there was the will to be proved, and the complex negotiations with the men to whom Sir Robert had entrusted his estates, and with the royal officials who would deal with the wardship of young William. (His wardship would not go to his mother, just as hers had not gone to her own mother: someone else would be granted, or buy, that privilege.) Some of the negotiations and petitions would have continued for years.

So this was a time not just of mourning, but of stress, expense, heavy demands on Joan in every sense. And it was a time of uncertainty too. One phase of her life was over forever. For better or worse, their sadly deficient son William was now the heir to Sir Robert's lands, and her task was to protect him, and find a way to see his responsibilities fulfilled. She and those close to her must have given much thought to how best to achieve that.

St Mary's Church, Radwinter, Essex

17 One sparrowhawk or two shillings

At the north west boundary of this parish [of Cobham], adjoining [the antient Roman road, or Watling-street-way] is a water, called St. Thomas's-well, probably from the use made of it by St. Thomas Becket in his journeyings through these parts.

Our HERBALISTS have taken notice of the following scarce plants, growing in this parish, viz.

Pneumonanthe, *Calathian violet.*

Trachelium majus, *blue and also white Canterbury bells, found under Cobham park pales, in the road from Shinglewell to Rochester.*

Chamæpitys, *ground pine of several sorts.*

Tragoriganum, *goats marjorom, or organy, near Cobham house.*

Lamium luteum etiam rubrum, *the yellow archangel, as also the red, found in Cobham woods.*

Lautana five viburnum, *the wayfaring tree.* (fn. 1)

Narcissus sylvestris pallidus calyce luteo, *the wild English daffodil …*

From an 18th-century account of the parish of Cobham[1]

Ickworth, Suffolk

Amass for Sir Robert Hemenhale on the third day after his funeral; and another on the seventh day; and another on the thirtieth day. And more masses, and more: hundreds of masses, most likely, recited in a gabble by the poorly paid clerics at Westminster Abbey, at Burnham Norton church, at the friary by the Carmelite monks, and perhaps at the chantry at Cobham too. And for some of them, at least, Lady Joan would have been present, on her knees, praying for her dead husband, and thinking about her own future.

She was still no more than twenty-one. And she had seen the deaths of her parents, her brother, the whole-minded one of her sons, and now her husband. The only people left close to her now – except perhaps a kind servant or two – were her Cobham grandparents and her ironically surviving idiot son.

She needed not just to care for young William, but to prepare for what would happen if he were to die. Perhaps she thought that likely: even today, those with mental disabilities rarely live as long as those with their full faculties. Sir Robert might have favoured his own estates over those his wife had brought to their partnership, but Joan had every reason to do the reverse, because if young William were to die, those estates would not go to her, except for her dower estate, the one to which she had been granted title on her marriage, and any unentailed lands that her husband had willed to her. The core estates, Hempnall and the rest, would go to Robert's heirs by entail. At that time this was his brother John, and should John die without the children he had not yet had, then the lands would go to a cousin.

However the evidence suggests that Burnham Norton especially meant much to Joan, not surprisingly since it had been her main home for ten years or more. It had most likely been young William's home too, and perhaps it was as much for his sake as for her own that Joan continued to spend some of her time there. She must also have spent time in Essex: her dower estate from Sir Robert was at Radwinter, only fifteen miles from Chrishall, so this was a major centre of her possessions. But perhaps most of all, she spent the months after the death of her husband in the company of her grandfather and grandmother, in London or in Kent.[2]

The Cobhams were not in extreme old age, but they were definitely elderly. They had married in 1332 or 1333, and if they were both born around 1320, which seems likely, they would have been seventy or so when their granddaughter was widowed. Although Lord Cobham had had an impressive career, in the king's council as well as in Kent, he

Stained glass on both pages from Canterbury Cathedral

must at this time have been drawing back from his public and political activities. The council that had deposed the earl of Suffolk and others of the king's favourites a few years earlier had now ceded power back to the king, who was undeniably of age now, no longer in need of any regency arrangements, and determined to regain his ascendancy. It seems clear that there were underlying problems that had not been resolved in the relationship between the king and his nobles, but effectively there was a truce between the two parties – uneasy, but definitely a truce – and it was no longer as necessary for men such as Lord Cobham to spend much of their time in London. And quite likely, after having taken the uncharacteristically bold step of joining publicly in the attempt to force a change of government, Lord Cobham was now keen to step back from the glare of the harsh sunlight it had thrown on him, and retreat into the shadows.

The family's ancestral home was the village of Cobham, and it was in Cobham church that Joan could find what she had never known in East Anglia, or indeed in Northamptonshire: commemoration of generations of her ancestors. Their heritage was very important to the Cobhams, as it is to most long-established families, and they could trace not only the Cobham line back in time, but the lines of Joan's grandmother, linked to the Courtenay earls of Devon, and her great-grandmother, Joan Beauchamp, descended from kings. Perhaps at this difficult time in her life she was to find a new stability from the sense of rootedness that Cobham gave her. It is certainly true that she took Cobham to her heart: she was to live in this area for much of the rest of her life, and it was in this church, among her ancestors, that she in turn chose to be buried.

Cobham was a quiet village a few miles inland from the North Kent coast, set on another of the great Roman roads that criss-crossed England, Watling Street. It was described in the eighteenth century as having 'a healthy and rather a pleasant situation, though the woods and foliage in Cobham Park give it in general a gloomy appearance'.[3] (There is a great house in Cobham Park today, but this was probably not the site of the house that the Cobham family owned in Joan's time.) This is undulating countryside, more hilly than Essex, though far from mountainous, and like Chrishall, Cobham lies on a ridge, with wide views across open countryside from its church.

Little is known about the medieval manor that the Cobhams lived in, but when John de Cobham died in March 1300 it was described as 'a messuage with garden worth 6s 8d per annum'. There were a hefty 585 acres of demesne lands, and eighty-five free tenants leased portions of the manor, which they paid for in cash, eggs and poultry. The estate included woodland, good and less good arable land, a fine garden and salt meadows.[4] The lord of the manor paid to the king for the freehold of this substantial estate a yearly fee of one sparrowhawk or two shillings. And for this sum, he must have possessed pretty much all the land that he could see in every direction.

The Cobhams were not just rich and well

established. Joan could also find in Cobham, to a much greater extent than she had known in East Anglia, the evidence of how an affluent and devout man might spend his gains to the benefit of his neighbours and his country. Next to Cobham church was the college and chantry that Lord Cobham had founded thirty years or so earlier. There was a quadrangle of buildings (which largely survive today, although they have been much repaired and renewed over the centuries) set around an open courtyard, and linked by covered passages to the church where the priests would sing the masses, for both the living Cobham family and their dead ancestors – and all other Christian souls – that were the main purpose of their existence.[5] Originally the chantry had five priests, of whom one was the master of the school that formed a part of the complex. In 1391 William Tanner had held that post for almost thirty years.

Five years or so earlier Lord Cobham had added provision for some lay servants, and he had taken care to endow the college with enough funds out of his own estates to ensure that it not only ran smoothly, but could handle any emergencies.[6] So there must have been an air of quiet affluence, or even of opulence, about the church and estate in these relatively peaceful times.

More recently Joan's grandfather had been involved in building the great stone bridge at Rochester and a chapel to go alongside it, and he had taken a hand too in strengthening the fortifications of the county town, Canterbury. But his main focus over the previous decade had been at Cooling (then sometimes also called Cowling), about five miles from Cobham. Cooling must by the time Joan came to stay have been the Cobhams' main residence, although they doubtless continued to come to Cobham church and hear those masses that were said by the priests, and it was Cobham church that remained the family burial place.

Cooling was very different. While Cobham was firmly set inland, Cooling was on the Hoo peninsula, the promontory that stuck out to the east of Cobham, between two great estuaries: the Thames to its north-west, and the Medway to the south-east. A line of clay and sand hills runs down the centre of the peninsula, but even today much of the rest of the land is damp and marshy, and in Joan's time it was much more so. Perhaps the marshes and mudflats around Cooling reminded Joan

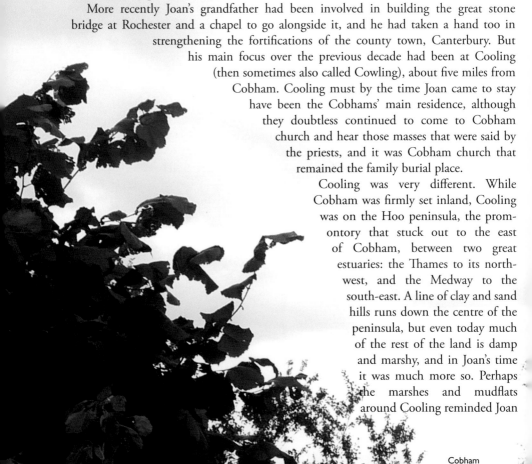

Cobham

of her home at Burnham Norton. Both are remote, open, bleakly beautiful in sunlight, and rather forbidding in stormy weather. (It was around Cooling that Charles Dickens was to set the scary opening scenes of *Great Expectations*, and the churchyard that features, where Pip first met the convict Magwich, is recognizably that of Cooling church, where the children's graves that Dickens mentions are still to be seen.)

The family had owned land at Cooling, and probably had a house there, for almost 200 years. But it was Lord Cobham's choice in his old age to turn this into his main residence, in spite of its inaccessibility. Not least because the site was a vulnerable one, subject to attack by the French or any other invaders, it had strategic importance, and in 1381 he obtained permission to crenellate it: to turn the manor house into a castle.

Huge amounts of work had gone into the buildings at Cooling in the decade before Joan came to stay there, and by then the work was largely finished. The castle was built around two islands – a more accurate description, at least in those times, than moated enclosures, although the water around them had the function of a moat. There was a navigable route to the Thames, which was about two miles away, so the castle could be supplied by sea, which was more practicable, most likely, than travelling to it overland. The twelfth-century manor house that had long stood on the western island – probably on land built up from the flat marshes round it – was now surrounded by a quadrangle of curtain wall, built of Kentish cob and rough flint, with towers at each corner. A gatehouse led to a drawbridge across the moat and to the eastern island – also fortified with a wall around its circumference – and the main gatehouse, which still survives intact (although the rest of the castle is a ruin today). Although the land around Cooling is very flat, banks and ditches were built up as part of the outer defences, so in those days, when there would have been fewer trees and much less habitation on this marshy land, it would have been a striking sight, visible for miles.

Lord Cobham was evidently proud that as well as providing a secure home for his family, the castle contributed to the defences of the country, and he had that fact memorialized in the plaque that was affixed to the castle gatehouse: 'Knouwyth that beth and schul be/ That I am mad in help of the cuntre/ In knowyng of whyche thyng/ Thys is chartre and wytnessyng.' [7]

Closed up in the castle, in its ring of marshes, with her elderly grandparents for company: it must have provided a kind of solace for Joan in the months after Sir Robert's death, but she probably knew from the start that this life could not continue, and that soon she would need to emerge and find a more dynamic way forward for herself.

18 The merlin, the trap

Quant je fus prins au pavillon
De ma dame, tresgente et belle,
Je me brulais a la chandelle,
Ainsi que fait le papillon.

Je rougiz comme vermillon
Aussi flambant q'une estincelle
Quant je fus prins au pavillon.

Si j'eusse esté esmerillon
Ou que j'eusse eu aussi bonne aille,
Je me feusse gardé de celle
Qui me bailla de l'aiguillon
Quant je fus prins au pavillon.
  Charles d'Orleans, 1394–1465

A very loose translation:

When as a bird is I was caught
Trapped by my lady, sweet and kind,
A candle burned me soul and mind.
No moth could greater pain have sought.

I turned bright red and flared to nought,
A spark that blazed and then declined
When as a bird is I was caught.

A merlin soars upon its wing,
If only I'd had one, I sing.
I'd have sailed beyond her salty sting
And never, never let her cling
When as a bird is I was caught.[1]

She found that way swiftly – alarmingly swiftly, by any standards. Sir Robert Hemenhale died in September 1391. By February 1392 his widow had married Sir Reginald Braybrooke.

That does not speak of devastating grief. Nor does it suggest that her grandparents had decided she must remarry, and found a suitable husband for her: if they had done that, surely they would have done it more slowly. Many people might have thought, once Joan had been a widow for a while, that it would be wise for a woman in her position to marry again. But no one is likely to have hustled her into marrying while the incense burned at Sir Robert's funeral still stained the air of Westminster Abbey, and the long legal business of sorting out his affairs had barely been started. It must have been something she chose for herself.

Did she cause a scandal by doing it? There is no indication that she did, although that does not mean she did not. Dry legal documents, which are all that we have to outline Joan's life, tend to be silent on such issues. But it seems clear that her grandparents were not against the match, that it caused no rift with them, and that they remained on good terms with Joan, and welcomed her new husband to the family. Indeed, in order to marry again, even though she was of age, she would have had to look not only for her family's approval but for the king's approval. The king was in a very real sense her overlord, and had the right to ensure that her estates would fall into the hands of a man who would serve his king and country well. She could be (and some women in a similar position were) fined heavily if she remarried without the king's consent.

That she got this approval was not because Joan had made a stunningly impressive new marriage, to a great noble or a rich merchant, because she had not done anything of the kind. Sir Reginald was a second son of a respectable landowning family, but he was not the heir to a fortune. Indeed, he seems not to have been the heir to very much at all. So it was probably because the Cobhams liked Sir Reginald, and thought he would make their granddaughter a good husband, and the king also liked him. He seems to have been the kind of younger son whom people feel deserves a good inheritance and a significant position in life; the sort of man whose friends say that they really ought to find him not just a pretty and likeable, but also a rich wife.

Obviously Joan liked Sir Reginald too – or even, was madly in love with Sir Reginald. Perhaps she had become deeply unhappy with Hemenhale, and her joy now was something her grandparents too found irresistible. Perhaps, even, she was pregnant, and everyone who knew her secret thought it would be as well if the couple got married as soon as they decently could, so that the dates could be fudged in the time-honoured way. People might have muttered and gossiped, but when it was a case of a young couple in love, and a rich and likeable young couple at that, one who might grow to have considerable influence in time, it would have suited most people to shrug and smile, and wish them well.

Perhaps she had been quietly involved with Sir Reginald for some time. We can think, if fancifully, of Sir Reginald in his armour and his surcoat at the great tournament in 1390, and Joan on her palfrey, caparisoned with the swans looped in their crowns, tossing him to him her silver chain. We can think of them

Stained glass from St Mary Magdalene's Church, Mulbarton, Norfolk

glancing at each other over the tables of the great feasts at the bishop of London's palace – he would have been there, he was the bishop's nephew – and bowing to each other in the courtly dances that followed. Maybe passion had overcome them then, and Sir Robert's death gave her an opportunity to regularize her situation. The church might frown on adultery, but that did not mean it did not happen. Even priests broke their vows; married women certainly did from time to time.

Indeed, if there was not some reason such as this, it is hard to understand why Joan should have remarried so shockingly fast. There was no obvious practical reason for her to do so. True, she had to ensure that her – and her son's – estates were properly managed, but there were plenty of ways to do that which did not involve acquiring a new husband. The lands could be leased out, or if she chose to farm them directly, she would have – must already have – had retainers and agents in place to do the day-to-day work: keeping the accounts, demanding that villeins fulfil their labouring duties, selling the crops and so on. And she had her grandfather to guide and advise her, and the surviving Hemenhales as well.

These were not times of war or crisis, when any woman might be forgiven for grabbing the first man who came her way for protection. If she stepped from her mourning within the walls of Cooling Castle and back out into the world with such speed, it must have been because she wanted to.

As well as the likelihood that the pair had met at some of the feasts and celebrations at the king's court, we know at least one reason for her to have had dealings with Sir Reginald. It was his family that had bought from her and her husband Castle Ashby and other estates in Northamptonshire and Huntingdonshire. Sir Reginald was not the Braybrookes' heir, and his father was still alive, but perhaps he had acted as liaison in the negotiations.

Who was this man who rode so forcefully into Joan's life? He came from a Bedfordshire family, which was the junior branch of a family that came originally from Northamptonshire.[2] So this was a marriage that drew Joan away from East Anglia, and back towards the centre of England. The Bedfordshire Braybrookes were clearly comfortably off, owning a good spread of land across Bedfordshire and Buckinghamshire, as well as having sufficient cash resources – indeed, very substantial cash resources – to buy the estates they had acquired from Joan and Sir Robert Hemenhale. They were not aristocrats, although their head was probably rich enough to live up to the status of baron if he had chosen to seek a title.

Sir Reginald's uncle, Robert Braybrooke, the bishop of London at whose palace the king and queen had held their feasts, was an influential churchman and courtier who had briefly been chancellor of England (just before the earl of Suffolk took the post) and also acted as chancellor of Ireland. Sir Reginald had begun his career as marshal of his uncle's household, and it was probably his uncle's connections that had helped him to move from there to a place in the king's household. The Braybrookes were also distantly related to Princess Joan, King Richard's mother, and he would have found this link extremely useful too. Starting as an esquire, he had readily found favour, and by the time of his marriage he had become a king's knight. In other words, he had a salaried position in the royal household, of which he was a full-time member. His duties probably included providing an escort to the king on his travels, and ensuring the king's security both at Westminster and elsewhere. And when the king had need of an army, he was of course expected to take a command in it.

So he was not a member of the king's council, or powerful in a political sense, but he was well connected, usefully positioned, and if not rich, at least solvent. In this course of his rise to favour he had acquired two manors, taking advantage of the confiscation of lands that occurred during the Merciless Parliament that had removed the earl of Suffolk and his associates, so at the time of his marriage he held Little Holwell in Bedfordshire and Banstead in Surrey. (Neither seems to have been a major property: Banstead, which he sold on his marriage, was worth 40 marks a year, but these gave him a sufficient income to live up to his position.) He had also been appointed the keeper of Salcey Forest in Northamptonshire, a role he passed on to his elder brother Sir Gerard on his marriage. And he left the king's household at the same time: so if Joan had wanted a husband who would devote himself to stewarding her own estates, she found what she needed in Sir Reginald, who did just that.

The Braybrooke family

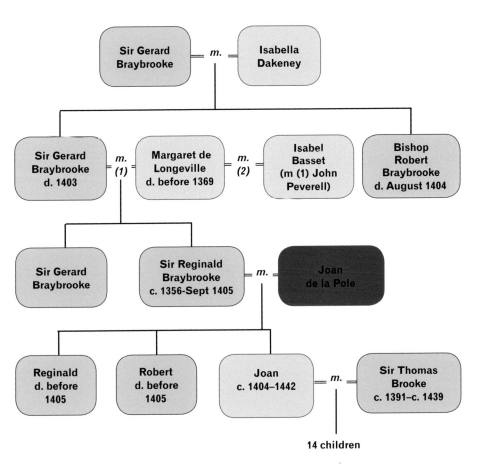

Sir Reginald was quite a bit older than his new wife: there were perhaps fourteen years between them, so Joan was about twenty-two when they married, and her husband in his mid-thirties. And all of this speaks of a man who was well liked, sociable, socially skilled, and from a family of similar men and women, one that anyone might comfortably enjoy becoming a member of. In short, he was in the mould of a promising husband, one with whom Joan would be happy, and under whose guidance her inheritance would be kept secure and built upon.

As far as we can judge (on admittedly thin evidence) this proved to be the case. Sir Reginald seems to have been the husband of Joan's who was closest to her heart. He fitted well into her life, and into her family. When she died, and her epitaph was drawn up, it ignored her other four husbands and set her down as the widow of Sir Reginald. True, the only child of Joan's who survived her was by this marriage (and might have had a hand in composing that epitaph), but even so, this speaks of the marriage that was at the centre of her life. It was also probably the longest of her marriages, though not by a great deal: it lasted no more than thirteen years.

Although it might seem more than a coincidence that the family of Joan's new husband had acquired some of Joan's own estates, the evidence suggests it was just that. The Braybrookes had a family interest of sorts in the Peverell estates, because Sir Reginald's father, Sir Gerald, had married – as his second wife, Sir Reginald's stepmother – Isabel Basset, who had been the wife of John Peverell, the brother of Joan's Peverell grandmother, and the owner in the last years of his life of Castle Ashby and the rest of the great Peverell inheritance. This lady, who had probably started life as the illegitimate daughter of a minor lord, had an eventful life, even a rackety one: after Peverell's death she had married at least four more times before ending up with Sir Gerald. Richard Bradestone, Robert Rigge, Sir Thomas Shirley and Sir John Woodhill: she got through them all in a scant eighteen years. Any man who becomes a woman's husband number six or seven (unless she is so astonishingly rich that he cannot fail to gain by doing so) has to be admired for his bravery. But Sir Gerald seems to have made a choice that worked out well for them both. That he had taken the trouble to gain back her first husband's lands suggests he was still motivated to please her when the opportunity came up, about twenty years after their wedding. Lady Isabel lived long enough for Joan to meet her, but she died in 1493. Her husband did not marry again.

Another fact also confirms that the estates were not acquired with any expectation that at some time Joan would join the family and effectively get them back. Chesterton, the Huntingdonshire estate, was settled on Sir Reginald's sister (who was, of course, called Joan) shortly after the Braybrookes acquired it. And Castle Ashby and the other Northamptonshire estate, Chadstone, were not settled on Sir Reginald when he married, although he was given the reversion of them. So his stepmother was able to enjoy her first husband's old house during her lifetime, and the young couple only received it well after her death, when her husband too died in 1403.

19 Laughing, jangling, weeping

the assembly should be made in a fair mead, well green, with fair trees … all about
… and a clear well or some running brook alongside. All the officers that come from
home should bring thither all that they need, everyone in his office well and plente-
ously, and should lay the towels and boardcloths all about on the green grass, and set
divers meats on a great platter … and some should eat sitting and some standing,
some leaning on their elbows; some should drink, some laugh, some jangle ….

Edward duke of York, *The Master of Game* (c. 1406–13)[1]

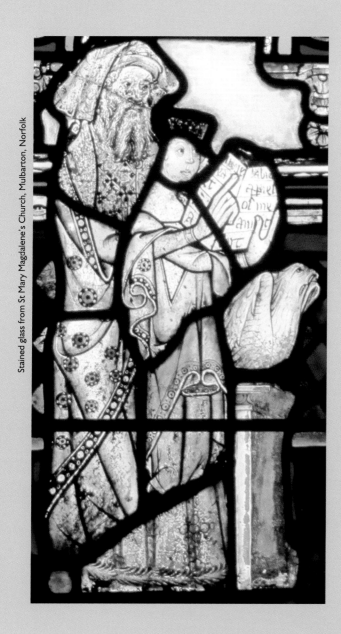

Stained glass from St Mary Magdalene's Church, Mulbarton, Norfolk

After his marriage, the only estate Sir Reginald Braybrooke owned on his own account (rather than his wife's) was Little Holwell, and that was one he held only by lease. His family have left no mark at Little Holwell, and it was almost certainly on Joan's estates that they lived.

Joan seems to have kept control of Polstead Hall, although many of the Hemenhale estates that had passed to her son were probably controlled by the Crown while he was a minor, after those legal arrangements that Sir Robert had made so carefully were unveiled and doubtless unpicked. And probably the Braybrookes spent some of their time in Burnham Norton, which seems to have remained as young William Hemenhale's home. They most likely spent much time too at Chrishall, and perhaps at Joan's nearby estate of Radwinter. They must have travelled to Bedfordshire and Northamptonshire to visit Sir Reginald's family there, and to check on those properties that Joan still controlled in that area, and perhaps also to stay at Castle Ashby, which was a family house, though not yet theirs. And they would have travelled to Kent to visit Joan's grandparents.

Whether she was pregnant on her marriage or not, Joan's priority was to produce an heir. She must have been delighted when she gave birth to sons: two of them, whom they called Reginald after his father, and Robert – perhaps not after her first husband, but after the bishop of London. Perhaps she conceived other children too, because she was to claim at her death that she had been a mother of ten. There is no reason to think she exaggerated, but it is not clear which of her husbands was the father of some of these children. Whenever she bore them, they were sadly to die very young.

And more sadly, neither Reginald nor Robert grew to adulthood. By 1405 at the latest they were both dead. This must have been a source of much grief to their parents. But these were times when such deaths were common, and when it was expected that mothers and fathers would cope with their sorrow. They might – they surely did – say masses, light candles, pray at the graves of their lost children. But to be flattened by such a loss was not only not expected, it would not have been tolerated in their society.

Sir Reginald was no longer a member of the king's household, but he still had close connections at court, and there was every reason for him to maintain them, and use them to help his wife resolve all the legal issues that had been thrown up by Sir Robert Hemenhale's death.

For most of the rest of the time, during the first years of their marriage, there was little need for a man at arms to provide active service, because there was little fighting taking place. This led to a superfluity of unemployed men at arms, which caused plenty of social problems, but it also meant not only that Sir Reginald was free to help his wife sort out her affairs, but that the king's court was crowded and busy, and plenty of men and women were to be met there. So the Braybrookes would have travelled to London and Westminster as well as moving around their own estates.

The couple probably stayed at Cobham's Inn when they came to the city, as Joan would have done since she was a girl. Nothing is known today of the house, except that it was large and grand enough to attract attention from those who wrote about the city. It probably had a small resident staff, and when members of the family came there they would of course bring their personal servants with them. It would have had a great hall, where colleagues could be met with and business could be transacted; private quarters

Clare Priory, Suffolk

for the family; accommodation for the servants, and of course stables for the horses. In a city, provisions could readily be bought, so it did not need to be as self-sufficient as, say, Polstead Hall; there was no need for the Cobhams to brew their own ale and bake their own bread in London.

Lord Cobham would have stayed at Cobham's Inn when he came to London, of course, but as he grew older he perhaps did so less frequently than he had been used to do, and slowly the great townhouse started to become more of a home to Joan and her husband.

As an adult, King Richard travelled around the country for much of the time, though mostly in the southern counties – he rarely ventured north. So his court was not always in

residence at Westminster, and for those who were used to attending court, it would make sense to come to London when the king was there, and as a result his advisers, his council, his courtiers, his friends, were also there. To the mass of the population, the king's presence would have made little difference – for Richard was not growing into a king who appeared frequently in public and courted the love of the common people – but to people such as the Braybrookes, this would be a major factor in determining their movements. (Of course there were other important factors too: the religious year, and the need to attend church for the great festivals; the agricultural year, and the need to oversee the harvest and the planting season; domestic events, and not least, Joan's pregnancies.)

Sir Reginald obviously knew the king quite well

as a result of his years at court, although there is little reason to think he was ever a friend of Richard, as opposed to being his well-liked servant. And Joan too, when she visited Westminster with him, must have come to know the king and queen better than she had before.

King Richard increasingly valued ceremony and display. He liked to wear his crown, and to dress in elaborate costume.[2] His manner was not informal: this was not a reluctant king, or one who chose to play down his own unique importance. He would often sit on a throne, surveying those gathered in his presence from on high. Those who caught his gaze were expected to pay him obeisance: lowering their eyes, bowing low, physically acting out their subordinate status. He required people to call him 'your highness' and 'your majesty' – as his predecessors as king of England had not – and to couch their petitions to him in every more flowery language. So this was not a court with an easy, relaxed atmosphere; it was one that even those who were not in a position to compare it with continental courts knew to be stiff and formal. And there were of course many foreign diplomats at court who could make such comparisons, and share them with others.

Stained glass
from Canterbury Cathedral

For those who themselves liked formality and display, all this might have been welcome; and those who did not had to learn to like it. If at times the atmosphere was stilted, there must have been compensations, and that was particularly so for a young woman with the resources to wear fine costumes, afford expensive jewellery, and invite interesting people she met at court to an imposing townhouse that was all but hers to command.

In 1393 the king and queen hosted another large tournament and pageant, so probably Sir Reginald and Joan both attended, and perhaps Sir Reginald played a part, although he was not one of the privileged few knights chosen to joust one against one with the opponents – on this occasion, the Scots. The England and Scots had always been deadly rivals, and if this was a ceremonial occasion, it was still one given a real edge by the enmity between the two camps. The Scottish earl of Mar challenged the earl of Nottingham to joust with him, but before they had completed the usual number of rides at each other, lances poised, Mar was thrown from his horse, and injured so badly that he was carried out of the lists. The English must have cheered Nottingham's decisive victory, and it was probably no great sorrow to them to learn later that Mar had died as he was being carried back to Scotland.

Joan certainly took notice at some point of another man who had a very visible role: a knight called Sir Nicholas Hawberk, who fought in single combat a Scottish knight called Cookeborne (or perhaps more properly Cockburn) in a second great staged challenge. They rode five courses, then Hawberk got his thrust in, and Cookeborne, like his unfortunate compatriot, was unhorsed and thrown to the ground.[3] Hawberk was not a well-known English man at arms. Indeed it is not clear who he was, but he must already have had some renown as a jouster, or he would not have been chosen to take such a prominent part. Possibly he was a Bohemian, a member of the queen's retinue. The common people might despise the foreigners who crowded the great halls at Westminster, but to those familiar with the ways of the court they must have provided stimulation and interest, just as the English writers and minstrels did. Men like Hawberk would have been friends of the Braybrookes, as perhaps were some of the richer London merchants who were also in a position to offer extravagant hospitality.

If the King loved tournaments and pageants when he was in London, and hunting for game when his court was in the country, there is less reason to think that he had great intellectual interests. But there were many learned men, both churchmen and laymen, who played a part in public life, and for those wished to join in them, there must have been intellectual discussions. Perhaps the debates across London supper tables were not as serious or intense as those at the great universities of Oxford and Cambridge, but the debates that first arose at the universities were also carried to London, and pursued, doubtless, by men and women there. And if they did not have as wide a range of debating partners when they returned to their country estates, still they could discuss the issues they had become aware of in private, between man and wife, or with a few trusted friends.

If it was not as obviously dangerous as facing an opponent at a tournament, there was still a danger to intellectual debate, and no one can have been unaware of that. The Church had always been jealous of its role as arbiter of people's thoughts, and indeed as controller of them. Its long resistance to making the bible available to individuals in their own language had its roots in the wish that they should look to priests to tell them how to interpret the word of God, and not try to find their own interpretations. The Church also had weapons that it could use to fight back if it perceived debates as threatening its own position. Just as there was a thin line between trying to guide the king to rule the country wisely, and criticising him in a way that could be described as treason, so there was a thin line between ruminating on the teachings of Christ in a way that could be considered truly holy, and questioning the teachings of the Church in a way that amounted to heresy. Heresy, treason: these were crimes that could cost someone their life. All those who set out on any kind of quest for knowledge, or reform, knew what chasms they trod alongside.

This was another dimension in which the presence of Bohemians at court must have had an impact, for it widened the sphere in which radical thinkers might have an influence. An influential philosopher or theologian in central Europe could expect to find an audience – if sometimes a wary and secretive audience – among thoughtful men and women in England, and similarly, thinkers and writers in England could share their ideas on this wider canvas. This was certainly true of the first stirrings of the movement for religious reform, where men (and women) across Europe were voicing similar concerns, raising similar issues, and fertilizing each other's debates.

John Wycliffe, who had done much to start the movement in England, was dead now. He had barely been tolerated in his last years, particularly after the Peasants' Revolt had alarmed many with its overt attacks on the church and its higher clergy. He had been removed from his appointment at Oxford University, although he had been allowed to live out his last years in peace in rural Leicestershire. Nor were his followers openly accepted, but provided they remained discreet in their worship, they were not persecuted either. Wycliffe's theological writings were probably as difficult for most of his contemporaries to fathom as they are today, but the rebelliousness they embodied certainly found its echoes in the wider world. Hatred of the corruption of the church, and a determination that men and women should be able to read the bible, and not only approach God's word through often incompetent priests: these were among the messages that came across to hundreds, if not thousands of thoughtful people. Some accepted Wycliffe's more openly heretical views, such as his rejection of transubstantiation (the belief that in the mass, the bread and wine that are used to symbolize the body and blood of Christ are actually miraculously transformed to that body and blood), but others drew the line more cautiously.

In Bohemia, a young priest and academic called Jan Hus was to pick up these ideas and popularize them, and most likely there were others before him, who opened channels between England and Bohemia that were to remain open for decades to follow. Some thought Queen Anne to be among them: a learned woman, she was claimed to possess copies of the Gospels in English, which rated as a provocative, even dangerous thing to do.[4]

It was around the 1380s that those who espoused these ideas had come to be known

Stained glass from St John the Baptist's Church, Thaxted, Essex

as the Lollards. The word meant 'mumblers', and that had a certain appropriateness, for those whose ideas would attract criticism had every reason to express them quietly. By 1390, the poet Gower was writing of 'this new sect of Lollardry',[5] although it never developed a tight agenda. The name was applied to a very wide range of rebels.

Was Sir Reginald a Lollard sympathizer – and was his wife? If so, they were cautious about it. Sir Reginald was still close to his uncle, and almost by definition a bishop was no radical. But nor was Bishop Braybrooke a reactionary. Thomas Arundel, archbishop of York, chancellor of England for two long spells under Richard II – and younger brother of Lord Arundel – was one of those, and there were others too among the ranks of senior clergy, but Bishop Braybrooke seems to have taken a different line. There was one notorious incident in 1387, when 'almost a hundred' Lollards rioted in London,[6] and little action was taken against them afterwards, so perhaps the bishop who chose to leave them be had a degree of sympathy with at least some of their agenda.

Braybrook in Northamptonshire, which was presumably the original home of the Braybrooke family, although they no longer owned the manor, was becoming a notorious centre of Lollardry, which was spreading from there across the county. A chaplain called John Woodward had made converts not just there, but in Chipping Warden to the south east – a spread of activity which must have encompassed many of Sir Reginald's family's and Joan's own estates.[6]

So Joan and her husband must have learned of the Lollard ideas, and most likely talked them over too. And perhaps all those funerals that Joan had attended, and especially the long weary rituals for Sir Robert, which would have fallen mostly to her to arrange, had focused her mind on some of the problems with the contemporary Church. Was it true that the Christ who had called on men to share their goods, and claimed that only the poor could expect salvation, had endorsed a Church where only the very rich, those who could pay others to pray for them, could look for an easy route into the hereafter? Was it right that so many priests should spend their lives in the empty repetitive activities of the chantry, saying endless masses for the dead, when living parishioners were left with no one to minster to their spiritual needs? If she had read the bible, or had it read to her, she would have taken note that it made no mention of most of the saints around whom much worship then centred; none of indulgences and pardons; none even of the pope. The more she read, the more she learned, the more she, like others, might have questioned. Some of the Lollards were plain working men and women, but there was a significant coterie of sympathizers among the upper classes too, and if Joan and her husband developed such views, they would readily have found others who shared them.

Those who were concerned at the state of the Church were often no less concerned about the wider state of the kingdom. The inequities in English society, and the shortage of acceptable ways of addressing these issues, had been brought into sharp focus by the Peasants' Revolt. Although more than ten years had passed since then, the demands that

not just peasants, but many more affluent and influential people had made, for fairer governance, fairer taxation and greater equality before the law, had still not properly been addressed. England was changing, in the wake of the black death, the slow collapse of the feudal system, the increasing influence of Europe; but King Richard did not seem to be changing in the same direction.

All of these ideas swirled together in an undercurrent which was apparent in much of southern and middle England, and must have had its echoes at court. The Braybrookes might well have been an intelligent and thoughtful young couple, and what we know of the later course of Joan's life suggests that during these years she might first have begun to give consideration to such matters. It is conceivable too that Sir Reginald, a capable and perhaps deep-thinking man, but one who had grown up without any great expectations of inherited wealth, and who had seen the machinations of the court at first hand, would not only have found much to question, but might have shared his questions with his wife.

At the same time Sir Reginald was no rebel, and certainly no traitor. He took care to support the king, and one of the greatest efforts he made to do so was when King Richard made an expedition to Ireland in October 1394. Richard was the first English king in almost 200 years to visit Ireland, and although his expedition gave him a worthwhile opportunity to strengthen the fairly nominal English rule, many men must have questioned whether it was wise to divert his attentions when France and Scotland posed much more obvious threats. Richard never showed any inclination to pick up the reins of his grandfather's campaign to retrieve the throne of France, however; he had rather to be pushed to do the minimum that was necessary to keep England safe from threats across the Channel.

It was not for Sir Reginald to second-guess the king's motives. His job was simply to act as a captain in the king's force. It was a large force, and as well as the household knights – Richard was amassing a sizeable force as a core part of his household, rather than a mere bodyguard, with archers from Cheshire at the centre of it – many captains from across the country were invited to bring their men. Sir Reginald was one of these. He was paid the usual wages of war, would have raised a troop of men from his and Joan's estates to serve under him, and arranged before he left that both his father and Joan's grandfather would handle his affairs in his absence. He must have been away in Ireland for all of the six months that the king spent on the expedition. The expedition was a success, on its own terms: both diplomacy and force were used to bring the rebel Irish lords firmly under English control.

20 Salcey Forest

The hunters dispersed themselves by the side of a wood, and the rocks and the trees rang with the noise of the horns. Some of the hunters fell in with the scent where the fox was biding, and oft they tracked and tracked across in wily fashion. One of the hounds took up the cry, and the hunters called him, and the others fell thereto panting hard and close together. They ran forth in a rabble right on his track. The fox ran on in front, and they found him at length and followed hard after him, and savagely they scolded him with an angry noise. He tricked them, and made quick turns in many a rough woodland, and dodged in and out, and sometimes would pause to listen by many a hedgerow. At length he leapt over a quickset hedge by the side of a little ditch, and then stole out stealthily by a rugged path, and tried to escape the hounds. Then, ere he knew it, he came suddenly upon one of the stations, where three hounds fiercely set upon him at once.

Sir Gawain and the Green Knight
(anon, late 14th century, in a modern translation[1])

Stained glass on both pages from St Peter's Church, Ardwincle, Northants

If there were days in London, and perhaps at Cooling too, where the Braybrookes talked politics and religion with trusted friends, there were also days, probably many more of them, where they pursued a simple (though affluent and privileged) country life. Rainy days, when Joan would sit with her maids and perhaps a visiting friend, doing needlework, chatting, singing a new song that one of them had learned, or an old and well-loved one. Crisp bright days, when they would head out to the mews to find their hawks, and ride into the meadows, loosing them to fly high into the clear blue sky, and dive again to find their prey. Hot days, for sitting in the flower garden, and cold ones, when they huddled by an open fire. And there were days too of hunting, when they could get together with neighbours and perhaps with some of their tenants too, to make a good party for the chase. There would have been wooded areas on many of the couple's estates, where either small-scale hunts to keep down the foxes, or larger gatherings in search of deer, took place regularly when the master and mistress were in residence. The Braybrookes probably also took part on occasion in the even larger hunts that were organized by the great aristocrats or for the king.

Sir Reginald might have given up the keepership of Salcey Forest, but it had only gone as far as his older brother. This was an administrative job, overseeing the maintenance of this substantial hunting ground – a small remnant of which remains even today – which was one of the royal forests, so it was reserved for the use of the king and those he invited to hunt there. This presumably included the keeper and his associates, provided they ensured that plenty of game was available for the king on the relatively rare occasions when he made a visit. Salcey was not Windsor; none of the king's main haunts was close. But it was not far from Castle Ashby, and nearer still to Milton, so it was in the centre of the Midlands area in which both the Braybrookes and the de la Poles owned plenty of land. And in September 1398 the king did come to Northampton,[2] and quite probably spent some time hunting there.

A royal hunt, or even a hunt authorized by the king, but not in his presence, was a major social event. This was not a few men scrambling through briars and across streams with their dogs in search of any game they might come across. It was orchestrated carefully, to all but ensure a great kill, and the role of the host and his guests was not to chase the quarry, but to station themselves to shoot at it when it was brought within range.

There were hunting lodges in the forest, and these could be supplemented by tents, for those who could not find a place in the permanent buildings, so everyone was lodged close at hand, and the hunt could begin early (although the day must have begun much earlier still for the huntsmen who did the hard work). For the guests the day started with a gathering, when plans were made, or the plans the huntsmen had already made were confirmed, over a hearty breakfast. The main quarry – typically a mature stag – was generally identified in advance, and it was part of the huntsmen's job to ensure it was brought within range.[3]

It was also a part of the hunt staff's job to handle the hounds: first the harriers, to clear the rascal (the young deer who were not the intended quarry), and then the highly trained hart hounds, to scent and chase the chosen deer. The hunting horns that were blown sent messages between the hunters, and helped them control this complex process in the wild and largely trackless forest. Harried and chased, at last the deer would break

cover, and the lords and their attendants could shoot them down with their hunting bows. Then the master of the harriers would finish the kill, blow the death on his horn, and reward the hounds, before the bleeding carcases were loaded on to carts ready to be taken back to the kitchens. Applause from the assembled knights and ladies; and a canter at dusk back to the lodge, for a supper of venison and a sharing of tales.

Salcey Forest

21 The sun and the clouds

How admirable and long-suffering is the king's forbearance! ... Previously the sun was hidden behind a cloud but now, soaring in arms above the mountains and bounding over the hills with his might, he has dispersed the clouds with his sun, whose light shines ever more brightly.

The 'Short Kirkstall Chronicle' on the parliament of 1397–8[1]

Stained glass
from
Canterbury
Cathedral

The tournament of 1393 was the last great pageant for some time. The next year the plague returned to London, and one of its victims was the queen.[2] The royal marriage had been regarded as a happy one, and the young king was distraught. Melodramatic by temperament, he refused for a year to enter any room she had been in, and he had his manor at Sheen, where she had died, completely destroyed. More than that, her death must have ended an era for the court. Although Richard married again not long afterwards, it was to a child – Isabella of France – and not only was his court never the same, those who knew him probably judged that he too was never the same. The queen had been considered a soothing influence, calming his tempers, mediating with his enemies – and after 1394 all this was lost.

Joan and Sir Reginald must have felt the impact of the changes at court. Quite likely they had been on good terms with Queen Anne, and felt her death as a personal loss. But the death of Joan's grandmother two years or so later was a much heavier blow for their family, and this seems to have had as devastating influence on her husband as the queen's death had on hers, albeit he did not react by tearing his castle to the ground. Margaret Courtenay had been an old woman, one who had seen her daughter and many other relatives precede her to the grave. But she too seems to have been a linchpin of her household, and a close partner to her husband. Lord Cobham arranged a huge funeral.[3] He ordered four sets of heraldic banners and 100 pennons from a London painter, so Cobham church was bedecked with flags that advertised the family's connections and its power. The family's many retainers, the priests and the pupils of the college, their tenants and friends: hundreds of people – Joan and her husband included – would have attended to say goodbye to a long-lived and (as far as we can judge) well loved lady of the manor.

After his wife's death, Lord Cobham seems less to have been the vigorous knight who had played a forceful part both in Kent affairs and at the king's court, and to have anticipated his withdrawal from public life, and eventually from life itself. At about this time he executed an elaborate deed of entail, which included the eventual transfer of lands to several members of the family.[4] It ensured that although Joan would inherit his main estates and his title, these would not pass permanently out of the Cobham family, should for instance her husband outlive her. There seems no reason to think that this reflected a dislike or distrust of Sir Reginald on the part of Lord Cobham. Far from it, he seems to have expected that the Braybrookes would eventually replace him at Cooling, and run the estates from there, perhaps even during his lifetime – which they were indeed to do.

But there were major upheavals to be negotiated before that happened.

Had Lord Cobham known, all through the ten years that followed the Merciless Parliament, that there would eventually be a reckoning? Had Joan and his other relatives anticipated one, or had they long forgotten that there was bravery in his choosing to join the king's opponents? Perhaps they had all thought the tremors well behind them, the pardons that Lord Cobham and his colleagues had been granted security enough, his reputation as a steady and reliable (and elderly) member of the nobility firmly restored. They all knew, of course, that the relatively stable days of King Edward's long reign had gone forever, and that Edward's young grandson's court had a much more jagged edge running under its smooth carapace of formality. They knew that any man who takes a prominent role in uncertain times is running a risk: even a passing familiarity with the history of England would have told them that few such men die in their beds. But perhaps, after a life when he had fought his share of battles,

faced his portion of danger, and come through relatively unscathed, they believed that even so, this venerable old lord would ride gently into the twilight of his great old age.

That was not to be. The earthquake struck in 1397, and rumbled on into 1398. The king had been slowly moving to consolidate his position and marginalize those who had once so openly opposed him; to strengthen his bodyguard, and ensure he would be secure when he struck. Once this was achieved to his satisfaction, he implemented his plans. He managed to assemble a parliament that was willing to do as he wished, something many thought he achieved by subterfuge. The composition of the parliament was unusual, all but unique: almost half the men summoned had never sat in a parliament before, and far more than usual were men directly retained (and paid) by the king. One chronicler described the king 'riding menacingly through the middle of London surrounded by five thousand armed men, most of whom were malefactors'. This was a parliament designed and drawn up to fit the king's purposes.[5] And those who saw those five thousand men, or were brought word of them by others who had witnessed their riding past, would scarcely have needed more warning that terrible events were likely to follow.

Richard started by ordering the arrests of the leaders of the lords who had challenged his favourites in the Merciless Parliament. These men were treated harshly. The earl of Arundel was executed; his brother Archbishop Arundel[6] and the earl of Warwick were banished; and the duke of Gloucester only escaped being found guilty because he had died before the sentence could be pronounced (many believed, murdered at the king's command). Once these great men had been dealt with, the king moved against the men who had supported them. Lord Cobham was one of these.

Treason can be a difficult crime to comprehend: a nebulous one, not readily pinned to the ground, but drifting in the air like smoke. What was being spoken of here was not the simple treachery of wartime, the kind that involves giving away secrets, unlatching gates and letting in the enemy. This was the kind of treason that festers in the crevices between loyalty to the king, and loyalty to the country; a kind that can find accusations against men who believe they have always acted in England's best interests. Lord Cobham seems never to have been a natural rebel. He was an establishment man, a holder of a succession of public offices, a loyal servant of the Crown first as a man at arms and then as a courtier and politician. He was no weaselly seller of secrets for personal gain. But all the same, the word that is used for such low-life criminals was now being applied to him.

Albeit the king had planned his move carefully, there must have been plenty of people, including some in the king's entourage, who sympathized with men such as Lord Cobham. And Lord Cobham himself had surely been alarmed, more than alarmed, at the first sequence of arrests. He hardly needed the warning of others to know that his position was a dangerous one. Little as he would have wanted to face that hard reality, he accepted that charges were about to be laid against him. He knew he must flee immediately, if he was not to face the same end as Lord Arundel, the death that he himself had engineered for Sir Simon Burley ten years earlier.

He went to the Carthusian monastery in London – the Charterhouse at Smithfield, just by the great showground that was also a place of execution – and announced his intention to renounce the public world. He surely meant it: this can have been no world he wanted a part of.

And he must have hoped, at least for a while, that his withdrawal would be accepted as punishment enough. His family – Joan, Sir Reginald, their servants and friends – must all have hoped for that too. But Richard could be a vengeful king, and he was surrounded by those who sought revenge on those who had seen other men brought down ten years before. Lord Cobham was not allowed to stay in the monastery. He was dragged out of its precincts, and committed to the Tower of London in September 1397. The Braybrookes must have been brought word immediately, and if they were conceivably able to do so, they would surely have come to London, to give what support they were able to the captive.

So perhaps they were at Cobham's Inn when, a fortnight after his arrest, Lord Cobham was brought from the Tower to stand before the lords in parliament. Westminster Hall, the usual venue of London parliaments, was being renovated, and the parliament met – and the king sat on what had become his habitual high throne – in the yard outside it. Joan and her husband could probably not have attended, since it was a parliamentary hearing, but there would have been many friends and sympathizers who brought them news of what took place.

The main accusation against Lord Cobham was simply that he had been a member of the 1386 council that had opposed the king's wishes, and had been one of the lords who in 1388 had ensured that Suffolk was exiled, and Burley and others condemned to death. He was committed for trial, then sent back to the Tower.

So he was close to Cobham's Inn, so close that his family and his servants could have called at the Tower on a daily basis – and quite likely Joan did. This was a respected lord, not a cheap pickpocket: he would have been housed decently in one of the stone towers in the great complex, and the guards would (for a price, of course) have been able to bring him messages, and perhaps some physical comforts too: warm blankets and a good thick cloak to ward off the chill of the stone, hot suppers, a missal to read. He was an old man, and probably frail. Joan and Sir Reginald would have known how much he needed what comfort they could bring him. But although they could ease his conditions physically, emotional comfort would have been harder to come by. Even those who know from long experience how many public careers end in disgrace tend to assume it will not happen to them. And these were charges that carried not just a sentence of death, but the prospect of a terrible, demeaning, public death, the worst end that any man could anticipate.

Lord Cobham stayed in his cell at the Tower until the January that followed: four months of a cold winter, four months for his family to bribe and plead. That would have been a winter of manoeuvring and lobbying, both among those who chose to support the king (and, many of them, gain titles and estates as a reward), and among the families of the accused men. Sir Reginald had friends at court, and although he would have needed to tread carefully, to ensure he was not enmeshed in accusations himself, he surely would have made representations where he could. The other Lord Cobham who was active at this time – Reginald, the second baron Cobham of Sterborough – was under investigation too, so he could be no help. Bishop Braybrooke might well have provided sympathy and support, but Joan must have wished she had many more influential relations. She probably wished too that Queen Anne was still alive.

And she probably learned, even before the trial took place, that there was a depth of resistance in the country. Many people who had never set foot in a parliament

The Jewel Tower, Westminster

had supported the reforms of a decade earlier, and were appalled that those who had played an honourable part in them were now under threat. They liked the five-thousand-strong army around the king no more than the Braybrookes did. If it was not clear how they could change the trends in the country, nevertheless they hated those trends, and wanted to see them reversed.

It was perhaps because of the rumblings of discontent, of unease, that when parliament was reconvened in January it was not held at Westminster at all, but at Shrewsbury, which was a long way from the Braybrookes' spheres of influence. Perhaps even so Sir Reginald rode over to lobby its members and learn what happened. If he did not, the Braybrookes would have made arrangements to have word brought to them.

So Joan was perhaps in London, where the news would reach her fastest, when she learned of the outcome of the trial. Lord Cobham had been dignified and courteous as always in the face of the charges. He had protested his loyalty to the king, but it had not saved him from being found guilty:

> And therefor they adjudged the said John Cobham a traitor to the king and kingdom, and that he should be hanged, drawn, beheaded, and quartered: and that all his castles, manors, lands, tenements, reversions, fees, advowsons, possessions, and every other manner of hereditament of the said John Cobham, which were his on 19 November in the tenth year of the king's reign [1386], or later, in fee simple; and also all the lands, tenements, and possessions with which other persons were enfeoffed to his use, on the same 19 November [1386] or later, should be forfeit to our said lord the king and his heirs, from the said John Cobham and his heirs for ever, of whomsoever they were held.[7]

It was the worst possible outcome, the one they must all have dreaded and feared.

But for all his faults, Richard II was not bloodthirsty. He had been seeking control, not vengeance. Perhaps the same messenger brought the news that the king had announced he was 'moved to pity', and that Lord Cobham might live out the rest of his life in perpetual exile on the island of Jersey. And although a finding of treason generally involved automatic forfeiture of all the condemned man's lands, parliament had not supported the king that far. It had pronounced that although Lord Cobham himself would lose his entailed lands, they could be restored to his heirs after his death.

So at Cobham's Inn there must have been relief, exhaustion, and not a little despair. Exile to Jersey was far better than death, although Lord Cobham's public response had been that he had hoped to see eternity a little sooner than it seemed he now would.[8] It was still a brutal sentence for an ageing man, a cruel ending to a life that had been crowned with honour before this terrible disgrace.

Next would have come the king's commissioners, to take possession of Cobham's Inn, Cooling Castle and all Lord Cobham's other estates, and tip his household and his possessions out into the road. Lord Cobham himself probably did not return to London or Kent, but perhaps Joan and her husband rode over to Portsmouth, or whatever other port he had chosen for his embarkation, and saw him take ship that chilly January, and sail off into his bleak exile.

22 Miserable oppression

While the king remained in Ireland attacking the Irish, imagining that he was achieving great things, God suddenly decided to humble his pride and bring succour to the people of England, who were now so miserably oppressed that they had lost all hope of deliverance and relief unless God were to reach forth and help them.

Thomas Walsingham's chronicle[1]

Ascramble, then: to meet up with Lord Cobham, if they could, before he went into exile; to rescue their possessions from the forfeited manors; to protest, plead, do what they could to keep their cart from tumbling into the ditch. Then came the long weary aftermath – and the long weary battle, in which Sir Reginald took the lead, to try to salvage what they could from the ruins.

He did this by continuing (at least in public) in wholehearted support of the king, and Joan most likely supported him in that policy. He could have afforded to do nothing else; there was no other way to retrieve anything. In this, he clearly had help from his uncle, and he did favours for Bishop Braybrooke in return. (For instance, when the bishop negotiated with the king to purchase the right to arrange the marriage of a minor lord, Sir Reginald stood surety for him.[2]) And he must still have been on amicable terms with the king he had served for so long. All this stood him in good stead, and the requests he made were kindly received. In May and December 1398 he was given a royal grant which:

by … letters patent committed to [Reynold Braybroke knight] for a set yearly farm the keeping of the castle and manor of Coulynge, the hundred of Scamelle and the site of the manor of Cobham and of one 'tylehost', two mills, 313 acres of land, 300 acres of pasture, pasture for two horses, two avers and eight oxen, 6*l*. of rent, one conyger and the manor of Cobeham which were of the said John [Lord Cobham], and by reason of his forfeiture and of a judgment against him rendered were in that king's hand.[3]

So although these lands no longer belonged to the Cobhams, Sir Reginald and Joan were able to go to live at Cooling Castle and to adminster the estates as if little had changed. (They had to pay quite heavily for the privilege, however: the fee was £105 13s.4d. a year, to be paid to the Exchequer.)

It seems likely that they did indeed spend much of their time at Cooling in the months that followed. Even if they held the reins of the estates once more, the upheavals must have unsettled the tenants, their servants, the peasants on the land. Reassurance and normality – even if the Braybrookes did not sense it themselves – were what was needed most. And why would they remain in London? Although they had the Kent lands under their control, they most likely did not also have Cobham's Inn. The atmosphere at court must have been poisonous. The king was even more autocratic in the wake of his successful purge; his guard of Cheshire archers clustered closer around him than ever. If the Braybrookes had friends at court, these too were probably choosing to retreat from Westminster as much as they dared, and wait in the quiet of the country for better times to come.

So many of the great men of the realm had been lost. Those who had risen to take their places, and the inflated titles that Richard bestowed on them, were seen as such small men by comparison that they were described by the cynical as the 'duketti'. These men might be squabbling and fighting for influence and position, but Sir Reginald was apparently not among them. He might have opted for tact and flattery, and swallowed his anger at what had happened to his wife's grandfather, as a tactic to win back control of the estates, but he seems to have made no attempt to go further and try to wheedle from the king some new appointment. No dukedom came his way, or any smaller prize either.

He had been fortunate in getting the estates back for Joan, and probably never asked for, or even wanted, any more.

Queen Anne was long dead now, and her successor, Isabella of France, was still a small child. Of course she had adult ladies in waiting, both French and English, but this was not a court known for its culture, its learned men and women, its serious conversation. It was certainly no court where the sane would have chosen to express radical views, on religion or any other subject. Even the fabulous entertainments were years in the past. Many people who had frequented the court a decade before had probably concluded that there was no place for them there any more. Despair in private, and blank courtesy in public; presenting themselves at court when summoned, and keeping well clear for the rest of the time: these were the tactics that plenty of people in the Braybrookes' circle must have employed.

Perhaps some of them guessed that the apparent stability imposed by the Cheshire archers, and by the arrogant new upstart lords, was a flimsy skin over a cold stew with a hot fire beneath it. They suspected it would not persist for long, that trouble would bubble up and over. Perhaps, like Lord Cobham had done, they were making their own preparations for the upheavals that might lie ahead.

So the Braybrookes might have been in Kent or East Anglia when the news came to them only months after the parliament that had convicted Lord Cobham, that a serious quarrel had broken out between two of the lords who had stood by the king and played a part in the prosecution. One was Thomas Mowbray, earl of Nottingham, who had been made duke of Norfolk as his reward; the other was Henry Bolingbroke, duke of Hereford, the son of John of Gaunt, and as such one of the great nobles of the realm, and heir to perhaps its greatest fortune. The two accused each other of treason. The charges were heard in parliament, and it was agreed it was impossible to judge the truth of them. So it was determined that the two men should fight in single combat to resolve the issue.

This was dramatic news; exciting news. If quarrels between lords were common enough, there was nothing commonplace about this way of handling them. True, single combat was an old and accepted legal process, but it was also an outdated one, and a quixotic and high-risk choice. Although parliament had endorsed the proposal, probably everyone who knew the protagonists guessed that the king was behind it. Some things about King Richard had not changed, and his love of a spectacle at which he might preside was definitely one of them.

If it provoked some excitement, though, this news must also have provoked unease among thinking men and women. A bitter argument between two great nobles was worrying enough. An attempt to marry that argument with the pomp and glamour of a staged tournament, with an outcome which could see one of those lords dead, and which even at best would do nothing to heal their raw wounds, but would instead stick public poultices on them: how could this be a wise way forward?

But it was the king's way, endorsed by his parliament. And even those thoughtful lords and ladies probably relished the gossip, not just about the quarrel in parliament, but about the plans for the showdown that was now to take place.

Making the arrangements took several weeks. It was announced that the event was

Stained glass from St Mary's Church, Saxlingham Nethergate, Norfolk

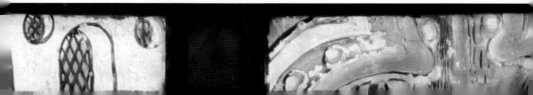

to take place at Gosford Green, outside the walls of Coventry, that September, in the presence of the king and his other lords. The two disputing lords made their preparations, and the king made his: he came to Coventry accompanied by what the chroniclers claimed were ten thousand fully armed men. This was perhaps an exaggeration, but it seems clear that the king made a huge effort to provide security. Of course, this security was primarily for himself: it was not for the crowds of gawpers, who would be unceremoniously shoved out of the way by the troops if they came too close. Nor was it for the two contenders, who were left to see to their own safety as best they might.

Coventry was some way from the Braybrookes' sphere of influence, but ten thousand men took a lot of finding. The king must have called on every knight at his disposal, so it is probable that Sir Reginald Braybrooke was among those summoned to escort him north. And Joan? Well, many thousands of people, both great and small, did go to Coventry to witness what would surely be one of the great events of the era. She might have been one of them, but equally she might have sensed that disquiet, that unease, and chosen to stay safe at Cooling.

Even if she did not go, she would have known she would hear plenty of tales of the combat, and that they would be as contradictory, colourful, confused as such tales are. And she would have been right, for this proved to be, if not a great event, certainly a major turning point of English history. The crowds were assembled, the troops in position around the jousting field, and the two noble lords were just preparing to make their first charge in the lists, when the king instead threw his sceptre to the ground and had his heralds stop the contest.

Shock; astonishment; exasperation; the would-be combatants and the crowd must have felt all of that, and more. They had to wait in the autumn sun for a full two hours, while the king took counsel of his advisers. Many must surely have thought – even if they dared not say – that if he had doubts about the course that had been chosen, he would have been wise to express them a good while earlier.

At last the king emerged, and his heralds announced his decision. There would be no duel. Instead both Nottingham and Hereford were to be banished from England for ten years. More shock, more astonishment; not a little fury, surely, not just from the two men who had both believed they would prevail, but from the thousands who had taken time and trouble to come to watch their battle, and were now sent away disappointed.

And more worry, in the days and weeks that followed, for those already deeply concerned about the way the government was heading. The Cheshire archers might be clustered tight about the king, but there was a threadbare look to the lords in his council. First the purge of the Merciless Parliament, then the purge of its purgers: it had cost the country more of its aristocracy than could be spared. How could it now spare John of Gaunt's son, the heir to a vast fortune and an even greater spread of lands? Or the head of the Mowbrays, immensely powerful in East Anglia? This was not a king with a huge family. Richard was an only child, his uncles now ageing or dead. He had not even a son to rise up alongside him (and with his new wife still a child, had little hope of obtaining one for years to come). What the Cobham estates were experiencing, with their lord in exile, was written larger across the whole country, with much of a generation of nobles

dead or banished. The wise counsel, the steady pressure to hold to sane policies, from those who had traditionally formed the counterbalance to the monarchy: all that seemed now to have gone.

But it happened, nevertheless. Mowbray and Bolingbroke left England's shores late in 1398. Mowbray died in exile a short while later.

Worse followed. When John of Gaunt died in February 1399, and his son should have inherited the duchy of Lancaster, the king announced that he was minded instead to make Henry's banishment permanent, and to confiscate the vast Lancaster estates and keep them for himself.

It was not only the radicals and whisperers, not only the watchers and thinkers, who felt alarm now. If the king was to get rid of Lancaster for good, then who would there be left to negotiate with him, to provide a reasoned opposition, to ensure the secure running of the country? Henry Bolingbroke was not a man who had marked himself out ten years before as an opponent of the king. On the contrary, he was the son of the king's loyal uncle. He had backed up the coup against the king's opponents, and grabbed his rewards. Men might have, and indeed had, accepted the king's driving through treason charges against men who had set themselves up as his critics, but it made no sense to class Bolingbroke among such men.

Bolingbroke was also a man with power, money, a depth of support in the country. Nobody who knew him (and the Braybrookes were among them, although they probably did not know him intimately) believed he would quietly accept this confiscation. Permanent exile? The loss of all his inheritance? For an unproved charge of treason? No, it could not, and surely would not stand.

Something had to be done – but who would do it? There were few if any lords left in England with the power and confidence to mount any protest against the king. Sir Reginald Braybrooke, not even a lord, but only a man with expectations, was certainly not the person to stand up. He probably concluded, as did his friends, that there was only one man who could take the lead, and that was Henry Bolingbroke himself.

So the rest of them had to wait, to see what move the man who should have been duke of Lancaster would now make.

They were waiting too, of course, to see what move the king would make. Richard surely knew his decision was a high-risk one. Did he have a plan, some way to ensure that it would be enforced without repercussions?

If he did, it was not apparent in the announcement he made next. He declared that he planned to lead a new expedition to Ireland.

Ireland? True, there was unrest across the Irish Sea, where the deal the king had imposed five years earlier was fast disintegrating; but there was frequently unrest across the Irish Sea, and it was not usually the major priority of English kings to deal with it. Many of the king's knights and courtiers, including Sir Reginald and his wife, must have thought this not merely an unwise decision, but on the brink of madness. Did it not occur to the king that he would be leaving the kingdom unprotected, and at a time when both lords and common people were waiting for Bolingbroke to make a move?

Perhaps it did not. Richard had been king for most of his life, and had inherited a throne held stably for half a century by his grandfather. If English kings had been deposed before, not only had it never happened in his lifetime, it had not happened in the lifetime

Stained glass from St George's Church, Shimpling, Norfolk

of almost anyone then living. And he seems not to have been a ruler who troubled to pay attention to the thoughts and reactions of others. He perhaps believed that he had sucessfully achieved the downfall of Henry Bolingbroke, and indeed of anyone else who might challenge his own way of ruling over England, and felt perfectly secure in the company of his expanded bodyguard and his remaining duketti.

That was quite mad, of course. But what was a man who was not Henry Bolingbroke to do, when this unhinged king called on him to join his loyal troops and accompany him to Ireland?

Sir Reginald Braybrooke had accompanied the king on his previous expedition to Ireland, and as a veteran who knew the terrain, he was certain to be called on to accompany him this time too. He was. He went.

That he did so does not imply that he approved of the king's choices – of any of the king's choices. He surely went because he had no realistic alternative. Whatever people hoped, or even believed, might happen when Henry Bolingbroke learned what his cousin had done to him, it had not happened yet. Unless he was to mark himself as a traitor, and face an immediate death for the crime, Braybrooke had to do as was demanded of him, muster his men, and head west to meet up with the king. His uncle was ordered to go too – Bishop Braybrooke had spent six months in Ireland two years previously as its lord chancellor, so he was heavily involved with Irish issues – and perhaps they rode across England and Wales together to Milford Haven, where the troops were being mustered.

What they discovered when they met up with the king must have dismayed them even more. Although the unrest in Ireland was very real, the expedition was being treated by the king almost as a royal progress. Bishop Braybrooke was not the only senior cleric to have been summoned: the king was taking another five bishops too, plus the abbot of Westminster. He had so lost his sense of perspective that he had ordered a large troupe of minstrels to accompany him. He was even taking the royal embroiderer. When men suggested – very cautiously – that perhaps this was unnecessary, they were told shortly that the king was not willing to be parted from his embroiderer, or from the crown jewels, which also made the journey.

Some people evidently believed the king intended never to return. Perhaps Joan, left to manage the estates from Cooling, was among them.

Sir Reginald and his uncle were in Ireland, both of them, in the company of the king, when Henry Bolingbroke, who definitely intended to claim his duchy of Lancaster, returned to England. A relieved country rose up to welcome him, and offered him rather more than that. King Richard had proved a disaster, he was told, and they would welcome his claiming the throne himself, and restoring to them a good strong government.

Henry was securely in control of England before Richard could get back to confront him.

That Robert Hemnale knight at his death held… in fee tail the manor, called 'Polstedhale' in chief by knight service jointly with Joan his wife (yet living), to them and the heirs of their bodies, that he died on Friday after the Exaltation of Holy Cross 15 Richard II, that William his son was his next heir and then of the age of four and upwards, that the said William was an idiot all his life, that he died on Monday before Christmas last.

Calendar of Close Rolls for the reign of Henry IV, 17 May 1403[1]

It was not that Sir Reginald Braybrooke and his wife had found themselves on the losing side of the civil war, because there was no civil war. The support for Henry of Lancaster was so overwhelming, that for Richard II so flimsy, that by the time Richard's troops reached England again, they were facing a fait accompli. It must have been somewhat uncomfortable for Joan until Sir Reginald came home, knowing that he was with the effectively deposed king. It was doubtless none too pleasant for Sir Reginald himself to be part of the army that the Richard abandoned around Carmarthen, probably about a week after his household and troops returned to the country they had left less than two months previously. But that was a temporary discomfort (compounded by the fact that they would never now receive whatever pay remained outstanding). The men dispersed, the minstrels and the embroiderer also made their way home (and applied in due course to the new king for work), and word came through before long that King Richard was in the custody of Henry of Lancaster's troops. That September of 1399, Richard was formally deposed. In October a parliament confirmed Henry as King Henry IV, and saw him crowned. And the following February it was announced that the former King Richard had died. It was convenient for almost everyone, and a wise individual did not enquire any further into exactly how his death had come about.

The Braybrookes had seen the end of a reign in which they had prospered. Joan and Sir Reginald would have known that as a man who had not been in a position to join Henry of Lancaster's triumphant progression through England to claim its throne, he was not in the forefront of those queueing up for preferment from the new king. But that could not be helped, and meanwhile the pair could celebrate the advantages of the change of regime, not the least of which was the end of Lord Cobham's mercifully brief period of exile.

Lord Cobham wasted no time in returning to England. He was among the lords who were present at the October parliament which saw Henry IV confirmed as king. Joan and her husband might have thought that following this, they would need to leave Cooling and let her grandfather take back possession of his great castle, and resume all the local tasks that she and Sir Reginald had been carrying out in his name. But perhaps the experience of his trial and exile had broken something in him, because this did not happen. Lord Cobham evidently decided to let Sir Reginald continue to fill the place in Kentish life that had been his, and he withdrew instead to the other side of England, to Maiden Bradley in Wiltshire. He also owned some estates in this area, but at this point in his life he clearly was not looking to become involved with their administration for the first time. Rather, he must have been inclined to move well away from any pressure from his friends and associates in Kent and London to take an active part in affairs, and instead to find a quiet place where he might live out his last years in contemplation.

This he found at the priory of St Mary and St Lazarus, an Augustinian priory which had developed from what had once been a leper hospital. Little is known about the priory, but it seems likely that in those days it provided nursing services to the elderly. So Lord Cobham would have been comfortable there, and could prepare himself for the eternal life which, for him, was still some years off.

Lord Cobham clearly did not feel that Joan and her husband were still in need of his guidance, but Joan might well have missed his presence. Perhaps her husband missed it less. He and Joan had evidently decided to make their life primarily in Kent, and Sir

North Kent coast

Reginald slowly began to involve himself with Kentish affairs. He began to serve on local commissions, and in 1403 he was summoned to attend a great council, as one of five Kentish men given that honour. These were not appointments that suggest Sir Reginald was in any way exceptionally able or ambitious. Probably he was neither. But they show him slowly starting to expand into the space that Lord Cobham had left empty, in anticipation that when the old man died, the title and position would come to him.

In December 1402 Joan's son William Hemenhale died. Perhaps in some ways it was a blessing, since this was an heir who would never have grown up to administer his inheritance, but Joan quite likely did not see it so. This was her first son, the only one who had lived into his teens, and his death severed a link with a major part of her life.

William's closest surviving relative was his mother, but the entailed Hemenhale lands were not destined for her; they passed on to more distant relations of his father. This might have been an opportunity for Joan to also end her links with Burnham Norton, and the other places that she had known and lived in during her first marriage. But clearly she did not want to, because instead she and Sir Reginald embarked on a long campaign to ensure that Polstead Hall and the other Hemenhale lands would stay in her possession. It took them many years to achieve this, and in the end Joan had to swap some of her de la Pole estates with the Hemenhale ones to ensure that she held on to Burnham Norton. With no son, or even daughter, to press her to keep their inheritance safe, it can only have been because she wanted these lands for herself. She must have felt great affection for Burnham Norton, and perhaps with many of the local people, to be so determined to retain her involvement with it.

A son lost; a daughter gained. Joan's sons by Sir Reginald were perhaps already dead by then, and this left her with not a single living child to show for all her pregnancies. Probably she did not dare to hope too much when she conceived again, around 1403. But this time her child was born healthy, and thrived from then onwards. It must have been some disappointment to both her and Sir Reginald that it was not the son they so much needed. But it must have been a pleasure too to Joan that the child she named Joan after herself (and after Sir Reginald's sister too) was one of whom she could feel proud. If she could have this healthy child, perhaps she could have more. Surely she hoped so.

These were years of many births and deaths in the family,

Stained glass on both pages from St Mary's Church, Martham, Norfolk

and one of the most significant was the death of Sir Reginald's father in February 1403. His elder brother was still alive, so Sir Reginald was not the main heir to the Braybrooke estates, but Castle Ashby and the other estates whose reversion had been settled on the couple on their marriage came to him and Joan. They did not move to Castle Ashby, though. They must by then have been well settled in Kent. Even if they visited the place from time to time, they were probably absentee landowners in Northamptonshire, and although the income from the estates would have made them a little richer, the inheritance must have made little real difference to their lives.

It perhaps had a greater impact on the couple when shortly afterwards Bishop Braybrooke also died, and with him the couple's last remaining close association with the previous king's reign. Braybrooke had been bishop of London for more than twenty years, and for almost all that time he must have been a major influence on his nephew. Perhaps Sir Reginald was not sorry that Lord Cobham had decided to draw away and not meddle in his handling of the estates, but he might have felt differently about his uncle. The bishop had a splendid funeral in August 1404 in St Paul's Cathedral, the greatest church in England, renowned for its tall spire and its brilliant stained glass, where Richard II's body had laid in state a few years earlier, and John of Gaunt's great tomb still stood.

24 Striking fear into minds

such wicked doctrine and opinions
From the text of
'De heretico comburendo'

The tomb effigy of King Henry IV in Canterbury Cathedral

Henry of Lancaster never sat very securely on the throne he had usurped, for all that he had claimed it relatively easily. His reign was punctuated by rebellions, in Wales, the North Country and in Scotland. He never troubled to follow Richard II to Ireland, but there was plenty of rebelliousness there too. There were several assassination attempts. When the King did anything that was unpopular with his nobles or commons, there were murmurs that other men had greater hereditary claims to the throne than him. (This was fundamentally true, which made the murmurs all the more difficult to counter.)

Much of Henry's policy – and he had a very different conception of the role of king from Richard II's – can be seen as a response to this situation, and not least among it was his attitude to the Church.

Critics of the vast, encrusted, corrupted edifice that was the Catholic Church in these times had two motives. One was purely religious. They thought – with much justification – that the Church had become, not an avenue to bring people to Christ's teachings, but a road that had diverted far from them. It had diverted in its religious emphases, which were increasingly not on Christ and the Trinity, but on the Virgin Mary, on saints, on miracles. It had diverted in its greed, and its desire to make people pay to support it, which had become a tendency to make people pay for the hope of salvation – buying off their sins with 'indulgences', funding masses for the dead, and much more besides, all of which sat more than uncomfortably with Christ's original emphasis on simplicity and poverty. Some people understandably thought it should have put stress not on buying one's way out of the consequence of sin, but on refraining from sinning in the first place. And it had diverted in its desire to control minds, which led it to discourage people from looking directly into the bible, and to force them to receive religious instruction only through anointed priests. All of this justified calls for reform, but a vast international body is not easily reformable, if it is reformable at all. Also, religion is not at heart rational, and the unquestioning acceptance that is at the heart of sincere belief does not sit readily alongside any acknowledgement of the need for change.

The other motive of critics was more political. They looked on the huge vested interest that was the Church. They saw the great expanses of land it controlled. They saw the obscene richness of many of the higher clergy, and the downtrodden poverty of the lower ones. They saw funds that were nominally meant for charitable works put instead to providing luxuries for churchmen. They saw the struggles of the monarchy to fund the public administration and the defence of the realm, the heavy taxation on the poor to provide those necessary funds; and they saw the relative freedom from taxation of the Church, and its tendency – understandable, inevitable, but also infuriating – to funnel funds out of England and towards the pope, in Rome or Avignon. They liked none of this, and they wanted to see it changed.

Supporters of the Church could also be seen as having two motives. Again, one was religious. They believed sincerely in heaven and hell, and the need for men and women to conduct their lives on earth in a way that would give them a hope of salvation, and a chance to avoid the eternal agonies of hell. They accepted that the teachings of the Church were fundamentally correct, and they believed that to question them, to go against them, would indeed lead people to damnation.

And they too had a pragmatic motive. Those with vested interests do not generally want to see revolution; they will support other vested interests, in order that those interests also support them.

These motives were not pure, of course; they were entwined, confused, not clearly spelled out, not least by those who possessed them. And the critics of the Church too believed sincerely in heaven and hell, and once they had taken notice of the Church's failings, were just as convinced as those within the fold that the route they had chosen was the route to heaven.

Under Richard II, the reform movement that had been given momentum by John Wycliffe, and bolstered by similar trends elsewhere in Europe, had been given much latitude. This was perhaps less because of the king – who arguably had nothing so definite as a policy towards the Church and its opponents – than because of John of Gaunt, who chose to use his influence and power to shelter Wycliffe, and let others too creep under his roof. Gaunt's tolerance had its limits. Although he evidently accepted the argument that there should be liberty for individuals to learn about Christ in their own way, he did not accept any rejection of transubstantiation. (The belief in transubstantion was to be a clear line between heretical and orthodox beliefs for centuries, and indeed remains a dividing line between different Christian sects today.) But even if he perceived that Wycliffe had gone too far, and embraced beliefs that he himself abhorred, Gaunt did not use his might to trample on him and on the movement of supporters that was developing into the Lollard tendency.

But Richard was no longer king, and Gaunt's son, made king, had different priorities. Probably, too, he had different beliefs. He did not support religious tolerance, and that was most likely from a sincere conviction that those who rejected the teachings of the established Church were damned, and if they were not discouraged – by force if necessary – they would lead others too to damnation. It was also from the pragmatic realization that he needed the established Church. Politically, he could not afford to encourage any movement for reform. Practically, he needed the support of the rich and powerful upper clergy.

He was faced, too, with a different situation, one in which an increasing number of people were questioning the Church and its teachings. This situation could have been left to ferment a revolution, but if the king did not want it to provide the yeast for that fermentation, then he needed to take firm action to quash the dissenters.

And King Henry had one further motive. His inclination was to extend the spread of the king's law. There was a wide area in which the Church's law held sway, and the king's agents – sheriffs, bailiffs, judges – had no influence. The Church's law had not operated effectively when it came to dealing with those who might kindly be called dissenters, or more harshly be described as heretics. (The root of the word 'heretic' is the Greek word for choice, but that too had been corrupted in meaning; now it meant, not a free choice, but a rejection of an enforced choice.) Henry seems to have seen the opportunity to let the secular law-enforcement mechanism work with the Church to enforce its privileges, and in doing so to creep into areas that had until then been the Church's to police.

It was in line with all these tendencies that in 1401, not long afer the beginning of his reign, Henry supported his archbishop of Canterbury (the same Archbishop Arundel, brother of the executed earl, who had been exiled by Richard II) in bringing before parliament a statute concerning the crime of heresy and the penalties that would be enacted for it.

De heretico comburendo (the Latin for 'the burning of heretics') was one of the most draconian laws of religious censorship ever enacted in England. It effectively confirmed the Catholic Church in its monopoly of religious belief and expression in England. No one was to be permitted to express any doctrines or opinions of which the Church did not approve. Preachers were from then onwards required to be licensed by the Church authorities, and no one was permitted to 'preach, hold, teach, or instruct openly or privily, or make or write any book contrary to the catholic faith or determination of the Holy Church'. Nor was anyone, 'of whatsoever sex, estate, or condition', permitted to provide any aid to such a preacher, or to possess any heretical book. If any such were in their possession, they were required to deliver them to the Church authorities.

If anyone was suspected of possessing heretical views, the Church authorities were given the power to arrest them – calling on the secular law enforcement officers for aid – and subject them to questioning. Those found to possess heretical views were to be given an opportunity to abjure (that is, reject) them, but if they failed to do so, then they were to be subjected to burning at the stake, 'that such punishment may strike fear into the minds of others, whereby no such wicked doctrine and heretical and erroneous opinions, nor their authors and fautors, in the said realm and dominions, against the Catholic faith, Christian law, and determination of the holy church, which God prohibit, be sustained or in any way suffered'.

Although the judgement of whether a person was a heretic was one for the Church, the statute explicitly laid down that 'sheriffs, mayors and bailiffs' – that is, all the secular enforcers of the law – were to aid the Church in enforcing the law, and attend on the carrying out of the sentences.

This was a law that would unnerve, at the least, anyone who had become a supporter of the Lollards – indeed, since the Lollards had nothing so formal as a membership, had become a Lollard. Plenty of people, both high and low, had been listening to criticisms of the Church and its teaching over several decades now. Many of these people had become sincerely convinced that the Church was mistaken, and that a different avenue was the one that led to heaven. They were now faced with an uncomfortable choice: to change their beliefs, or at least cease to express those beliefs, or put themselves outside the law.

It was a law that was to remain in force in England until 1559. For that century and a half, it set an indelible stain upon the country.

At first, people – people like the Joan and her husband, who probably felt at least some sympathy with the reformers – might have hoped the law would not be strictly enforced. That was a mistaken hope, for this was no empty threat. That was proved by the burning at the stake of a Lollard priest in the same year that the law was enacted. William Sawtre had the dubious honour of being the first known person executed for heresy in England when he was burned at Smithfield in March 1401. Many people watched his execution. Many more, who did not need to watch to know that this was an agonizing form of death, would have heard of it, and shivered, as they were intended to do.

Shivered, yes: but did they change their beliefs? That is not so easily done, when a person has given careful thought, listened to others they respect, and come to conclusions that have grown from rationality to conviction, to a sincere and firm belief. Many, perhaps most of them, believed no different after the statute was enacted than they had done before it. But they would have been markedly more careful in sharing those beliefs with others.

All Saints Church, Filby, Norfolk

Il a aujourd'hui un mois,
Que mon ami s'en alla.
Mon cœur demeure morne et coi.
Il a aujourd'hui un mois.
« A Dieu, me dit, je m'en vais. »
Ne puis à moi ne parla.
Il a aujourd'hui un mois.

[It was a month today
That my lover went away.
My heart stays dull and grieving.
It was a month today.
'Goodbye,' he said, 'I'm leaving.'
None further did he say.
It was a month today.]
Christine de Pisan (1364–c. 1430)

Middelburg, Netherlands

As well as playing an active part in Kentish life, and overseeing the rest of what was now an enormous inheritance, with lands from the de la Poles, the Peverells, the Hemenhales, the Braybrookes and of course the Cobhams under his and Joan's control, Sir Reginald must have spent a fair amount of his time with the king's forces. There is no reason to think he became an intimate of King Henry, but as an affluent landed couple, who were effectively acting as the lord and lady of Cobham (Braybrooke was even described on occasion as the 'lord of Cobham', although the third Lord Cobham was still alive), the Braybrookes would naturally have attended the court on occasion.

Henry IV was a man who had never been expected to become king, and he had not made the kind of diplomatic marriage that was common for English kings. But the mother of his children, Mary Bohun, had died in 1394, and in 1403 the King made a grand remarriage to Joan of Navarre, a Spanish princess who was the widow of a duke of Brittany. So there would have been Spaniards and Bretons, most likely, among her household; but life at court was probably shaped less by the queen and her associates than by the king's sons. He had daughters as well, but they were younger, still small children when their father took the throne, and both were married young to foreign nobles, and left England to live with their husbands.

The king's four sons were young too, but they were growing up fast. Henry, his heir, was only thirteen when his father took the crown. He began to fight young, and was wounded quite badly by an arrow that struck his face at the battle of Shrewsbury in 1403, against the Welsh rebel Owen Glyndwr and the Percy lords from Northern England. There were three other sons, and the king's father John of Gaunt had also had a family with his second wife, born illegitimate but legitimized after their parents' marriage, so in comparison with King Richard, who had had no siblings and no children of his own, this was a court crowded with relatively young close relatives of the king.

If it was a more martial, more male-dominated court than King Richard's had been, it also had its share of ceremonial, and probably Joan as well as her husband attended both the king's coronation and his marriage to Queen Joan, as well as the funeral of Richard II. In 1404 Sir Reginald was appointed as one of the knights of Kent to attend the parliament held at Coventry, which became known, rather unflatteringly, as the Parliament of Dunces after the king decreed that no lawyers should be nominated to sit. Sir Reginald must have hoped that this would be the first of many times he would sit in parliament and have a hand in the governance of the realm, initially as a knight, and then if all went well, later as a lord of Cobham.

But first, there was fighting demanded of him.

There is no evidence that Sir Reginald fought in the King's Welsh and Northern campaigns, although that is not proof that he did not. But we know that he was called on in 1405, when the king had an army assembled, and ships requisitioned, to carry out a campaign along the coasts of Flanders and Northern France.

This was a campaign that was contentious from the start. Indeed the London merchants had petitioned the council to beg the king to abandon it, because they thought that military intervention was likely to do more harm than good. Trade in wool, and increasingly in finished cloth, with Flanders was vital to the English economy, and it was essential to the English to maintain control of the trading routes. But in 1385 the duke of Burgundy (the overlord of large parts of the Low Countries) had chosen to fortify the strategic port of Sluys. This was considered by the English to be a threat, and a likely precursor to a larger Burgundian attempt to take control of the Channel. So the English campaign was designed to reassert control over the sea between England and Flanders, to discourage piracy, and to take advantage of Flemish discontent with their Burgundian overlords. These were difficult and to some extent contradictory objectives, which is presumably why many thought the campaign unwise. It probably did not help either that its command was given to Prince Henry's younger brother, Thomas of Clarence, a bright but inexperienced lad of seventeen.

Still, Sir Reginald responded to the call to arms, and took his men down to Sandwich, the small Kentish town (all but deserted after attacks of the plague and piracy) where the troops were being assembled. They spent a wearing two months or more there in the spring of 1405, while the force grew to around 5,000 men and up to a hundred ships to carry them, and Prince Thomas wrangled with the Treasury over funding for the venture. Joan must have chafed meanwhile: her husband was not so far from her home, but not with her there, and probably not even able to visit.

It was mid-May before the expedition set off, and perhaps a week later it landed, after sailing along the Flemish coast and not just reconnoitring, but making a 'mocking demonstration', as one historian called it, within sight of the Flemish ports of Dunkirk and Nieuport.[2] Mocking demonstrations never achieve much, so perhaps this was a sign of Prince Thomas's youth.

Sluys had a fine deep harbour, in which the English had scored a memorable victory in a naval battle at the start of the long war with the French, sixty-five years earlier. On this occasion there was no great French fleet to engage with the English flotilla, but there were a few merchant ships at anchor, which the English gleefully (although again, perhaps not altogether wisely) set on fire. They did the same with the outer fortifications of the town, from which its intended defenders had fled. But the strong stone walls that formed the inner fortifications, inside which were a good force of Flemish, French and German mercenaries, were a different matter.

In other circumstances the English might have set a siege which would slowly starve out the defenders. This was the most reliable, least risky option for those who needed to capture a well-defended town or

Stained glass from Evreux Cathedral, France, left and Canterbury Cathedral, right

castle. But word reached them that the duke of Burgundy was putting together a sizeable army of his own to bring to Sluys, and they wanted to be within those stone walls before it arrived. So Prince Thomas ordered an assault.

They spent five days hurling themselves against the new stone walls. It achieved nothing. When Prince Thomas finally ordered a retreat, about sixty of his men were dead, and many more had been injured. Sir Reginald Braybrooke was among them.

So he was not with the prince's troops as they sailed across the broad harbour and raided a few villages on the other bank. He was not with them as they sailed back across the Channel, having spent a good deal of money and achieved little more than nothing. He was carried to Middelburg, a fortified town a few miles inland from the great harbour, and word must have been sent to his wife that she was unlikely to see him come home alive.

He was not dead when word would have reached her. Badly wounded though he must have been, he was to survive almost another four months, before he died on 20 September 1405. If Joan ever left England, then surely she did so on this occasion, to go to nurse her husband on his deathbed. No record of what she did survives, but we can at least imagine that she did so: that she took the hazardous journey across the North Sea, sailed in to Sluys harbour as her husband had done, was escorted to Middelburg by an esquire who had stayed with him, and had the opportunity to wipe the sweat from his face, feed him nourishing broths, and do everything else that was possible to ease his pain. We do not know the nature of his wounds, but quite possibly there were times when she – and he too – believed that he would survive, disfigured or handicapped, but able to continue a worthwhile life. Eventually, though, it would have become apparent that however skilfully and lovingly he was nursed, there was no possibility of recovery, and a long slow final decline would have taken place.

In those agonizing months, Braybrooke must also have had an opportunity to settle his affairs, or at least to order others to settle them for him. It was presumably his decision that he should be buried, not among his own ancestors, but with his and Joan's sons in Cobham Church. Probably he gave some thought to his wife, and what she might do after his death. She was not a young girl any more, but in her mid-thirties she was far from old. He probably knew that however much she would miss him and mourn him, she was not the kind of woman who would choose to retreat to a convent. She needed a son still; she would marry again. Perhaps he even suggested to her whom she might marry, because the man she was

to marry next must have been known to him, and was quite likely a close friend of his.

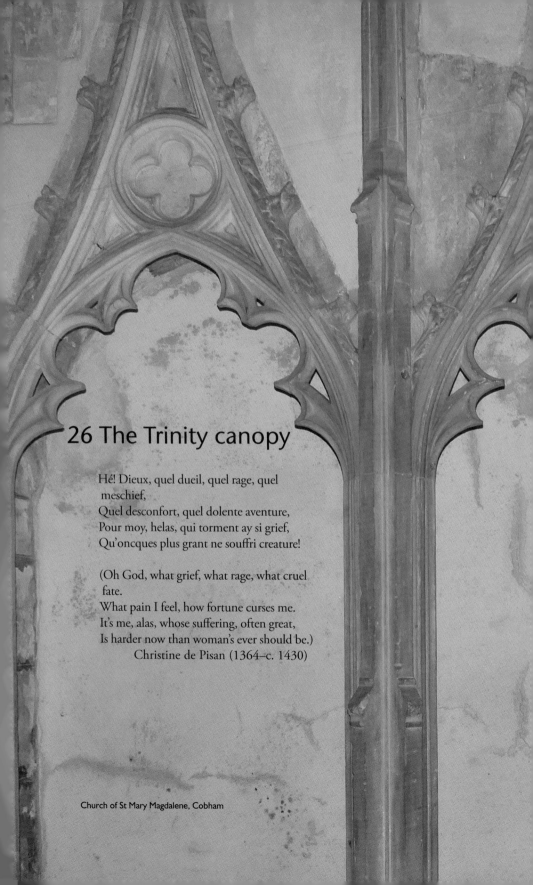

26 The Trinity canopy

Hé! Dieux, quel dueil, quel rage, quel
 meschief,
Quel desconfort, quel dolente aventure,
Pour moy, helas, qui torment ay si grief,
Qu'oncques plus grant ne souffri creature!

(Oh God, what grief, what rage, what cruel
 fate.
What pain I feel, how fortune curses me.
It's me, alas, whose suffering, often great,
Is harder now than woman's ever should be.)
      Christine de Pisan (1364–c. 1430)

Church of St Mary Magdalene, Cobham

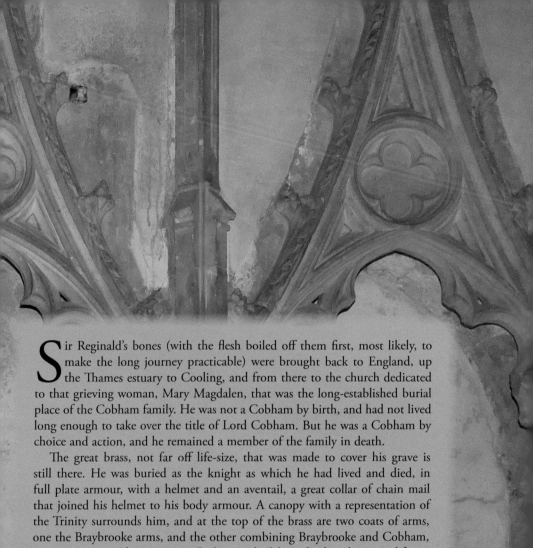

S ir Reginald's bones (with the flesh boiled off them first, most likely, to make the long journey practicable) were brought back to England, up the Thames estuary to Cooling, and from there to the church dedicated to that grieving woman, Mary Magdalen, that was the long-established burial place of the Cobham family. He was not a Cobham by birth, and had not lived long enough to take over the title of Lord Cobham. But he was a Cobham by choice and action, and he remained a member of the family in death.

The great brass, not far off life-size, that was made to cover his grave is still there. He was buried as the knight as which he had lived and died, in full plate armour, with a helmet and an aventail, a great collar of chain mail that joined his helmet to his body armour. A canopy with a representation of the Trinity surrounds him, and at the top of the brass are two coats of arms, one the Braybrooke arms, and the other combining Braybrooke and Cobham, to commemorate his marriage. Perhaps it had been by his choice in life, or perhaps it was Joan's choice after his death, that unusually the brass should show not just Sir Reginald, but also the two sons that she had borne him, and had already seen to their graves. Little Reginald stands on one side of his father, and Robert on the other, both praying miniatures of the men they did not grow up to become. This is the inscription, probably made like the brass some time after his death, when Joan had become Lady Cobham in her own right:

Here lies Reginald Braybrooke, knight, son of Gerard Braybrooke, knight, and husband of Lady Joan, Lady of Cobham, heir of John de Cobham, founder of this College. The said Reginald died at Middelburg in Flanders on the 20th day of the month of September in the year of the Lord 1405. On whose soul God have mercy. Amen, AMEN.

27 To escort a princess

As he dozed on a bed curtained with white canopies, he suddenly heard a slight noise at the door. He lifted up his head, and drew up the edge of the hangings, and looked warily to see who it was. And he saw the lady, the loveliest to behold, and she softly drew the door closed after her, and came towards the bed.

Sir Gawain and the Green Knight[1]

It would be trite to judge that Joan's years with Sir Reginald Braybrooke were the happiest of her life. Probably there were happy times, but they would have been shadowed, if not obliterated, by the loss of their sons and the trial of her grandfather. The terrible last months when he lay dying in Middelburg must have been hard too, whether she chose to go to him, or to stay alone, leaving him also alone, and conduct their affairs from Cooling. There was little in this to cause her to judge that God had been kind to her. And his death must have led to a long cold winter, her second winter of mourning among the bleak North Kent marshes after this, her second widowing.

She had no mother alive, no father, only one grandparent living, and he in seclusion at the other side of the country. No brothers or sisters, no son. One small daughter, whom we must hope provided some consolation. What else? A fortune, of course. Perhaps a servant or two to whom she felt close, or a kindly chaplain, and a friend or two from among those who had been friends to Sir Reginald too. A lapdog; a hawk. It was not enough. Seeing this, it is perhaps easier to understand why she wanted more, badly enough that again she wasted no time at all in remarrying.

Perhaps there was a sliver of ice in her heart, that held her back from mourning so intensely that for months and years following Sir Reginald's death, she would have found it unthinkable to seek another partner. Perhaps after all she had not loved him with real passion, but there had been problems in the marriage of which we know nothing. Or perhaps she was, quite simply, the kind of woman who cannot resist a handsome man in armour. Because the husband she chose next was a man who clearly cut a dash on horseback, who was renowned by his contemporaries and remembered through the centuries for his skill in the lists. He seems to have been the kind of man who could easily make a lonely widow lose her sense of caution.

It is certainly arguable, though, whether this next swift marriage amounted to rashness. She did have to make plans for the future, and might well have felt all but obliged to make further efforts to have a healthy son before she became too old to conceive. She did have to steward her inheritance, or find someone who would do so for her. There was no question, it seems, of her grandfather returning from Wiltshire and resuming the management of his lands in Kent. He was in extreme old age now, and quite possibly not capable of doing so even if he had wished to. It was Joan's responsibility to ensure that those who farmed those estates were supervised, with a husband if she chose, or with managers and agents if she did not.

Did she even choose this husband herself? Some historians have written of Joan as if all her decisions were made for her by others, and suggested that since she now had no close relative to negotiate her next marriage, her new husband might have been 'found' for her by the king, or someone to whom he delegated the task.[2] But there is no reason to think that Joan was incapable of finding a husband for herself, or that anyone else would have intervened so swiftly, rather than giving her a year or two to mourn and recover. It seems more likely that the reason for this rapid remarriage was that she already knew an unattached man she judged to be suitable – one whom it is entirely conceivable Sir Reginald had suggested to her. Sir Reginald would surely have known the man she married next. They had both been knights associated with the court, under both King Richard and King Henry. They might well have been good friends, and it could be the case that Joan was doing what her last husband had suggested, even arranged, that she do after his

Painted wood from St Botolph's Church, Trunch, Norfolk

death. It is kinder to Joan to imagine that she was marrying the friend her husband had asked to watch out for her, rather than imagining she was seduced into skimping on her mourning. But that not does mean it was not so.

Whichever was the case, within a year of Sir Reginald's funeral Joan was Lady Hawberk, the wife of Sir Nicholas Hawberk.

Sir Nicholas is something of an enigma. A few things are known about his career, but nothing certain is known about where he came from. Although there was a family of that name in Leicestershire, they bore entirely different arms from Sir Nicholas,[3] which indicates that he cannot have been one of them. His is not an English-sounding name, and it could even have been a pseudonym: a hauberk is the name for a shirt of chain-mail (that is, for what was by then an old-fashioned form of armour), and it is a suspiciously appropriate name for a man who made his living with his sword and lance.

It has been suggested too that Sir Nicholas's arms have a German look to them, so perhaps he was one of the knights who accompanied Anne of Bohemia to England for her marriage to Richard II. A foreigner landing in England without good contacts would have found it difficult to get established in the king's court and wider society, but the same was not true of a man who arrived with the queen's effective mark of approval.

And since Sir Nicholas evidently did settle in very well, and thrive in England, it makes sense that he had a connection such as this to get him started.

There were plenty of foreigners in England during Joan's lifetime, in London especially: merchants, bankers, diplomats, men at arms and more. But a man with an inheritance on the Continent is unlikely to have chosen to abandon it and come to England permanently, unless a major difficulty at home had forced him to do so. Such a man might have been called on to escort the queen to her new home, but he would have turned round and gone back to his family once she was settled. So Sir Nicholas most likely did not have any great inheritance, although he came from a background that had enabled him to undertake the costly training, and acquire the costly equipment, of a man at arms. Perhaps it was known to his contemporaries – because they had learned it from reputable people who knew his background at first hand, the queen included – that he was a younger son of a good family. But many people at times feel a degree of unease and suspicion about foreigners, and there

Stained glass from St Peter's Church, Ringland, Norfolk.
Photos by Mike Dixon

were probably also those who wondered whether Sir Nicholas had had problems in his past that he wanted to leave behind, and this was why he had not returned to Germany.

He had not only stayed on during Queen Anne's lifetime, he had stayed on after her death. A couple of years later, in 1396, he had married an Englishwoman – a noble Englishwoman, daughter of one lord and widow of another – and this had naturally given him reason to continue to stay. Then by the time she had died (in September 1400, around six years before he married Joan) he had acquired possessions and appointments, and again it must have seemed wiser to build on what he had, than to go back to a home country where he would have been a stranger.

So whatever was the truth about his origins and past, he had been living primarily in England for fifteen years or so when Joan married him. Probably she had been acquainted with him since the early 1390s. As he first achieved notice as a king's esquire back in 1391, Sir Nicholas was perhaps around Joan's own age; quite a bit younger than Sir Reginald, but not so much so that they could not have been good friends.

Joan would certainly have noted Sir Nicholas as one of the knights given the privilege of holding a single combat at the great tournament in 1393 – and he won the bout. He must have been famed before it as a particularly talented jouster, or he would not have been awarded what was surely a heavily sought-after role, and the victory would have given him considerably more fame.

So we can suspect a degree of flashiness, and a degree of the charm that is needed for a man who is not rich to thrive at court. He evidently had diplomatic skills, and the ability to get them recognized, first by Richard II, and then even more notably by King Henry. In 1401 he had been one of the men who took Richard II's child-widow Isabella back to her family in France. He was also an escort when Blanche of Lancaster, King Henry's daughter , travelled to Germany to marry Louis III, the Elector Palatine.[4] That he took on both missions suggests he had a particular affinity with regal young ladies – that he knew how to make himself liked by them, and how to manage them well enough to please those responsible for them.

Sir Nicholas does not seem to have been given the use of manors by either king in the way that Sir Reginald had been, but he had received some preferment. In 1396 he was made sheriff and constable of Flint, a county on the Welsh borders (known then as the Marches) that was then relatively well controlled by the English.[5] The woman he

married first was also then living in the Marches. Maud de Mohun was the daughter of the second Lord Mohun of Dunster, Somerset, but she had been married to John, Lord LeStrange, whose main seat was at Knockin in Shropshire. Although it is always difficult to disentangle the dates and ages of people with similar names, it seems that she was first married back in 1372, so if Sir Nicholas got a pedigree and perhaps a bit of land with his rich widow, he did not get youth as well.

This sounds, indeed, like the sort of marriage a fortune-hunter might have made, although Maud had already had sons by Lord LeStrange who were set to inherit the bulk of the LeStrange lands, so there was no question of their going to any children she had with Hawberk (if she had still been young enough to conceive when they married; perhaps she was not, because there is no evidence that the couple had children). And she had been a younger daughter of Lord Mohun, although his elder daughters died relatively young, so she did become his heir. So it had not been a grotesquely unsuitable marriage on her part, but it had not been a particularly advantageous one for her, while it had been a remarkably impressive one for Sir Nicholas.

A charming, competent man, skilled at jousting, a likely asset as a captain in the king's army: probably many people would not have looked askance at his marrying upwards socially and economically, very much as Sir Reginald Braybrooke had done. But marrying a second rich widow? And leaving the part of Britain in which he had established himself, and moving right across the country to Kent in order to do so? It would have been understandable if some people had seen that as rather dubious.

But clearly Joan was not among them. She probably knew more than we can know today about Sir Nicholas's past, and so would other people that they both knew. Did she know about the murder he had committed? This was not a dark secret he had left behind in Germany, it was one that had happened in England. He killed one Peter Imaynesson of Richmondshire in Candlewick Street in London on 4 May 1390, and that November another of the king's knights, Baldwin de Bereford, petitioned the courts for a pardon for him.[6] The pardon was granted, so there was no crime set on his record, but some people would have remembered this over the years.

One sign of the unease, if not outright disapproval, that some might have expressed is the fate of Sir Nicholas's grave. Like Sir Reginald, he was buried in Cobham church, and the brass that covers his grave is in many ways a twin to Sir Reginald's, in a style so similar that experts think Joan might have commissioned the two at the same time, or at least from the same craftsman. His head rests on a jousting helmet, as Sir Reginald's does not. His brass too shows two sets of arms, his own unusual arms, and those combined with the Cobham arms. But both have been defaced – one local historian suggests on purpose, by heralds who felt that Sir Nicholas was not rightly entitled to them.[7] Perhaps this was done shortly after the brass was laid down, although since there is no record it might equally have happened years, even centuries later.

So this was in some ways a brave marriage for Joan to make. It was not one that she made in order to obtain more land or powerful connections. But the man she married was by no means a completely unknown quantity to her: he had obtained the friendship and approval of others, including another woman from the nobility who chose to marry him, two successive kings of England, and most likely her own previous husband. We have no reason to think her a stupid woman, and although we might guess that Sir Nicholas was an attractive and likeable man, there is no reason to think she married unwisely, deprived of her usual good sense by his charm or his ability to thrill the audience on the jousting field.

One reason that she chose Sir Nicholas might have been that she knew she was acquiring a husband who would devote himself, much as Sir Reginald had done, to taking care of her estates, simply because he did not have great estates of his own to demand the bulk of his attention. Perhaps Joan, now comfortably settled in Kent, and working to retain her connections in East Anglia, was very reluctant to up roots and go to live where a husband dictated, so it made sense for her to choose a partner who would be happy to live at Cooling. Certainly Sir Nicholas did so. Perhaps he too had no desire to spend more time in the bleak and old-fashioned little border fortress of Knockin. Anyway, Maud's son by Lord LeStrange was by then just of age, so although Sir Nicholas had been the boy's guardian after his father's death, by this time there was no obvious role for him in Knockin. His appointments in Flint were not so very impressive, or so very demanding, as to dominate his life. Probably he had always spent more of his time in Westminster than in Wales or the west of England, and it suited him to be within close range of London – and to have the use of Cobham's Inn in the city.

Was the marriage a success? It is difficult to say, mostly because it proved to be brief. Joan must have become pregnant very shortly after their wedding, and she gave birth to a son, whom the couple called John, perhaps early in 1407. She was no luckier with her children by Hawberk than she had been earlier, though. John too was to die as a small child.

And sadly, Sir Nicholas was not long in following his infant son to the grave. He died on 9 October 1407, only a little more than two years after Sir Reginald's death, when the couple can have been married not much more than a year. So it is little wonder if he made no lasting impact on Kentish society, left no memorial beyond his grave in his newly adopted county. He had had no time in which to do so.

Stained glass, left, from St Mary's Church, Saxlingham Nethergate, Norfolk; right, from St Margaret's Church, Stratton Strawless, Norfolk

28 The fish in the ring

De Terre fu fait et fourme et en Terre et a terre suy retourne.
Lord Cobham's epitaph[1]

The winter of 1407 to 1408 was the coldest for a century, a time when the snow lay permanently on the ground, and the ponds and rivers stayed frozen for months. This was a time when Cobham church must have been almost permanently decorated with the banners that Lord Cobham had ordered for his wife's funeral. Joan and Sir Reginald's sons; Sir Reginald himself; Joan's son with Sir Nicholas, and then Sir Nicholas himself: it was a long sequence of great funerals, of great losses for Joan. And the brasses cannot yet have been set in place, the candles would still have been alight on the unfinished graves, when in January 1408 Lord Cobham's life came to an end.

He died at Maiden Bradley, where he had lived perhaps longer than he had first expected when he withdrew there about eight years earlier. But it seems he had always intended to be buried among his family at Cobham, and he was indeed brought there, as far as we can tell, to lie under a brass that he had, unusually, apparently commissioned about forty years before his death.[2] The reason was simple: he knew how he wanted to be commemorated. Clearly the achievement of which he was most proud during his lifetime was founding the college at Cobham and enhancing the church there, so the figure on his brass is shown holding a church in his hands, as a visual reminder of what he had done. (It is a stock image of a church, and does not look much like Cobham's St Mary Magdalene, but the inscription makes it clear that it was Cobham it signified.)

The surviving documents suggest that Joan paid out only a modest sum to bring Lord Cobham's body home and see him buried, so the procession to escort her grandfather's bones across southern England was probably more chilly than grandiose.[3] Joan might well have become sick of great funerals, and perhaps she had come to have religious beliefs that militated against the kind of expensive ceremony that had been arranged for her grandmother. She would have done what she felt appropriate, and this, it seems, was what she judged appropriate for her grandfather (or possibly it was what he had specified himself). He had his memorial in his college and his castle, and in the memories men and women held of him.

Joan can have seen little if anything of her grandfather after he moved to Maiden Bradley, so if this brought a finality to her loss, it was a loss that she had essentially suffered some years earlier. Of course she now became the full owner of the Cobham inheritance, and as such a very rich woman; but she had lived very comfortably before, and both her previous two husbands seem effectively to have administered the estates, so the change was mostly a legalistic one. Lord Cobham's death did however mean that she became not Joan Hawberk, but Joan, baroness Cobham; and if she married again (to a man whom the king deemed suited to the honour) her husband could expect to become Lord Cobham, and to be summoned to Parliament as one of the king's lords in that capacity. It made her an even more desirable property in the marriage market.

A sketch of Lord Cobham's brass from *Kent Archaeology*

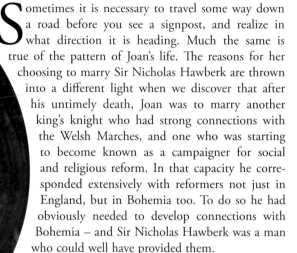

Sometimes it is necessary to travel some way down a road before you see a signpost, and realize in what direction it is heading. Much the same is true of the pattern of Joan's life. The reasons for her choosing to marry Sir Nicholas Hawberk are thrown into a different light when we discover that after his untimely death, Joan was to marry another king's knight who had strong connections with the Welsh Marches, and one who was starting to become known as a campaigner for social and religious reform. In that capacity he corresponded extensively with reformers not just in England, but in Bohemia too. To do so he had obviously needed to develop connections with Bohemia – and Sir Nicholas Hawberk was a man who could well have provided them.

Alongside the defaced coats of arms, another feature of Sir Nicholas's tomb is well worth considering. Incised into the stone that holds the brass is a curious symbol, a fish curled up into a ring.[4]

This is known as a symbol of early Christians. Of course Sir Nicholas was a Christian; almost everyone in England claimed to be a Christian. But this symbol is not often found on medieval tombs, so perhaps it had a special meaning at the time. Perhaps those whose Christian beliefs were not of the mainstream, but more specific – like those of the Hussites in Bavaria, or the Lollards in England – would have recognized this as an indication that he was one of their own.

Sir Nicholas was not known as a Lollard to the general public, as far as we can tell, but after the passing of the De heretico comburendo law that was no wonder. Many people who sincerely wanted more religious freedom would have been very wary of expressing that opinion – during their lives, at least. When they were dead, a symbol that some would recognize might generate some tricky questions for their families, but it could do nothing to endanger them.

Sir Reginald, Sir Nicholas, Sir John Oldcastle (Joan's next husband): all of them were similar types of man, and not only in that they were appropriate, if not hugely impressive, husbands for a woman of her class. They would have run across each other in military campaigns, in tournaments (Sir John was a keen jouster like Sir Nicholas, and perhaps Sir Reginald was too), in attendance on the king at court, and at Parliament too. Both Sir Reginald and Sir John had been nominated to represent the Commons in the 1404 parliament.

The English nobility was a very limited group (of well under a hundred lords) at this time, and although there were more knights at the level just below nobility, still this was a small group, of men near the top of a small society in a relatively small country. All the English lords and many of the knights would have known each other to some degree, but an accident of shared appointments under the same commander, or simply a liking for each other, would have caused some men (and of course women too) to have developed closer friendships with some than with others. Perhaps Joan's swift remarriages are more understandable if we think of her husbands as a band of brothers in arms, men who knew each other, shared experiences and beliefs as well (not all of them beliefs they wished to broadcast widely), and supported each other. Left alone, Joan might readily have turned to her dead husband's close friends and colleagues for support; knowing she was left alone, those friends and colleagues might have gone out of their way to support her.

Whatever the truth of it, after Sir Nicholas's death – and her grandfather's death too – it was not long before Cobham saw another ceremony. The date of Joan's marriage to Oldcastle is not known, but it would have been before July 1408: again, almost as soon as was decent.

Stained glass from Canterbury Cathedral

29 Fifteen earls and 1,500 knights

And also, how King Alexander had conquered many different regions, lands and cities, and, among others he had conquered a great city, and asked for advice from Aristotle on how he could most securely fortify the same city, by a wall or otherwise. To whom the said Aristotle replied by saying that the best security and guard for each realm and city is to have the whole and cordial love of the people, and to maintain them in all their laws and rights.

From the speech by Henry Beaufort, bishop of Winchester
(and half-brother to the king)
at the opening of the 1410 parliament[1]

It is a dangerous job indeed to try to colour in the bald outlines that are all history has left us of the men and women of the Middle Ages. If the attempt to sketch out shadows and subtleties provides us with a three-dimensional picture of sorts, it will quite likely not be a picture that their contemporaries would recognize. But it is easier with Sir John Oldcastle than with most other men and women, because there is only one kind of character that makes sense of his dramatic, tragic history. That colouring gives us a sense of a large man in every way (except the physical, which we can barely judge, beyond an impression of power and rude health): one strong, charismatic, decisive. It would be unfair to describe him as a man who did not think, but perhaps much less unfair to judge him one who did not think deeply or acutely. He was a man for bold outlines, grand gestures; he was no academic, pausing and questioning, exploring different angles before tentatively heading into action. These qualities made him a leader of men, although he did not always lead them in the right direction. On the battlefield, he would have been – as his contemporaries clearly judged him to be – an impressive commander.

Much of this is also true of the picture that could be drawn of King Henry V – still Prince Henry, at the time Joan married Oldcastle. And indeed in many ways the two men were similar. It was this, surely, that made them both friends of a sort and enemies. But only one of these two men was to achieve a kind of greatness – and it was not Sir John Oldcastle.

Henry must not infrequently have been exasperated beyond bearing by his brilliant, uncontrollable colleague. But in the king's dealings with him, a rare humanity is always apparent. Henry found it in himself to be tolerant, compassionate; he never, even at the times when Oldcastle least seemed to deserve it, lost a sense of respect for his adversary. If Sir John Oldcastle had managed to find in himself the same respect for his king, perhaps his story would have had a different ending. But it was not only, perhaps, his natural tendency to reject authority, to hate any form of control of his actions, that led him to fatally disrespect Henry. It was also a kind of blindness, an inability to see the other's point of view, that made it impossible for him to steer a safe course through life. When he did compromise, it was only briefly – much too briefly – and there is the sense that there was another hand behind those compromises. It was a hand that failed to hold the reins firmly enough to keep him on track. Perhaps – but only perhaps – it was the hand of his wife.

Joan had had plenty of experience in dealing with different husbands when she married Sir John. Perhaps she had not always dealt with them successfully, but deal with them she undoubtedly had done. And we might guess – it is little more than an informed guess – that she managed only moderately with Sir Robert, hampered no doubt by her own extreme youth and inexperience, and that she managed much better with Sir Reginald. (Sir Nicholas was too briefly in her life for a judgement to be possible.) The verdict with Sir John is much clearer. If she tried to control him – and quite likely she did not even try, and the faint tugs on the reins that history shows are not hers at all – then she failed. This was a man too large for her, too fundamentally uncontrollable. Regardless of her character and intelligence (about which, again, we can only guess), Joan's money, in brutal terms, would have earned her some power in her relationships with her previous husbands, some respect and consideration from them. Sir John was not a monster, and there is no reason to think him cruel or vicious. He was a moral man – almost too much so, or at least, too black and white in his morality. But that fundamental blindness to others, that inability to respect, leads to a sense that he was not a considerate husband.

His priorities were not fundamentally focused on her, whatever attempts he made (in the earlier, easier days of their marriage) to steward her estates diligently and responsibly. And when it became apparent that to pursue his priorities would all but destroy her, he went on to pursue them anyway, and let her all but be destroyed.

We can see Joan as choosing Sir Reginald, choosing Sir Nicholas; but it is easier to see Sir John choosing Joan, than her choosing him. She acquiesced, of course; he did not marry her by force. And he would doubtless never have thought it a conceivable judgement that he had done her wrong by marrying her. But he married her, surely, because she gave him what he needed: money, the position as one of the king's barons that came with that money, space to live out his life in the way he chose. He did not marry her because he wanted a life's partner, because he was not the kind of man who worked in partnership. He was a man who led, and in the last resort, he led both himself and others to a tragic doom.

His intentions were fine, though. What we see in him of idealism, of a consciousness of a better world he hoped to achieve, is impressive indeed. If only his character had been tempered with more self-awareness, more awareness of the thoughts and needs of others, then he too might have been great.

But it was not.

Oldcastle was not the enigma that Sir Nicholas might have seemed: his background was respectable and well known. His family came from Almeley in Herefordshire, some way south of Flint where Sir Nicholas had held his appointments, but also in the border region where there were regular military campaigns to keep order and resist the challenge of the rebellious Welsh. One biographer of Sir John described his family as 'of no great account',[2] but that is rather unkind: his grandfather and his uncle had both represented Herefordshire in parliament (as did Sir John himself) and his uncle had also been sheriff, and held various other appointments there. But the Oldcastles were not a hugely rich landed family: they seem to have owned little land outside Almeley.[3] Oldcastle himself was primarily a professional man at arms. His appointments were mostly connected with keeping the peace in the Welsh Marches: he had been captain of Builth Castle (which came under attack from the Welsh during his tenure), and commanded a sizeable troop of men at Hay. These were not the kinds of task that would gain a man a fortune, and although he seems to have been a distinguished and highly regarded soldier, and had been granted some modest rewards by the Crown, Sir John had evidently not become rich from his endeavours.

Opinions vary about his age, since his date of birth is not known. But most likely he was about Joan's own age, or possibly a few years younger.

So once again, Joan was clearly marrying – choosing to marry, to the extent that it was her own choice – not for land and power, but to obtain a husband who would benefit from her own land and power, use them well, and enable her to live the life she chose. Once again she presumably made it a condition of the marriage that Sir John would make his life with her in Kent. After his marriage he left Almeley and spent most if not all of the time (at least, for as long as he was able to do so) with Joan at Cooling and in London.

A woman in her late thirties, who has been married three times already, is by no means in the same position as a young girl in making a marriage. She brings to it, inevitably, the bundle of her past experiences, both bad and good: her joys, her sorrows, her agreements and disagreements with her previous partners. She brings her children, alive and dead; she brings hopes for her future that are tempered by all that has happened in the past. And the man she marries, if she chooses someone of a similar age, will bring his own experiences, his existing situation in life, and thoughts and beliefs that have become well rooted and cannot easily be changed.

Oldcastle was not a highly educated man. He must have been able to read, and to write a little; there is no reason to think him stupid, any more than Joan might have been stupid. But he was no lawyer or priest, not taught at an university to debate fine points of logic. He seems to have been no diplomat. He was not the kind of man, like his predecessor in Joan's bed, to be appointed to escort young princesses across Europe. He was a man who gained the friendship of kings and the hand of a rich woman, however, so he must have had a charm of his own.

And he was evidently a man of strong beliefs. He was not widely known as a rebel at the time of his marriage to Joan, any more than Joan's grandfather or her previous husbands had been, but by a year or two after their marriage he was clearly marked out as a Lollard. It seems unlikely that he had developed these views from scratch during those years; he had more likely held them for some time.

His religion was like Wycliffe's only in its general tendency. Oldcastle did not spend his time wrangling with abstruse issues. It seems more to have been simple and robust. His were beliefs about religion, and about politics too, that had evidently been forged by the experiences that were common to a degree to all English people over the previous twenty years and more. When kings can be deposed, and a more acceptable king put in their place, one whose hereditary claim to the title is far from evident, then it is difficult to believe that there is something inevitable, let alone divine, about the hereditary rights of kings. When there are two rival popes – as there continued to be until 1417, although by the 1410s moves were being made to resolve the situation – then it is difficult to believe in the absolute authority, given by God, of either of them. When corruption is apparent, and goes unchecked, both in the Church and in the king's administration, then it breeds cynicism: or its mirror image, a desire for simple absolutes, a faith that has no truck with corruption or debasement at all. And this can lead on to fanaticism, to intolerance, to a tendency to see things in stark black and white terms, and to condemn as black all that is not evidently white.

What Oldcastle's beliefs were, we know from the confessions that he wrote out later in his life. He believed that Christ was the only true head of the Church, and by deduction, that the pope could not hold that position. He believed that 'God asks no more of man than that he shall obey his law. Should any prelate require any other kind of obedience, he contemneth Christ, and so becometh an open antichrist.' (He was several times to be quoted as finding his opponents, the pope included, to be effectively antichrists.) He believed that men and women should seek Christ directly, and not via the mediation of clerics. In his church there were three classes, of priests, knights and commons, all with their own roles to play.[4] He believed that the bible should be available for men and women to read, and quite likely his own household did so. It also had other religious

Stained glass from St John the Baptist's Church, Thaxted, Essex

books. His belief was not a puritan or ascetic one; he had the books illuminated. And it was not a pacifist one, a notion that had no place in his era.

Sir John had been married at least once before. Some biographers claim he had been married twice, but nothing is known of his second wife, he evidently had no children by her, and others have understandably concluded that she did not exist. Unlike Sir Nicholas, he had not previously married into the nobility. His first wife was apparently Welsh, although her mother was heir to lands in Buckinghamshire. She was Katherine, the daughter of Richard ap Ievan, whom he had married by 1394, and by whom he had had four surviving children, two sons and two daughters.[5] Sir John's father had died in 1397, so by the time he married Joan he had been possessed for some time of the family estates, and had a thriving young family, and no great need of further children. Joan did apparently bear him a

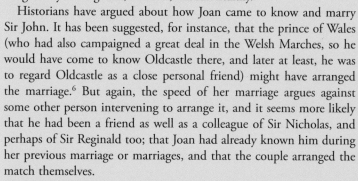

daughter, but like so many of her children, this baby did not survive. Her daughter by Sir Reginald, however, was still healthy.

Historians have argued about how Joan came to know and marry Sir John. It has been suggested, for instance, that the prince of Wales (who had also campaigned a great deal in the Welsh Marches, so he would have come to know Oldcastle there, and later at least, he was to regard Oldcastle as a close personal friend) might have arranged the marriage.[6] But again, the speed of her marriage argues against some other person intervening to arrange it, and it seems more likely that he had been a friend as well as a colleague of Sir Nicholas, and perhaps of Sir Reginald too; that Joan had already known him during her previous marriage or marriages, and that the couple arranged the match themselves.

Although the wider world did not yet seem to know Oldcastle as a Lollard, if his beliefs were already firm at the time of his marriage, then he would have been in touch with others of similar inclinations, and Joan would presumably have known his thoughts and convictions. And quite likely she shared them, and this was among her motives for choosing him. Also, he was an impressive man: strong, charismatic, attractive, and all this might well have drawn her to him, as it was to draw many others. Perhaps he made it clear at the time of their marriage that he would use the opportunities it brought him to pursue his ideas of reform, and in time to try to bring them to fruition.

There was undoubtedly a risk in seeking any kind of reform, particularly of the Church. Those with different beliefs also held them sincerely in many cases, and resisted any change in the orthodoxy. There were plenty of people, too, who had comfortable lives within the Church establishment, and a vested interest in seeing it unreformed. But the risk that was involved might then have seemed a slight and manageable one, particularly if Oldcastle and his friends were to focus, at least initially, on the structure and administration of the Church rather than on its doctrine. After William Sawtre's burning, there had been no great campaign against the Lollards. Indeed there had been no other execution for heresy in the intervening years. So although in theory all people in England were expected to support the Catholic Church and believe what it dictated that they should believe, plenty of people did not do so, at least to some degree, and found their unorthodoxy unpunished and effectively tolerated.

Stained glass from, left, St John the Baptist Church, Thaxted;
centre and right, St Lawrence's Church, Little Waldingham, Essex

Whether she expected it or not, on her marriage Joan became the wife of a radical Lollard. She and Sir John seem to have lived mostly at Cooling, and although the great castle had been Joan's main home for years by then, we can imagine Sir John transforming it almost beyond recognition. Ever since old Lord Cobham had shifted his home from Cobham to Cooling, it had been the administrative centre of wide estates, a place where many men (and some women too) would come, a place where the broad square courtyards bustled, the stables were full, the quay solid with boats, the kitchens and brewhouse steaming. It was a place where Lord and Lady Cobham would have entertained their associates, and after them Joan with Sir Reginald and then Sir Nicholas. But Sir John, surely, made it his own.

We can imagine Joan, perhaps bemused, perhaps exhilarated, finding her home becoming the magnet for men across England who supported the cause of reform. Heavy-accented preachers from the Midlands gave fiery sermons (fiery enough that rumour of them spread), not in Cobham church, where the unsympathetic might hear them, but in Cooling church, amid the empty marshes. The towers and halls of Cooling Castle must have been full of knights, esquires,  merchants too, talking, arguing, planning how they might use the new resources that Sir John (through his wife) had brought to their cause, to force great changes on the government and on the Church. We can imagine Joan emerging – perhaps bewildered, perhaps enthused – from her private chamber, with her longstanding maidservants, perhaps equally bewildered, and being greeted by strangers who assured her that her husband was a wonder, a hero, the man to transform England. Perhaps she believed it. Perhaps she was happy to take a step backwards, and leave her husband to stand in the blaze of sunlight. It would have been easier for her if she had, if she was.

Sir John Oldcastle became Lord Cobham on his marriage. (I shall call him Sir John in this account, though, to avoid confusion, and because it was a name by which he continued to be known.) It does not seem to have been inevitable that a husband of Joan's would take that title, so it was perhaps a mixture of his own achievements to date, his perceived suitability, and the need for someone to represent the Cobham interests in parliament, that ensured he became one of the king's barons. In that capacity he was summoned to parliament in October 1409. The king who confirmed him in his new title, and whose servants brought him that summons, must have had no conception of how Sir John planned to use it.

The parliament did not assemble till the following January, and meanwhile Sir John crossed the Channel and took part in a tournament at Lille. This was a trip mostly for pleasure, nothing to do with war, and certain to include dances and feasts of the kind she quite likely loved, so it is probable that Joan accompanied him. If there was a golden stage in this fourth

marriage, a time when she gloried in what it had brought her, then this was it.

Sir Nicholas had fought showy single combats in the lists, but he had not been hers when he did so. Sir John was hers, her husband, even if she was no longer a pretty young girl who might be chosen to ride ahead of the champions in their procession. It was for her to watch, doubtless with much pride, as he rode out into the lists, his pages and esquires checked his armour and helped him fasten his helmet and mount his courser, and he readied his lance for the thundering charge. He was pitted against a well-known French nobleman, Anthoine de Craon.[7] No record survives of which of them won the bout, but Sir John emerged from it uninjured and presumably with spirits undoused. The count of Nevers, their host, laid on three days of feasts and ceremonies. Perhaps Sir John had attended this kind of event before, or perhaps it was only now, with Joan's money and his new rank to support him, that he was able to indulge himself in this way. They must both have had a fine old time.

And then they came back, to get ready for the parliament. It must have taken much preparation, because Sir John was clearly determined that this would be the time to present proposals for a radical change of the government and the Church in England.

It would be a mistake to imagine that in this, he represented a small radical fringe. On the contrary: although only a minority of the English probably shared the Lollards' religious beliefs (and many in the country-side had quite likely not even heard of them), there was a majority who wanted change. Sir John was among the men who wanted to dynamize that majority. We cannot know now who all the planners of the action were, or indeed even be certain what role Sir John took, let alone what role, if any, his wife took. Those planners agreed that the focus of their proposals should be firmly on reform, and not on belief. (Then, when the Church as well as the state had been reformed, they might have looked for more latitude on what people professed to believe.)

Perhaps they started in Cooling. Then they probably moved to Cobham's Inn, which was large enough to host meetings, private enough to shield them from those who might be unsympathetic, and a great mansion that all London (and many beyond it) would have known. It was confirmed that the parliament would be held at Westminster, so in the weeks and days before it was opened, the lords from across England, and the knights of the shires and burgesses of the towns who had been chosen by their colleagues to represent them, were all coming to London or Westminster, and finding temporary lodging for the period that they would need to be in the city.

The leaders of the movement must have contacted them all, because they put together a proposal that they felt confident in presenting as coming from all the Commons of England. It was agreed that it would be presented by the Commons, not by the Lords, but there was clearly support for it among the Lords as well. Sir John was not alone, although there he might

Left, from the doorway of Westminser Abbey. right, Westminster Hall by Wenceslas Holler (1647)

well have been in a minority. The bishops and abbots who sat in the Lords would almost by definition have been opposed, so the rebels must have taken some trouble to keep any rumour of what they were planning from these men.

The proposals derived from ideas that had evidently been circulating for several years. But it must have been in these exciting weeks that the wording was agreed, written out, circulated, and men asked – not just a few men, but all the knights of the shires and burgesses of the towns – to commit to supporting it when it was laid before parliament. And as well as contacting the men who would attend the parliament, the leaders probably consulted widely among the network of Lollard supporters who were known to them in London. This strong network seems to have included many tradesmen and professional men: men of some standing, and some influence among their friends. The few surviving reports say little or nothing of women, but there must have been women too among the Lollards, and perhaps Joan had a hand in contacting them.

What the king thought, they evidently did not enquire. They did not brief the king in advance on their proposals. They must have known that this would be a parliament in which Prince Henry and his supporters would try to wrest more power from the ailing king (something that would be resisted by the king and his counsellors), but they apparently did not try to enlist the prince's faction in support either. Nor did they attempt to pack the parliament. (Prince Henry perhaps did, but that is a different issue.) They did not need to, because by the time parliament was assembled, and the great opening speeches were made, they had their support, and it was as solid as the walls of Cooling Castle.

One man spoke against the proposals when they were put forward. He must have been the only one, because the chroniclers who wrote accounts of their presentation (and, since they were monks, were deeply unsymathetic to the proposals) were able to name no one else. Those chroniclers are important, because the details of this petition and any account of the reception it received were omitted entirely from the official records of the Parliament.[8]

That gives as clear an indication as any of how this great proposal was received.

It was submitted as a petition to the king. A petition was, in this era, the way in which the Commons (and the Lords too) presented proposals to the king in parliament, so this was the equivalent of a modern parliamentary bill, and it is sometimes described as the Lollard Disendowment Bill. The word 'Lollard' does not appear in it, but contemporaries were clearly well aware that those of the Lollard tendency were behind the proposals, and it was probably widely known that Sir John Oldcastle was central to them.

The starting point of a medieval parliament was almost invariably a request from the king for a grant of money. This meant taxation, either direct (a tax on individuals related in size to their possessions, or more rarely – like the one that had sparked the Peasants'

Revolt three decades earlier – a fixed poll tax, levied equally on everyone) or indirect (a tax on trade). Indeed the need for money was generally the reason that a king called a parliament: he was not obliged to consult the Lords and Commons in parliament, and sometimes failed to do so for years at a time when he had no particular need of extra funds. And the Lollard Disendowment Bill was essentially concerned with money. It set out a radical scheme for how the king could change the economy of the country, by essentially disendowing (removing the assets of) the church in England.

Its early paragraphs say:

> truly that our liege lord the king may have, from the temporalities occupied and proudly wasted by bishops, abbots and priors within the realm, fifteen earls and 1,500 knights, 6,200 esquires, and a hundred almshouses more than he has now at this time, well maintained and faithfully sustained by lands and rents. And in addition, when this has been done, our lord the king may have £20,000 and more clear for his treasure for the defence of the realm each year, as can faithfully be shown. And you may reckon that each earl will be able to spend 3,000 marks from lands and rents each year, and each knight 100 marks of rent and four plough-lands in his own demesne, and each esquire forty marks with two ploughlands in his demesne, and each almshouse 100 marks, under the supervision of good and faithful secular ministers, since the priests and clerks have almost destroyed all the almshouses within the realm. And also it should be ordained that every town throughout the realm should support all the poor men and beggars who cannot work for a living, in accordance with the statute made at Cambridge; and if it happens that the aforesaid commons cannot sustain them, then the said almshouses can help them.
>
> And in order to show how this might be done, you should know that the tempo-ralities of bishops, abbots and priors amount to the sum of 332,000 marks a year. That is to say, the temporalities of the archbishop of Canterbury with the two abbeys there, Shrewsbury, Coggeshall and St Osyth, are worth 20,000 marks a year; the bishop of Durham and the abbey there, 20,000 marks; the archbishop of York and the two abbeys there, 20,000 marks; the bishop of Winchester and two abbeys there, 20,000 marks; Clerkenwell with its members, 20,000 marks; and thus the first 100,000 marks is accounted for.

The petition goes on to list various other abbeys and individual prelates, and suggest how much could be obtained from them, and concludes:

> Yet we still have not mentioned colleges, chantries, white canons, cathedral churches with their temporalities and the churches appropriated to them, nor the Carthu-sian monks, nor the French monks, nor glebes, nor the Bonhommes, nor the leper houses called hospitals, nor hermitages, nor the crouched friars.
>
> And therefore all the faithful commons desire, for the worship of God and the profit of the realm, that these worldly clerks, bishops, abbots and priors, who are such worldly lords, should be obliged to live on their spiritualities; for they do not at present live or perform the office like true churchmen or curates should,

and nor do they help the poor commons with their lordships like true secular lords should, and nor do they live in penance, nor undertake bodily work, as true men of religion should, in accordance with their profession. But from each estate they take luxury and ease, and they turn away from work, gathering up to themselves profits that should go to faithful men; and this life and evil example of theirs has for so long been vicious, that all the common people, both lords and simple commons, are now so vicious and infected by the boldness of their sins that hardly any man dreads either God or the devil.[10]

This was stirring stuff. Indeed it was the stuff of revolution: but it was not a revolution being started on the streets and in the fields, it was a revolution being proposed by the Commons in parliament. Its proponents were not the peasants and bondmen who suffered the worst in this profoundly unequal society, but solidly respectable, affluent men who had been selected by their peers to deal in the governance of the realm. The bluntness of the language, and the evidence of detailed work that had gone into the calculations, bear sharp witness to the strength of feeling in the country at large about the state of the Catholic Church.

The sums could have been quibbled over (and have been since) but the gist of the proposal was unmistakable. The Church had totally lost its way; it was entirely corrupt, so much so that these distinguished and influential men, the leaders of the bulk of the people of England, believed there was no remedy but to reform it fundamentally. They saw no way of remaking the economy except to

Stained glass from St Mary's Church,
North Tuddenham, Norfolk. Photo Mike Dixon

reconsider entirely the role of the Church, and find new and better ways of performing the functions it had taken to itself.

Politics is the art of the possible; the successful politician puts forward a proposal whose time has come, whose necessity is widely acknowledged, and which is almost certain to be accepted. Did and could the Commons believe this might be the case with their radical suggestions? Perhaps they did. They had had such wholehearted support from those they had confided in and consulted with that perhaps they managed to overlook the fact that there was another grouping in the country, with many men of great influence within it, who were certain to fight the proposal with every last sinew of their being.

Bishop Beaufort, the King's half-brother, who had opened the parliament in the temporary absence of a chancellor, and all the other prelates whose livelihoods were under such direct threat, were definitely among them. Did the Commons know in advance that the king would also be such a vehement opponent of their proposal that he not only refused to consider it or to debate its broad outlines, he ordered them never to bring such proposals to him again, and had the debate expunged from the parliamentary record? Or did they have at least some reason to hope that he, or perhaps Prince Henry and others of the younger generation of royals, might also have some sympathy for what they hoped to achieve?

Perhaps some at least of the Commons believed that the sheer weight of pressure behind these proposals would force the king to give them proper consideration.

Cooling Castle

and choose to implement them at least to some degree. Even Bishop Beaufort, in his speech at the start of the parliament, had acknowledged with Aristotle that it is essential for the good governance of the realm that the king and his people should be in broad agreement. Or perhaps, if they knew that it was unlikely the entire proposal would be accepted, they believed that they would achieve something worthwhile simply by setting out these suggestions openly, and ensuring that they would be debated.

Medieval parliamentary sessions were probably as rowdy as medieval church services, and medieval churches were not havens of grey peacefulness, they were a splurge of noise and colour. Although there is no record of what was said and done in that expunged debate, it was doubtless not a polite and considered one. The Commons must have been angry, very angry, when the king anounced that these proposals were completely unacceptable, so unacceptable that he would not even spend time discussing their details. Some of the Lords, Sir John Oldcastle included, must have been angry too. We can imagine heated arguments, men storming out, the ushers forced to intervene to hold back the furious, and quite possibly significant numbers of armed men being drafted in to enforce the peace. What was removed from the record was not a small suggestion from one man, it was the combined request of all of the Commons. There were surely reasons for the blank record, which went beyond the unacceptability (to the king and Church) of the proposals.

But only one side could win that battle, and it was not the Commons. The king was ultimately an absolute ruler, required to consult, but not to obey. This king was not one for ceding power, he was one for gathering power to himself. When he said no, the 'no' echoed across Westminster and far beyond.

So there would have been much concern and anger outside Westminster Hall as well, once the news filtered out of how the petition had been received. But the Lollards and their supporters had not planned this as the trigger for a revolution. The petition could have gained such wide support only if its proposers had made it clear that they were putting their faith in the parliamentary process, in getting the approval of the king. London could be a tumultuous city, but it was also one where the city authorities were well used to quelling unrest and enforcing the peace. Perhaps there were more troops than was usual out on its streets in the hours and days following the debate, but there is no record of any widespread disorder.

After rejecting the petition in its entirety, the king's further response was to have the law De heretico comburendo read out in the Parliament. There had been nothing in the petition about the issues that represented the line between acceptable belief and heresy, although there was admittedly plenty in its thrust of rejection of the authority of the clergy. But this response made it clear that King Henry saw this as a Lollard proposal, and wanted to drive home the fact that the Lollards would not be tolerated in his England. Perhaps the situation had been allowed to drift up to that point, but he was clearly determined people should not forget that it was the law of England that men and women remain full members of the Catholic Church and share its beliefs.

The Commons responded in turn with a request that De heretico comburendo be modified, since they felt its provisions for incarceration without any royal writ were too onerous. The king not only refused this request too, he replied that he was minded if anything to stiffen the penalties against heresy.

30 The toad and the spider

And when they had heard the king, they went forth. And lo! the star, that they saw in the east went before them, till it came, and stood above, where the child was. And they saw the star, and joyed with a full great joy.

Matthew 9–10, in the Wycliffe translation of the Bible

Stained glass
from Canterbury
Cathedral

There have been strong women throughout history who have found a way of making their mark. But many have done so only because they were born to a position that made it possible, and many more must have found it impossible. Whatever she wished or did not wish to do so, Joan, Lady Cobham could not have attended parliament, even to listen, let alone to take part in its debates. She could not have set her name to its petition to the king. She could not become a preacher, let alone a priest. The biggest role she had was to provide financial backing.

That she must have done, although perhaps not willingly. Her husband had substantial control of her estates, and since he paid out money to many people over the next few years, and did not have great resources of his own to do that with, it was presumably her money that he used. Joan herself, her daughter, her tenants, perhaps felt the effects of his doing so. Maybe she was not happy. But equally, maybe she had been as enthused as he by the great wave of support the Disendowment Bill had engendered, and wanted to do at least this much to forward the cause.

In the wake of the parliament, though, that cause was sunk.

When people suffer a major reverse, they may respond in any of a full spectrum of ways. Some resign themselves to the fact that they have lost, and think (or at least behave) in future in a way that accords with the winning side. Some accept the loss, but think it temporary, and pull back from confrontation until they judge that the time is right for a reintroduction of their proposal. And others are stiffened in their determination, and set themselves firmly in opposition to those who have defeated them.

Sir John Oldcastle was evidently in that last class. He certainly did not accept that he should not be a Lollard in future, should not argue for reform of the Church as well as for beliefs it did not tolerate. And nor did he accept that the failure that had been seen in the parliament represented a permanent rejection. He surely believed there were reasons to hope that the ban on reintroducing such proposals would not outlive the king who had imposed it. Everyone who attended Westminster had seen that the king had a disfiguring disease which was destroying his health.[2] They knew that he was likely to be able to rule in person for only a little longer, and perhaps would live for not much longer anyway. The king was blessed with an intelligent and forceful heir (and a clutch of reserves among his brothers). Times would change, and perhaps when Prince Henry managed to take control (he and his supporters had not managed it at that parliament, and indeed in the wake of their attempts he was now firmly out of favour), such proposals would be received more temperately.

Knowing the prince as he did, Sir John probably knew that he was hoping to revive Edward III's ambitions in France, and take advantage of disarray among its nobles to claim its throne for the kings of England. If he was to launch a campaign in France, he would need a lot of money, and the Lollard proposal had carefully focused not on beliefs, but on the amount of money that it might liberate. Would Prince Henry not be sensible to think further about that prospect, about all those knights who might be created and funded, about the depth of public pressure for change? And who knew then how he might respond?

Did Sir John retreat from promoting his views in public at least for a while, out of

The Oldcastle family

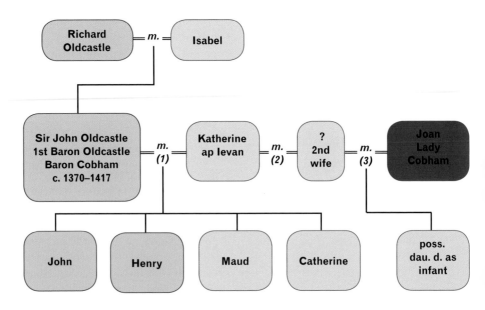

policy or simply out of a sense of self-preservation? It seems likely that he did not. He was accused later of using violence, or at least the threat of violence, to force people to do as he wished, and the seeds of those accusations must have been sown in the difficult time after the parliamentary record was censored. In the Hoo, at least, his rule was predominant. People there had to act as their lord chose, and their lord apparently chose to keep his Lollards and have them continue to preach the views that he shared with them. So anyone around Cooling who would have preferred to see the Lollards suppressed would have had to tread extremely carefully – indeed, they would have been wiser to move away.

Possibly his wife was intimidated too. She might have greatly wished that her husband would be more moderate, more cautious. But if she did, there is no indication that she did anything about it.

Equally, she might have wholeheartedly endorsed his choice of response. Cooling is an out-of-the-way place: the Hoo peninsula leads nowhere, and the church in its marshes is bleak and lonely. It would have been little less so even when Cooling Castle was occupied by a great noble family. If a person wishes to pursue radical views, there are worse places to do so unobserved than Cooling, or indeed than Burnham Norton, which is equally desolate. Perhaps it was not by coincidence that some of the places Joan apparently chose to make her home were remote and hidden ones, where ideas best kept private could be explored in relative safety.

But there was a clear and close danger in harbouring radicals there in times such as these. It probably became known not just after the parliament, but during it, that the king intended to take action to firmly suppress the Lollards. He let the message emerge from the Palace of Westminster that he considered his words in parliament to be insufficient for the purpose, and they would be backed up now with deeds. It was years now since William

Weycroft Hall, once the home of
the Brooke family. Photo by kind permission of
the Axminster TASK Centre, www.task-centre.org.uk

Sawtre had been burned at the stake, and evident that people had forgotten the harsh lesson his burning had represented. Another man would be burned now, and further action taken too.

Since Sir John was clearly known to be a prime mover of the proposals, it must have seemed possible, even probable, that some of that action would be against him and his family. It was not really conceivable that he would be the man to go to the stake – it was more likely a labouring man would be made an example of – but it was certainly conceivable that the king's officers would ride up to Cooling Castle and ask hard questions about its inhabitants, and in particular any Lollard preachers who figured among them. Those officers were likely to be as heavy-handed as officers of the law typically are, so this would not be pleasant for those inhabitants.

It was perhaps with this prospect in plain view that Sir John and his family made some plans designed to ease their path through what were likely to prove difficult times ahead. Among them was the marriage of Joan Braybrooke.

Joan was six years old, barely out of infancy. Royalty and the upper aristocracy occasionally married off their sons and daughters when they were still in the cradle, but this was not the norm among the rest of society. And when they did so, there was often a pressing reason: the impending death of the child's father, perhaps – which was one reason why Joan senior had been married young, although not when she was only six – or a particularly good offer that they wanted to take up without delay. By no means every young aristocrat was married young. The king's sons proved good examples of that: they were all now adults, or not far off it, and not a single one of them had yet taken a wife.

Young Joan's mother and stepfather were in good health, and the child herself had substantial expectations. She was, after all, Lady Cobham's only living heir, and Lady Cobham had quite possibly (indeed probably, judging by her daughter's marriage agreement) concluded that she would now have no further children. Her parents could easily have looked for a lord for her, a young man from one of the great, long-established noble families of England, like those from which some of her ancestors came. They probably would have been given short shrift if they had suggested marrying her to one of the young princes, but there were few others in England who would have rejected a girl with her prospects of inheritance.

Thomas Brooke, the man the Oldcastles chose, was not in this echelon of society. The Brookes were of the gentry, not the nobility. They were quite sizeable landowners in Devon and Somerset, and young Thomas was the eldest son. (It was not a large family: he

had just one younger brother.) He was then aged about 19. Not long afterwards Thomas held an estate called Blundeshay in Whitchurch Canonicorum (a small village in south-west Dorset) which was estimated to be worth £44 a year. And before his father died he and Joan were living at the family's main seat, Weycroft Hall in Axminster, a solidly impressive stone manor house. So the groom had a good contribution to make (a rather larger one that Sir John Oldcastle had brought to his own marriage), but this was hardly a match so impressive in material terms as to make the Oldcastles rush to sign the betrothal deeds.

They had other motives, clearly. It was not long before young Thomas came to be known as a Lollard and a keen supporter of Sir John Oldcastle, so this probably played a part. Thomas and his father (another Sir Thomas Brooke) undertook to pay Oldcastle 1,300 marks on the day of the wedding, which was to take place rapidly, before Whit Sunday that year, and maybe Sir John had become so short of ready money in the wake of his exertions in London that this was a significant factor. (In return, as well as coming with grand expectations, little Joan was endowed with Lord Cobham's estates in the West country, and Hempnall in Norfolk, which her mother and father had acquired from the Hemenhale estate, so that cash was exchanged for plenty of land.) And perhaps her mother in particular felt that if Sir John was to tempt the king and the Church too to confront him, it would be well to send the child a good way from Kent and London. and the trouble that was being courted there, as quickly as possible. In addition, her own preference might have been to see her daughter not brought to the court as the wife of a lord, but raised in a Godfearing way in a quiet country village.

So the betrothal negotiations took place under the storm clouds of the coming crack-down on the Lollards, and in the knowledge that the Oldcastles were not tempering their stance to protect themselves from the deluge, but if anything tempting the king and the archbishop to turn their eyes to Cooling. However the king's first move was not against them.

John Badby, a tailor from Evesham, had already been in in prison for over a year on charges of heresy. In March 1410 Archbishop Arundel ordered that he be taken out of his cell and tried. The man refused to recant his heretical beliefs, and instead claimed that the eucharist was 'worth less than a toad or a spider, which are living animals'.[4] He was evidently making a point of being as obnoxious to his judges as possible; like Oldcastle, this was clearly not a man to renounce his beliefs or even temper his expression of them under pressure. He was sentenced to execution by burning, and the sentence was carried out almost immediately, at Smithfield on 5 March.

That was so swift that if the Cobhams had not been in London, they could not have witnessed the execution. But perhaps they were still in London, since Sir John had been there for the parliament. Both of them must have been not only dismayed for Badby (although they, like Badby himself, must have sincerely believed he was headed for heaven), but concerned for other friends and colleagues. Was this to be the first of many executions? How would the London crowd react? How would men in a position to influence future events react – men, for instance, like Prince Henry? Perhaps they sent trusted supporters to watch and report back to them; perhaps they went to Smithfield themselves.

Stained glass, left, from St Mary's Church, Saxlingham Nethergate, Norfolk; right, from Canterbury Cathedral

Many people did so, since this execution, like most, drew a large crowd. The king himelf did not attend it, but two of his sons – Henry and John – were ordered by him to do so. The heretical tailor was bundled into a barrel in preparation for his burning. This was a choice so unusual that many might have wondered who had chosen it. It was unlikely to reduce the suffering of the condemned man, but it was a kindness to anyone squeamish who had been ordered to watch. They would not have to watch his skin blister and burn, his flesh melt; his screams would be muted, and no one would see his face. Others might have pointed out, more brutally, that this was defeating the object of the burning. If it was to deter others from heresy, it had not only to be horrific, but to be seen to be horrific.

What followed the lighting of the faggots under the barrel was certainly interesting to the Lollards among the crowd, and indeed to anyone looking for insights into the likely next king's character. When Badby began to scream for mercy, Prince Henry ordered the barrel to be removed from the flames. He had it opened, and went over and spoke directly to the badly burned man. Probably only a handful of people actually heard the conversation, but it was widely repeated afterwards, so before long all London (and not long after that, all the rest of the country) knew what had been said. Prince Henry had told Badby that even at that point he could recant, and he would not only be spared, but would be granted a small pension of threepence a day.

Badby indignantly refused. So the prince ordered the fire rekindled and the heretic went to be judged by his Lord in the hereafter.

Sir John already knew Prince Henry well, although he had probably never discussed religion with him, and Joan must have had some acquaintance with him too. Neither would have blamed him for having the fire relighted; he could not realistically have done anything else. The young prince was a hardened fighting man, not one to faint on seeing another man tortured, but this made it clear that he did not take pleasure from it. He had probably caused Badby more pain than the man would have suffered without intervention, but that was surely not his intention. He was evidently someone who believed in negotiation, and he had a fair sense of what would represent a suitable offer. Threepence a day was a labouring man's wage, enough for someone to live on modestly, so Badby could have retired from preaching and lived out his life in obscurity if he chose. It would have been rash to conclude from these unusual events that Prince Henry was secretly a supporter of Lollard views.

Perhaps Prince Henry would have judged Badby's terrible death enough of a lesson to the Lollards, but Archbishop Arundel had different views. Several other Lollards from London were arrested in the wake of the burning. The Oldcastles must have had informers and messengers, who reported these events to them not only in London, but after they had returned to Cooling. It can have come as no surprise to them when less than a month later, it was their turn to be the focus of the archbishop's attention.

On 3 April, just before parliament was due to reassemble after a recess, Archbishop Arundel informed the dean of Rochester that a 'pretended chaplain' called John, who had evidently been living at Cooling (quite likely, with the Cobhams in the castle) had been preaching without a licence. This John had propounded heretical views in the churches of Hoo, Halstow and particularly Cooling. The dean was ordered to investigate and to place the churches under interdict, which effectively meant that no services could be held in them.

An interdict was not a burning, but it was both a warning and an inconvenience. The plan had evidently been for young Joan to marry Thomas Brooke at Cooling. The betrothal had already taken place, but not the marriage ceremony itself. While the interdict lasted, it would be impossible to hold it there.

There were times when it made a kind of sense for Sir John to be implacable, and even for his wife to support him in his implacability. This was not one of them. If the marriage was to take place, they had to be realistic. They had to negotiate to get the interdict lifted, and had perhaps to make promises that Sir John would have preferred not to make. Whether it was his choice or his wife's, that was what they did.

They must have enlisted the people who could best intercede for them: the master of Cobham College, perhaps, or sympathetic priests among those serving at Rochester Cathedral. Perhaps the dean himself was by no means as inclined to take a hard line as Archbishop Arundel. Joan had negotiated in tricky situations before, or seen others do it for her. She was probably temperamentally better suited to the task than this husband of hers, so perhaps in this it was she who took the lead.

Whoever made the representations, they achieved their aim. Two days later the interdict was lifted, and Joan Braybrooke was married at Cooling church. Perhaps the original intention had been that the 'pretend chaplain' would conduct the service, but the Oldcastles would not have been so rash as to continue with that scheme.

But they were rash enough, it seems, to keep the suspect preacher in their household.

31 The dunghill

Listeth, lords, in good entent,
And I wol telle verayment
Of mirth and of solas;
All of a knight was fait and gent
In battail and in tournament ...
Geoffrey Chaucer,
'The tale of Sir Thopas'[1]

St James's Church, Cooling, Kent

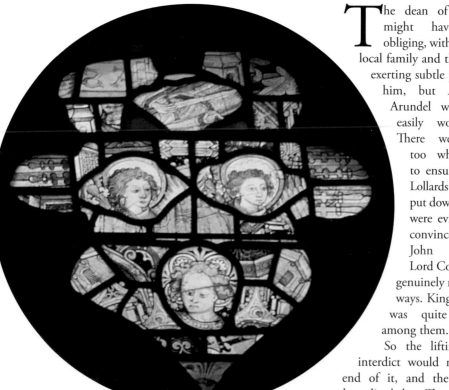

The dean of Rochester might have proved obliging, with a powerful local family and their friends exerting subtle pressure on him, but Archbishop Arundel was not so easily won round. There were others too who wanted to ensure that the Lollards were firmly put down, and who were evidently not convinced that Sir John Oldcastle, Lord Cobham, had genuinely mended his ways. King Henry IV was quite probably among them.

So the lifting of the interdict would not be the end of it, and the Cobhams surely realized that. There must still have been much traffic between Cooling and London – between Cooling and the great network of radicals and Lollards that had come together behind the Disendowment Bill – and the word that travelled down the roads to Kent would have been that they were being watched. The archbishop was a practical politician, and he would wait till he had the evidence to back up his move. But once he had it, he would act.

The only way to prevent that action was to ensure that the archbishop never got his evidence. But it was not in Oldcastle's nature to settle for moderation and caution, and if his wife would have preferred those to thundering defiance, well, her husband was not listening to her, and she lacked the weapons to make him listen. Or rather, perhaps, she had the weapons, but they were drastic ones, ones that would have ended her marriage and destroyed her husband if she had used them. And she did not choose to do so.

Perhaps, even, she did not dare to do so. It is a fair bet that most of those members of the Commons who had endorsed the Lollard Disendowment Bill looked on in horrified incomprehension when John Badby let the barrel be reclosed over his head, and resigned himself to the agonies of the fire in the sincere belief that they would earn him life eternal. They knew the Church to be fat on corruption, and genuinely wanted it reformed, but they did not share Badby's passionate beliefs. Indeed probably rather a lot of them (and even more of the less educated peasant and labouring classes) had given little if any thought to the finer points of the doctrine of transubstantiation and similar issues of religious disagreement. They were content to believe what the clergy told them to believe, albeit they wished those clergy were less lazy and greedy.

But these were not the men and women who were to be found at Cooling in those days. Sir John's supporters, his ardent admirers, were of a different cast. The preachers who roamed the country, declining either to apply for a licence or to preach in a way that would have earned them one, were of a different cast. Some were fanatics, while some probably fell short of that. But all were firm believers in the Lollard view of Christianity, and in its wider programme of reform. These were not people who would listen to Sir John's wild assertions of defiance, and gently ask that he reconsider. They were people who would applaud his stance, and encourage him to persist with it. They were not weedy academics weaned on small beer, they were strong men, many of them blooded in the battles with the Welsh. In a castle still packed with Sir John's supporters, it might have taken more courage than Joan possessed to suggest a different way forward. And if she had, well, these were not the men to stand by and let her betray them. They would have prevented her, and she probably knew it.

So Joan acquiesced, or so it seems. Perhaps privately she was seriously worried. More likely than not, she had no more wish to see her husband end up on the pyre than she wished it for herself or her daughter. Joan had not come from a family of extremists. Her family was full of men and women who adjusted their behaviour (and perhaps to an extent their beliefs too) to the requirements of their society. Perhaps she did what she could to ensure that what happened at Cooling stayed private within its walls. But if she differed with her husband, she probably did not make it known to the wider world.

She might not have liked it one bit when later in 1410, Sir John wrote to a number of religious radicals in Bohemia. Quite possibly these were contacts that he had made through Sir Nicholas Hawberk, since he seems never to have been to Bohemia himself. However he knew how to get a letter to Wok of Waldstein, a nobleman like himself, and Wladislas of Zwierzeticz, another follower of the reformer Jan Hus, congratulating them on their endeavours. These

Glass on both pages: St Peter and St Paul's Church, Swaffham, Norfolk

endeavours were just as dangerous as his own, because the authorities in Bohemia were no more friendly to radicals than those in Westminster. The letters were in Latin, in a clerkly hand, so he almost certainly had help in writing them. This was the kind of initiative that diplomats and spies would have learned of.

And she probably liked it even less when he went on to write to King Wladislas of Bohemia, urging him to protect the reformers in his country. King Wladislas was not known as their supporter, far from it, so there was no guarantee at all that what Sir John wrote would remain private. It was all too probable that it would become known to those who were not sympathizers, the English ambassador included. But if Joan held her breath when these letters went with their carriers across the Channel, at least in the short term there were no repercussions.

If the radical preacher Archbishop Arundel had heard tell of was one John Lay, then he was still in the Cobhams' household three years later. So, it seems, was another radical preacher, Robert Chapell. But no one came to Cooling Castle to apprehend them. After Badby's horrific burning there was no further rounding-up of heretics. Quiet descended; nothing happened.

In 1411 a message came to Sir John Oldcastle from Prince Henry. An army was to be assembled, and sent to France. The prince, who had recovered from his setbacks the year before, and was steadily taking a larger and larger part in his father's administration, was in charge of the arrangements. Sir John was invited (in reality, commanded) to muster his forces and bring them to serve in that army.

Although this was to be a fair-sized force, it was not so large that every knight in England was called on. The prince had evidently consciously selected Sir John, and Sir John and his wife might well have asked themselves why.

The prince surely knew of Sir John's role in the Lollard Disendowment Bill, about the unlicensed preachers at Cooling, and the archbishop's actions. So he must have known too that Sir John was not just a reformer, but an espouser of extreme, and probably heretical, religious views. Many on the moderate side of the debate would have chosen to give a wide berth to Cooling and its master, but here was Prince Henry showing Sir John favour, offering him a position that could gain him credit and renown.

Did this mean he was privately not unsympathetic to the Lollards? It might have done, but it also might not. The prince clearly liked Sir John, and valued him as a man at arms and a commander. He did not intend to lead this campaign in person, but he had involved himself closely in it, and was naturally anxious to appoint men who would make it a success, so perhaps he was prepared to overlook other issues in choosing the best men at arms. He and his advisers might also have reckoned it would be no bad thing to remove Sir John from Cooling, indeed take him right out of England, and disperse the nest of known radicals in the castle.

Lollard supporter or not, Prince Henry was evidently a supporter of Sir John Oldcastle, and that could only be a good thing for Sir John and his wife.

And as well as being a command that could not easily be refused, it must have seemed a tempting proposal for a man who liked fighting. It was many years now since the English had fought in France. King Richard had never shown an inclination to do so, and if Henry IV had had an inclination, he had had sufficient crises to confront in England that he was scarcely able to act on it. But his son had apparently persuaded him that this was a good moment to change that policy.

The French at that time were in a disarray more profound than anything England had seen in recent years. Two rival camps, the Armagnacs and the Burgundians, were tussling for control. The English negotiated with both at different times (and sometimes at the same time), and at this point they selected the Burgundians as their allies. The reasons were at least partly pragmatic. The duke of Burgundy had offered a tempting package in return for their support, including his daughter as bride for the still unmarried Prince Henry, and a clutch of towns to strengthen the English bridge-head of Calais in north-west France. So the English force was to join the Burgundians. It was led by the earl of Arundel, son of the man Richard II had seen executed, and nephew to the archbishop.

Sir John mustered his men (they must have included most of those who had crowded out Cooling over the previous couple of years) and led them off for what was likely to be several months, at least, in France.

His wife was left in unaccustomed peace. Her daughter had probably left the household by then, and moved to the care of her husband's family. A preacher or two might have lingered, but with the master absent, his men absent too, there were no great congregations for fiery sermons. It was a time for Lady Cobham to get her breath back, recover her equilibrium – and perhaps her finances too, without the drain of Sir John's and his supporters' demands – and return to something like the life she had known between her marriages.

The last time she had seen a husband off to war, he had never returned. She probably thought on that as well. And prayed.

The period of quiet in England that followed the short flurry of official attacks on the Lollards persisted throughout the campaign in France. The king's reign was coming to an end, as those who attended his court surely knew, but it was ending slowly and uneventfully. Those who wanted change were waiting until the new king succeeded.

Sir John returned from France around the end of 1411 – with a good payment from the duke of Burgundy – and in mid-1412 a peace was signed between the two rival French parties. The duke of Burgundy's troops had done relatively well. They had entered Paris, and pursued their rivals south. But the truce had not resolved France's underlying problems, and those who had been in the country doubtless realized that more fighting was likely, both between the French factions, and between them and the English.

In March 1413, three years after Badby's burning, the man who had done his best to dissuade him from his martyr's death ascended to the throne. King Henry IV died, and his son became King Henry V. He had not married a daughter of the duke of Burgundy, and nor had England been awarded the towns in France that the duke had promised to them. Henry was negotiating with both sides in France, and also planning to wrongfoot them both by making his own plans to leapfrog them and claim the French throne.

The Oldcastles must have been concerned, above all, to know what King Henry's approach would be to the Lollards. Would he continue his father's hard line? Or now that he was free to set his own policy, would he choose to reverse it, and allow a degree of tolerance?

These were not times when the international tide was flowing in the direction of tolerance. During Henry IV's last days a council held in Rome had condemned many of Wycliffe's writings as unfit to be read by good Christians, and deserving only to be burned. In Bohemia, indeed across Europe, there was a backlash against those with radical new ideas, those who sought reform in both the church and the secular government. Even so, a new young king had a degree of latitude. And those who were acquainted with him knew Henry V to be an intelligent man, one well capable of setting his own course; and a tough-minded one, one equally capable of ensuring Archbishop Arundel did as he wished. He had had nine years or so of expecting to inherit the throne, and no one doubted he had made plans for what he would do when the country was his.

It was Arundel who made the move, however, and did it so fast that people must have wondered whether he was acting at Henry V's request, or at least with his endorsement, or whether he was trying to pre-empt any new policy of the new king's. That same month of March 1413, Arundel's convocation – his council of inquiry – summoned John Lay before it. This was probably the same man as had been preaching at Cooling and other places in Kent three years earlier. For those three years Lay seems to have carried on with his radical sermons, and the Oldcastles and their friends had carried on listening to them. Now, abruptly, those years were over. They could scarcely imagine the convocation was about to tell Lay that he might continue as before. Archbishop Arundel had already made his opinion of Wycliffite teachings extremely clear. He had prayed publicly that Wycliffe's bones might be exhumed and thrown on a dunghill.[2]

Perhaps Lay, and the Oldfields, were already in London; they might have remained there after the old king's funeral. Or perhaps they travelled there from Cooling in response to the summons. Whichever was the case, Sir John and his wife were in the city when Lay presented himself before Arundel's convocation.

He answered its questions with apparently guileless honesty. He came from Nottingham. He had been in London for two days. That morning he had celebrated mass with Sir John Oldfield (Lord Cobham) and his household, presumably in the chapel at Cobham's Inn. The questioners must have exchanged glances when this information was laid before them.

The convocation's registrar demanded that Lay show his licence to preach. Lay protested that he had not brought it with him. He was told to go to fetch it. And he went: perhaps to Cobham's Inn, although it can scarcely have been with the intention of picking up a licence to show the convocation, since he almost certainly did not possess one. He did not go back to the convocation afterwards. Possibly this was at Oldcastle's urging, but quite likely Oldcastle would have preferred him to go back, and to force a public confrontation.

John Lay disappeared into the spider's web of Lollards, and the convocation's servants, coming to Cobham's Inn to find what was keeping him, were probably told he had not been seen there. They were not amused, and nor were their masters. Arundel responded by ordering further enquiries into local Lollard activities.

These new inquiries brought to the attention of the convocation an illuminator from Paternoster Row in the City of London. Among this man's stock was a pamphlet of unbound sheets containing several Lollard tracts: banned documents, whose possession was sufficient in itself to justify a charge of heresy. This book was not his own, the illuminator declared, when he was hauled before the panel to explain himself. It had been brought to him for illustration by Sir John Oldcastle.

Oxborough Hall, Norfolk

32 In the king's closet

I am fully persuaded that there is no abiding place upon earth, but that we are all pilgrims, either on the way to happiness, or tending to misery.

From the statement drawn up by Sir John Oldcastle on his first imprisonment[1]

Rash he might be, and confident in his own opinions and beliefs, but even Sir John Oldcastle would not have taken lightly a summons to be questioned on suspicion of heresy. However, when the inevitable summons came he perhaps did not see it as a mortal threat. He knew this new king, knew him well and regarded him as an ally, even a friend. He might well have persuaded himself that Archibishop Arundel would find his leash a lot shorter than he had anticipated when the king learned that it was one of his own commanders who had now been ordered to account for his actions and beliefs.

And he was probably reinforced in that belief when the summons he eventually received came not from Arundel at all, but direct from the king. It was by then apparent that Henry V had no intention of leaving his clerics to handle issues of heresy without his oversight. He intended to be an active king, the very opposite of Richard II, maintaining or even extending the level of control that his father had claimed for the Crown. He had not granted the archbishop and his convocation any blanket authority to make their own judgements on such issues. They were expected to consult him, and to defer to his decisions.

The king was then at Kennington, which had been a royal manor for centuries, known for its gardens and its rabbit warrens, as well as for its occasional use as a prison for noble offenders. He commanded to attend him there not just Sir John Oldcastle, not just the members of the convocation, but 'almost all the prelates and nobles of England'.[2] Knowing that he was to be questioned by the king himself, Sir John was probably confident, even jaunty when he rode there, presumably with an entourage of his fighting men, and perhaps with his wife as well. He might have hoped this would prove to be Arundel's undoing.

The meeting took place in the king's closet: that is, in the king's private office. With the prelates, nobles and the king himself as audience, members of the convocation produced the pamphlet that had been seized in London, and read out some of the more extreme passages. It is not clear what they contained, but there is no doubt that by the standards of the Church at the time they rated as heretical.

They were, said King Henry, the worst examples of heresy he had ever heard. What do you think to them, Sir John?

Sir John did not answer lightly. For once in his life, and surely taking note of this steer, he gave a careful and measured answer. So the convocation had seized this book? That was right and proper of them, he acknowledged. It was what they had been established to do.

So he agreed that the material in the book was heretical? Why then had he been possessed of it?

Well … possessed might, he agreed, be the word. But he had never used this volume. He had not read more than two pages of it.

Perhaps King Henry believed him. At least, King Henry chose to have the interrogation end there. So you have questioned my valued captain, he said (or at least implied) to Arundel's men; you have heard his frank answer; there is no more to be said or done.

A temporary victory to the prince, and a temporary victory too to Sir John. But Arundel was evidently not willing to let it rest there. Even King Henry had said the book contained heresy. Sir John's answer might be disarmingly frank, but that did not mean it was honest. The archbishop ordered further investigations.

King Henry let them proceed.

Whate Sir John did at this point is not recorded. Perhaps he went back to Cooling, or perhaps he remained in London, sending out spies, receiving messages, arguing in secret meetings. He probably knew when the dossier of charges the convocation was drawing up was consiered complete. He knew when the convocation rode back out to Kennington, where Henry had remained, and presented it to him.

And although this time he was not present in the king's closet, he probably received an account of the meeting that took place there from one or more men who were. So he knew he was accused of 'being a notorious favourer of error and heresy; of holding, asserting, and defending erroneous and heretical conclusions in many dioceses [by which they meant, London, Kent and Herefordshire]; of receiving, sheltering, and protecting unlicensed preachers; of sending them out to preach, attending their "shameful meetings", and oppressing any who resisted them with threats and fears and the power of the sword; of declaring that no prelate might lawfully make constitutions for the regulation of preaching; and finally, of holding heterodox views concerning the sacrament, penance, pilgrimages, image-worship, and the power of the keys'.[3]

It was a lengthy, detailed, and utterly damning list.

Sir John did not, however, copy John Lay and go to ground. Sir John was probably aware too that the king's response had been that he had no wish to see action taken against a close friend and valued knight, and that Archbishop Arundel was to hold off until he, King Henry, had had an opportunity himself to talk to Sir John, and persuade him that he was mistaken in his opinions. He would have known the archbishop had had no option but to agree. And perhaps he thought – how could he have

Stained glass from St James's Church, Southrepps, Norfolk

thought it would go from there? Perhaps he gave that no deep thought at all, but simply relished the idea of having a chance to meet with the king – not entirely alone, for a king was never alone, but at least without Archbishop Arundel and his damned convocation – and outline to him his own views, his plans for the country, his desires, perhaps even his expectations, of what the king might be persuaded to do.

What did Joan think? That, alas, is even more obscure. However involved she had been to that point, she did not attend the meetings that followed between her husband and his king.

But she, and all those around them, had taken in, no doubt, the implications in the very fact of the meetings. If Sir John had been boasting of his closeness to King Henry, of the king's respect for him, these were not empty boasts. They were the simple truth. Sir John was now one of the king's barons, but he was not a member of the king's council, not one of the great nobles at the core of the administration. Although he was regarded as a fine soldier, he had not commanded large armies. A man of his rank could not take for granted that complaints against him would be investigated in depth by the king in person. But that was precisely what was happening. Sir John was being treated to an extraordinary degree of the king's personal attention. That cannot have been lost on Joan, or on any of the Lollards who were waiting anxiously to see how the situation between the rebel, the king and the archbishop would be resolved.

The two men met repeatedly over the next two months, and between those meetings Sir John presumably returned to his wife and his entourage, and told them what had taken place. King Henry did not offer him a pension of threepence a day, but he did take care to pay him some money that was owed to him (or that it was said was owed to him). Quite likely the king had learned that Sir John was feeling the pinch financially (because his wife had closed her purse?), and this king always knew how best to tempt men. The king also made it clear that if Sir John would be reasonable, he would have his personal protection from the archbishop and his hunting dogs. All that was required of him in return was an affirmation that he acknowledged and accepted the doctrines of the church.

All that King Henry got in exchange was a lengthy recital of Sir John's own views. He was grateful for the king's efforts, anxious to remain the king's faithful servant, unwilling to defer to the pope and his clergy, and utterly convinced that what he believed was right.

In front of the convocation, confronted with the pamphlet, Sir John had seemed to be capable of diplomacy. But given this chance to harangue the king, that capability seems to have deserted him entirely.

The fanatics in his entourage might have clapped to hear this. The more moderate men – and women – in it must have quailed. To say to a king what he does not want to hear is to court his anger. And to anger a king is a brave, but also a foolhardy thing to do, even if it is done (perhaps especially if it is done) by a man whom that king both respects and considers as a friend. To persist well beyond the point when it might have seemed conceivable that he would win the king round, beyond the point where the king was willing to show patience, up to the point of making the king bloody furious with him: there might be a kind of suicidal bravado in that, but there was no good sense in it at all.

The sequence culminated in a meeting that August at Windsor. The king swore at Sir John and accused him of unforgivable obstinacy. As if to prove those charges justified, Sir John responded by storming off without obtaining permission to leave the king's presence.

When Sir John relayed this encounter to his family and friends, he was surely met with a shocked dismay. Henry might not be a king like Richard II, one who believed in peering down on his subjects from a high throne, but nor was he a king who took disrespect lightly. The king had tried to draw the line as far on Sir John's side as he reasonably could, but Sir John had still crossed it. This spelled an end to the fireside chats, and even the most blindly optimistic of Sir John's intimates must have known it spelled the start of something much, much darker.

But was it the end of confrontation, or was it rather the start of a different level of confrontation? Probably Sir John was looking back on the parliament of 1410, and the glorious moment when all the Commons of England had joined together to put forward the Lollards' petition. Perhaps he was even looking back to the Peasants' Revolt – which had failed, but which many must have believed had come close to succeeding. He knew that a king governs only to the extent that (and for as long as) his subjects permit it, and that when a king loses their consent, he can also lose his throne. The proposals that had been placed before parliament might have been expunged from its records, but they had not been, could not be, expunged from people's minds. There had been three more years for them to be talked about in the country at large. Perhaps Sir John believed (in retrospect it is clear that he must have believed) that if Henry forced a violent confrontation, there would be a great groundswell of support for Sir John himself and his views in the country, sufficient of one to ensure that this was a confrontation the king could not win.

He clearly wanted change in the country. He wanted revolution. Perhaps he sensed that provoking the king and Arundel into a violent response was the necessary spark to set it alight.

But once alight, it would need to be kept alight, to be fed with kindling. And perhaps he knew too that he and his supporters had not yet built up a sufficient store of kindling to be sure that the fire would build into a conflagration.

At that time Sir John did nothing, beyond retreating back to Cooling. Or perhaps he was not doing nothing, he was doing plenty, but all of it was the kind of action that does not make the pages of history books.

He was surely brought word that King Henry had placed his case back in the hands of the Church, and freed Archbishop Arundel to take whatever action he considered appropriate. The king had also sent writs to the sheriffs of every county, ordering them to take steps to arrest any unlicensed preachers in their territory, and all those who were aiding and abetting them.

The archbishop's summoner travelled to Cooling, presented himself at the great stone gatehouse where the previous Lord Cobham had inscribed his notice about the defence of the realm, and demanded admittance so that he might present a citation from his master.

Perhaps Sir John and his wife had discussed what they should do in these circumstances. Perhaps they had not, and they discussed it then. Or perhaps they did not discuss it all, but Sir John announced what he would do, and his wife was left to support him or to stay silent.

Sir John ordered his men to keep the gate shut, and tell the summoner that he would not be received. The summoner asked that Sir John come out of the castle, so the citation could be read to him in the road. Sir John sent back word that he would not do that either.

However many men Sir John had introduced into the castle establishment, there must have been many within it who had worked for the Cobhams for years, even decades before its then master had moved in. These were not all simple labouring men, they included stewards, bailiffs, lawyers: sensible and well-educated men who had accommodated themselves as well as they could to their new master, but were by no means uncritical admirers of his. Perhaps these men approached Lady Cobham and warned her of their deep disquiet. They could not see how this process could end other than in disaster. Perhaps she could not either. But she either felt powerless to change it, or she was persuaded of her husband's rightness, and did not even wish to change it.

It was not long before the news came to Cooling that the archbishop had responded by having the citation nailed to the doors of Rochester Cathedral, a few miles distant. Posted up on the great Norman door on 6 September, it ordered Sir John Oldcastle, Lord Cobham to present himself to the archbishop at Leeds Castle in Kent a week later, on 11 September.

Some of Sir John's men went to Rochester and tore the notices down. New ones were put up, and these too were torn down. Sir John also set his men to strengthening the fortifications at Cooling. They were strong enough anyway to withstand anything less than a siege.

The archbishop pronounced Sir John contumacious – a legal term for rebelliousness, which was certainly justified – and excommunicated him.

This was a man who cared nothing for the established Church, so to be cast out of it was perhaps not the terrible fate it would seem to one of its devout believers. But it had enormous symbolic significance. And it was another step on a path that would surely culminate in accusations of heresy and treachery.

Sir John did two things at this point. First, he wrote out a long statement of his beliefs. He included the Apostles' Creed, with which he presumably agreed, and which was, and remains, a core statement of orthodox Catholic beliefs:

I believe in God, the Father almighty, Creator of heaven and earth,
and in Jesus Christ, his only Son, our Lord,

who was conceived by the Holy Spirit, born of the Virgin Mary, suffered under
    Pontius Pilate,
was crucified, died and was buried;
he descended into hell;
on the third day he rose again from the dead;
he ascended into heaven, and is seated at the right hand of God the Father almighty;
from there he will come to judge the living and the dead.
I believe in the Holy Spirit, the holy catholic Church, the communion of saints, the
    forgiveness of sins, the resurrection of the body, and life everlasting. Amen.

What followed – his beliefs on the Church, on the obligations of its members, on their right to resist the demands of the clergy – was considerably less orthodox. This document ended with an appeal to the king to have the whole document examined by 'the most godly and learned men of the realm'. Which men he intended by this is an open question. He cannot realistically have meant the prelates who had already questioned him, and shown themselves entirely unconvinced by his beliefs, He also announced that he planned to send this statement to the pope, and to appeal to his judgement. It must have seemed even less likely that the pope whose office he wished to see abolished would be persuaded of the validity of his views.

This document prepared, Sir John did the second thing. He left Cooling – and presumably his wife – and went to find the king. He found him, it seems, at Westminster. He demanded to be taken into his presence, and remarkably King Henry agreed to receive him.

Sir John did have proposals to make, proposals that he perhaps even believed the king would consider. He declared that he was willing to have a hundred knights and esquires hear his case, in the conviction that they would clear him of all charges of heresy. Alternatively, he was prepared to submit his faith to trial by battle: to meet in single combat any man living, except the king himself and the members of his council. What he was not prepared to do was to submit to Archbishop Arundel's demands, and abjure his own beliefs.

This suggestion was not quite in the realms of absurd fancy. It was not so long since Henry of Lancaster, the king's father, had prepared to face his own opponent in single combat. Throughout history, it had been a solution resorted to when there was no other way of determining which of two adversaries was in the right. But from the view of the English establishment – the king, his councillors, his bishops and archbishops – this was hardly such a situation. The might of that establishment was all ranged against Sir John and his entirely unorthodox beliefs.

So it was scarcely a surprise when the king rejected the proposal. The archbishop had the right to try the case now, he said. There would be no further hearing before a different panel of wise men, no combat in the lists, and definitely no appeal to the pope. He then had his men arrest Sir John Oldcastle, Lord Cobham, and take him into custody in the Tower of London.

33 The head and tail of the antichrist

this same raven of treachery – with those his crows who, as arranged, were to flock to him from almost every part of England – there, in the near neighbourhood of the city, next to St Giles's Hospital (which is within a mile of the palace) resolved to take the field by night, as though to provoke his king and liege lord, as an opponent, into settling their respective beliefs by contest and into fighting a pitched battle.... what amazing, lamentable, and bitter madness....

Translated from *Gesta Henrici Quinti,*
The Deeds of Henry the Fifth[1]

Lambeth Palace

Nothing in Sir John's recent actions had carried the hint of a more cautious person pulling back on the reins, so if Joan was a more cautious person, and had tried to do so, she had had no effect. Perhaps she had not even been consulted; perhaps those noisy young men at arms who clustered thick about her husband had barred her from making any tentative protests. And conceivably Sir John, knowing all that he was risking, had determined to keep her at a distance from it, so that she might say with utter conviction that she had not even been aware of his plans, let alone supported them.

But when he set off, and she learned (if she had not known before) that he intended to shout his defiance at the king, she could hardly have failed to realize that this was likely to bring him to the Tower. So it was frightening indeed, but hardly surprising, when word came back to her that this had happened.

Joan knew the Tower all too well. And she knew, presumably, that the evidence of Sir John's heresy was so clear that the convocation could hardly fail to find him guilty. The usual practice after a guilty verdict was to execute the offender without delay. It was entirely probable that she would never see her husband alive again. Even if she had been horrified at the events of the previous few years, she could hardly have welcomed the prospect of her husband being led to a public execution.

She, and the others in the Cooling establishment who had not accompanied Sir John to Westminster, might well have expected that the repercussions would wash up to their walls with their defiant new patches of strengthening. But it seems this did not

Painting from St Mary's Church, Pulham St Mary, Norfolk

happen. Perhaps the archbishop's men knew that the Lollard clerics had by now moved to safer quarters. Probably nobody thought it would improve the situation if they were to question Lady Cobham.

Where she went, what she did, we have no record of. She might well have stayed on at Cooling. Or perhaps she travelled back up to London with the men of her husband's entourage who had brought the news to her, and diligently set about renewing her and her servants' contacts among the guards at the Tower.

Whichever place she chose to wait in, her wait was not long. On 23 September 1413 the prisoner Sir John was brought back in front of Archbishop Arundel.

He was not treated harshly, far from it. Arundel was a sensible man, and he had taken good note that Sir John was regarded as a dear friend by the king – a sorely misguided dear friend, perhaps, but still a dear friend. He offered to lift the excommunication, and in the long debates that followed, that day and on succeeding days, he provided every possible opportunity for Sir John to step back from the brink.

Sir John did not do so. There was much on which he agreed with the Church, but there were crucial points on which he did not, and on these he expressed himself unwilling to shift. And as Arundel and his colleagues persisted, he instead became more vehement, less reasonable, so hopelessly intransigent that the differences could not conceivably be glossed over. Transubstantiation he would not accept, and he had to accept it, if he was to be acknowledged as no heretic. The authority of the pope and his clerics he would not accept. In the end he became not so much vehement as hysterical. The pope was the head of the antichrist, he declared to the court, the archbishops and bishops its members, the friars its tail. He would accept no mediation between himself and St Peter, whose only true successor he considered himself to be. Finally he turned to the spectators and warned them that his judges were seducers of the people and would lead them to hell.[2]

However much she shared his beliefs, Joan must have been cold with terror when she had this reported to her.

This outburst must also have been the last thing that Archbishop Arundel had wanted, that the king had wanted, that any of those placed in judgement had wanted. None of them wanted to make Sir John a high-placed martyr to the Lollard cause. They wanted a fudge, of the kind that had been used throughout history to maintain some semblance of unity in the Church. This was not fudgeable, it was not forgiveable, it could lead to nothing but a finding of heresy. That finding was made, and it was extended to cover all 'favourers, receivers, and defenders' of the condemned man.

Even now, though – even after this unforgivable outburst – Sir John was given every opportunity to salvage the situation. It had been the practice to perform executions immediately after sentence was pronounced, but this was not done in his case. Instead he was given forty days' grace, in which he might consider the situation from his cell in the Tower, and perhaps bring himself to make a late recantation. Archbishop Arundel was not the man to show such mercy to a man who had called him the antichrist, so probably Sir John owed this piece of generosity to the king.

Such great, such unusual efforts were being made to be generous to Sir John, that it seems quite probable some effort was made to reassure his wife as well. No one used the scope of the pronouncement to threaten Sir John at second hand: as far as we know, he never faced the prospect of being made to see his wife executed in his place. If Joan had a role, it was to be used as a mediator, one final person to make the pleas to see reason that Sir John had failed so far to hear. Perhaps she was encouraged to visit him in the Tower for that purpose. Perhaps she did so.

Alternatively perhaps by then she despaired so greatly of his actions that she chose to keep herself aloof. Or perhaps she privately supported her husband to the hilt, knew what he and his friends were planning next, and was praying that his plans might achieve success. Because they had anticipated this much, it seems. That would not have been difficult: any common man would have known a man taking Sir John's line would surely end up in the Tower. But many men would have judged it the end of the story, with the burning as the epilogue. Sir John and his friends had a rather different ending in mind.

There have been villains and blackguards imprisoned in the Tower, and there have been men imprisoned there who are judged by posterity (and sometimes by at least some of their contemporaries too) to have been brave, honourable, even great. Men (and a few women) have known its cells and walked free. Others have walked out, but into exile, like the previous Lord Cobham. More than a few have walked no further than the executioner's block. What only a handful have ever done is to escape.

But that was what Sir John Oldfield planned.

No one escapes without planning, so it stands to reason that Sir John planned it, and that many other people helped to make the plan, and helped to execute it once it was made. The towers in the complex that were used to hold prisoners are all of them strong, and even someone who got out of a cell, out of the tower that contained that cell, had still to breach several layers of outer defences, so no escape was possible without help from those both inside and outside the Tower. The network of supporters that had been so strengthened four years earlier must have stretched its tentacles into the Tower establishment. There were men among its guards – there must have been – who were willing to take the extraordinary risk of helping Sir John get free.

There were others who probably did not help, but who nevertheless made the escape possible, because Sir John was being treated kindly, and few – even the king he had angered so – would have wished it otherwise. Sir Robert Morley, the keeper of the Tower, was probably not part of any plot, but he might have judged it appropriate not to keep this noble lord, this good friend of the king, fettered and chained to the wall.

That was not the story Oldcastle's supporters put out, which had him miraculously breaking free of his chains. (Nor was it the story his opponents put out, which had it that he had been freed from his fetters because he had promised to recant, and had then ignobly broken that promise.) This escape, it seems, was to be a trigger for the great rising that was to follow. And to give yeast to the rising, it was necessary to make the escape seem much more than a pedestrian matter of planning and persuasion. If Sir John was not quite claimed to walk through walls, at least he needed to be made to seem superhuman, more than life-size – in essence, king-sized. He was already known across England as a great champion of freedom and equality. Now was the time to transform his fame into legend.

This had to be done, because of what was planned next. Sir John's supporters might have loosed their grip on the hard political realities in some ways, but they had not failed to consider what would need to be done, if the changes they were determined to bring

Stained glass from St Mary Magdalene's Church,
Pulham Market, Norfolk

about were to be achieved. King Henry V was not the man who would let them happen, that was clear by then. So the rising that needed to follow had to get rid of King Henry. It had to do this, difficult as it might be, because it could not conceivably achieve its objectives otherwise. And it would not replace him with one of his brothers, or even the duke of York, since all these nobles were likely to be no more sympathetic to their aims than the king himself. It would replace with him Sir John Oldcastle, Lord Cobham.

Improbable it might be, but they could have seen no other path to the future they were determined to achieve. Since the real king was one who clearly had no truck with Lollards, the Lollards would replace him with a king who supported their cause. The only way to do this was to remove all the other candidates for that position, so their plan was to first kill King Henry and all his brothers, since there could be no justification for a regency otherwise. And while they were at it, they would kill the bishops and arch-bishops and other magnates of the realm. These were the men who had blocked them from making the Lollard Disendowment Bill a reality, so these men had all to be put out of the way. Then they could proceed to carry out the programme – that genuinely popular programme – that the previous King Henry had dismissed so cavalierly. They would demolish the monasteries, churches and cathedrals, and drive their priests and

monks from the ruins. And from the wreckage, they could build up a new, fine, equal society that, of course, gave the Lollards freedom to practise according to their beliefs.

Did all the Commons of England support this plan? They had certainly not been told of it. Only that fanatical central group understood the full radical insanity of what was intended. Did they think that the Commons would support it, when it was brought into action? Well, they probably convinced themselves that there was a pattern of events that would achieve what they wanted. First, and in secret, the royal family would be done away with. Then a vast rising of Lollards would take London, and raise that superhuman figure, the escapee from the Tower, to their head. And with that achieved, that man would announce his intention to restore calm and bring about a new world, and would call on his (genuine) friends among the king's army to help him.

This was a scheme that made the Disendowment Bill itself seem quite realistic. It was astonishingly audacious, and more than that, it was quite astonishingly abhorrent. Even when Henry IV had seized the throne, he had not openly murdered his predecessor and all his supporters (although admittedly, many believed he had had King Richard killed secretly). The good knights and burgesses who had all supported the bill when it was presented in parliament had none of them advocated murder. Sir John and his band of intimates had presumably persuaded each other – as tight, secretive bands can do – that this was the only way forward, but they had blithely overlooked the fact that the support they had in the country was not for this agenda at all.

It would have been a harsh reward, too, for all the forbearance that King Henry and his archbishop had showed to Oldcastle. But Sir John had this much in common with his king: neither of them ever shied from doing all that they believed to be necessary.

The escape actually happened, and if even the best-laid plans never proceed exactly in the way of the original scheme, the obstacles that arose were fought and overcome. The doors were unlocked, the gateways opened, the drawbridges lowered, and somehow – it is impossible now to know how – Sir John Oldcastle got himself free of the Tower, and into the safety of the anonymous streets of London. He did not go to Cobham's Inn, that was far too obvious. Instead he went into hiding in the house of a parchment-maker in Smithfield, one William Fisher. This man must have been one of the Lollard supporters, but one whom his colleagues believed was not yet marked down by the authorities.

Joan probably did not see him at all.

It might have made a fine story if it had ended there. In a different world, Sir John would have let the network of Lollard supporters spirit him out of London, and to somewhere he could live undetected – in the marshes around Burnham, perhaps, or the wilds of Wales. Or he could have gone abroad, to France or the Low Countries. But that would have required him to be a realistic man, one who acknowledged his limitations and knew where to draw the line. And he had by then ceased to be that at all.

So he stayed in London, and waited for the next stage of the plot to unfold.

Some historians believe that the rising was never a serious intention. It was so incredible, so unlikely to succeed, that they cannot accept that notionally sane men and women would have planned it. It was a story put about by the Church and the king's agents, they argue; a public picture that hides a more murky (but less incredible) reality. All governments need to create enemies, and to show those enemies vanquished. The escape from the Tower, which was certainly real, was a serious embarrassment not just to Sir Robert Morley but to the king and all his associates. The response, designed to divert attention and to justify a massive crack-down, was to create a rumour of a dangerous plot which needed at all costs to be foiled.

But if that was so, why did Oldcastle not immediately leave London? Why had he not let himself be led quietly, under cover of night, from Smithfield to the roads west, or east, or north, to a place where he might live out of the rest of his life in peace and obscurity? If he had done so, there would have been no grain with which to bake this loaf.

Instead he stayed at Fisher's house in Smithfield – according to the accusations laid against Fisher three years later, until the Wednesday after the following Epiphany (that is, Wednesday 10 January 1414, after the Epiphany of 6 January). He stayed there while the hapless Sir Robert Morley was removed from his post in punishment (although the king later relented and gave him it back) and while Archbishop Arundel had the sentence against him pronounced throughout England.[3] What Joan did meanwhile, there is no record of. But there were men across London, and way beyond, searching for the escapee, and presumably some of them were detailed to watch his wife. Even if she had wanted to do so (and perhaps she did not) she could not have risked going to meet with him.

From his place of hiding, Sir John continued with fleshing out the plans for the rising. A group of men disguised as mummers were to go to Eltham Palace, where the king had been staying for Christmas. As entertainers for the Twelfth Night festivities, they should have been able to get past the guards. Then once inside, they would throw off their disguises, pull out their knives, and fall on the king and his relations. Sir John was not to be a part of this group, because he would be needed elsewhere. He would be finalizing the plans to meet the thousands of Lollard sympathizers who would converge on the fields near St Giles Hospital, slightly to the west of central London. They would do so under cover of night, on Tuesday 9 January. Supporters in the city would head out of the gates, and there join those who had come from across the country. With the Londoners and the country men together, the plotters were persuaded they could raise a hundred thousand men. (Nor were they relying only on religious fervour: word had gone out that those men

Stained glass from Canterbury Cathedral

who answered the call would be paid.) Sir John Oldcastle would greet this multitude in St Giles Fields, and deliver the news that an irrevocable revolution was already under way, that the king was no more, and that they should follow him to true salvation.

These men did not have to agree to kill the king, because by the time they learned of this part of the plan it would already have been achieved. Oldcastle's chief lieutenant in this endeavour, a knight from Shropshire called Sir Roger Acton, would join him at the head of this vast army. They had almost certainly recruited other knights too, men whom they thought capable of turning a mass of unruly peasants and labourers into a formidable fighting force. That army would be so powerful, so strong in its righteousness, that it would draw all England to it, and carry Sir John to the Crown.

No king is perfect, and to the Lollards King Henry V undoubtedly was not. But Henry was not hated in the country, and nor was he stupid. Not for the first or the last time, Sir John Oldcastle's greatest mistake was fatally to underestimate his king.

The king had his own spies and agents. Over the months (indeed, years) that the Lollards had been under surveillance, some of those agents had infiltrated their movement. So Henry knew what was planned well before it took place.

He had his own supporters (many of whom were just as fixed in their convictions as the Lollards were in theirs), and he had the opportunity to make his own counter-plans. Henry did not go to Eltham that Christmas as it had been proclaimed that he would do. When the mummers arrived there, they found an empty palace. Instead the king had moved to Westminster, where he was better able to make preparations unobserved by the Londoners.

Tuesday night, the night for which the main action was planned. A January night, cold and dark; a night full of men, moving in silence, hoping, fearing, sick with exhilaration.

The Lollards had meant the city gates to be open, but the men detailed to do this were apprehended, and when the London Lollards arrived at the gates, they found them firmly barred, with the king's troops guarding them.

So there would be no men from London slipping down the dark roads outside the London city walls and up to St Giles Fields. And somewhere between Westminster and St Giles Hospital (the surviving accounts are almost as confused as the events they describe) the bulk of king's army was drawn up in the dark, waiting for the men from the countryside who could not be penned so easily. Every other road that led to St Giles had a smaller force stationed on it.

Sir John was not mistaken: he did have a great depth of support. The Lollards did have their own dense web, woven spider-sticky across much of England. Thousands of optimistic men who wanted to change their country beyond recognition left their beds in the dark that night, put on their thickest jerkins, took up their knives and picks. Moiling into groups, they made their quiet way down the roads to St Giles. When they made out the forces waiting for them, their spirits lifted: how many there were! How professional, how well equipped!

How bitterly opposed.

They managed to warn many of the latecomers, so there were plenty who learned the gist of what awaited them, and turned back in time to return to their beds with none but

their wives the wiser. But the king's net swept up a good catch, and carried the lot of them straight to prison.

It was probably a chill dawn before the sergeants realized that Sir John Oldcastle was definitely not among the catch. Nor was Sir Roger Acton. In the layers of treachery upon treachery, someone involved in the king's plans must have got word to them beforehand. They, and their immediate entourage, had had enough time to flee.

Word went out, of course: Sir John was public enemy number one, he must be apprehended at all costs. But his men must have made contingency plans, and the escape route down which he had been hustled closed blankly behind him. All the searches the king's sergeants made in the days that followed turned up less than nothing.

34 The parchment maker and the plot

I know thy works, and thy travail, and thy patience, and that thou mayest not suffer evil men; and thou hast assayed them that say that they be apostles, and be not, and thou hast found them liars …

Revelation II.2, in the Wycliffe translation of the Bible[1]

Lady Joan had possibly not seen her husband for months by the time of this second escape. Perhaps she had not met with him since the previous September, when he had first been committed to the Tower, and almost certainly she had not seen anything of him since his escape from it. However greatly they underestimated the king, both she and Sir John must have known that she was – had long been – under surveillance. For him to meet with her was so dangerous it could not be contemplated, and any messages that came to her would have travelled along routes so convoluted that no outsider could hope to follow them.

Whether she had spent it in Cooling, in London, or moving between the two, it must have been a dismal autumn and early winter for her. We can imagine her surrounded by two groups of men and women, fighting politely but firmly for influence over her. One on side, the Lollard supporters (the priests had left by then, but their servants and retainers must have included many firm believers, recruited by Oldcastle over the years) who worked to ensure she remained one of them. One the other side, those longstanding Cobham retainers who continued on her payroll, who had waited out the disconcerting years of Sir John's asecendancy, and were waiting now to comfort and protect his lady when (as they surely believed he would be) he was brought to the pyre. And in a ring outside them circled the king's men and the archbishop's men.

The escape from the Tower must have been disconcerting enough, with that outer loop of hostile solders and orthodox clerics thickening and tightening fast around her household. In spite of the circle of jagged pikes it was most likely followed by word through the Lollard network: Sir John is safe, he sends you his best regards, he has plans, and you will hear more anon.

Another wait: weeks of waiting, over a chill Christmas and New Year. Then she heard the more. The rumble of rumours, perhaps a message or two slipped into the hand of a servant in Cobham high street or Rochester market. Perhaps even optimistic at first, at least from Sir John himself: our plans have not worked out quite as we intended, but I am free, undaunted, regrouping even as I write. Horrified from the messengers who brough the public news, since the king and his men took pains to spread widely the claim that the plot had been designed to assassinate him and his brothers. Disconcerted, defiant, frightened, from those in

Cooling Castle

the network who were seeing their brothers, fathers, sons hunted down and hauled to the Tower. And also perhaps despairing. I am a haunted fox, cowering in the undergrowth. Send supplies, send money, help to save me!

Although the king's men must have doubted their quarry would take shelter in any of the Cobham houses, they were probably all searched. So Joan had to stand by as aggressive troops rampaged through her private rooms, emptied her coffers, clambered into the attics and down to the cellars – and treated the traitor's wife most likely with casual disgust.

There were surely men around her husband, the usual horde of them most likely, plotting and planning in dark parlours. But she was almost certainly much alone. Even those who had supported the Lollards' original plans would have been wary of siding publicly with her now. Indeed for months, ever since Sir John was escorted to his cell in the Tower, most reasonable men and women must have been convinced his story could only end in tragedy. And even those who showed sympathy could not necessarily be trusted.

For her, it was a strange kind of tragedy. Sir John was not dead, and she was no widow. She could not mourn. All she could do was to hold her head up, keep silent in public, and in private, do her best to comfort those who turned to her. This was not just a disaster for her, it was one that rippled across her estates, her servants, her extended family. Whatever happened next, none of them would emerge from the experience unchanged. And it was an experience that she had brought upon them, however little she had anticipated how the cloth of events would unfold.

The king and his officers were moving fast. They had not been taken by surprise, after all: they had known of the rising, and planned to respond to it. But realistically they had bungled the response. It should have been their priority to take Sir John and Sir Roger Acton, and instead they had captured neither of them. Within hours a commission of inquiry, stuffed with prominent nobles, had been appointed. A huge reward was offered for the capture of Sir John: 500 marks for information that would lead to his arrest, 1,000 marks for anyone who succeeded in making that arrest, and freedom from taxes of all kinds in perpetuity to the city, borough or township in which he was seized.[2] This was no threepence-a-day operation; these were life-changing sums which would have been seriously tempting to many. But vast as the rewards were, not a soul came forward with information.

The courts meanwhile got to work. That Friday week sixty-nine men were condemned to death. Some were found guilty of heresy, some of treason, and more than a few of both. On the following day, 13 January, thirty-eight of them were drawn on hurdles from Newgate to St Giles Fields, the place where they had planned to start their rising. Four pairs of new gallows had been set up. They were hanged in groups, and the bodies of those who had been convicted of heresy were burned for good measure. The stench of burning flesh must have hung heavy in the winter air for days. More executions followed.

Joan must have known more than a few of these men. A man called John Browne, who had been an esquire serving under Oldcastle, was arrested and executed; so was a well-known priest called John Beverley. But only a tiny minority of all the rebels suffered these terrible punishments, and there were other men she surely knew to be implicated who remained free.

Joan was not insignificant or peripheral. But she was a woman, an aristocratic woman, known to many, and probably well liked and respected. The aim of the king and his officers now was to close down the entire incident, eliminating those who were likely to cause trouble in future, and creating no further cause for dissent or rebellion. They clearly did not judge Joan to be central to her husband's planning, or a potential danger for the future. It would have been counter-productive to arrest her, and unthinkable to execute her for heresy or treason. So no punishment was inflicted on her, beyond that of facing the ruin of her life.

For two weeks her son-in-law Thomas Brooke was also left untouched, but on 23 January he was arrested and sent to the Tower. Possibly this was a precautionary measure on the sheriffs' part, because there seems to have been no firm evidence against him. The aim might simply have been to keep him in custody to ensure he gave no help to his wife's stepfather. This was a case when Joan could give help, or ensure that others gave it; at the least, to send provisions and pay bribes to ensure Brooke was decently lodged in the Tower and had good food to eat and warm clothes against the winter chill. His friends rallied round too, and on February four of them made a pledge of 1,000 marks that he would be the king's 'true prisoner' and make no attempt to escape. After this he was no longer kept in chains, and was allowed to move around the precincts of the Tower. But it was many months before he was freed.

The first frenzy was over by then, and the king was letting it be known that he would show some leniency. On the same day that Brooke was arrested, a man found guilty was pardoned, so there was hope now for all who remained alive – Sir John apart. No leniency was ever likely to be offered to him.

Nor was any on offer for his lieutenant. Sir Roger Acton was captured that February, found guilty of treason, and hanged at Tyburn after being hauled naked through the London streets. His body was left on the gallows for a month, until a brave trumpeter obtained permission from the king to take him down and bury him.

Months passed, and still no herald proclaimed the capture of that notorious traitor, Sir John Oldcastle. Perhaps from time to time he sent word to his wife: a message to tell her to keep up her courage, to arrange for him to receive money and supplies. (Apologies for all he had done: no, he would not have sent those.) She must, in humanity, have been relieved that he was well and free, but in some ways his freedom placed her in a more difficult position than if he had died. Tried, executed, buried: it was all done with now for Sir Roger's widow. But Joan was not a widow, she was a wife of the man who was fast passing beyond notoriety and into legend. Hated by some, adored by others; dismissed by some as a failure, but still looked to by others as their last best hope for change: he was all that and more. And for years to come there would have been people turning up at the gates of Cobham's Inn and Cooling Castle, claiming to bring messages from him, some believable, some not. There were tales throughout England of sightings of Sir John: again, some believable and some of them not. Dozens of messengers and spies had been rewarded for their part in bringing men to justice, but still nobody had claimed the great reward for tracking down the leader of the rebellion.

35 The accomplices

knowing that he, the same John Oldecastelle, was a traitor of our said Lord the King …

> Inquisition held as to an Accomplice [William Fisher] in the treason of
> Sir John Oldecastelle; and Trial and Sentence thereon, 1416

the Hoo peninsula, North Kent

Crises by definition do not last forever. Disasters are not absolute, for those who survive them. Gradually, normal life resumes. Things do not turn back to how they were before, but things continue, even so.

For Joan, the continuance meant dealing with a lot of legal issues. Summonses had been issued, calling on Sir John to present himself for trial, they had three times been ignored, and on 14 June 1414 Sir John was duly declared an outlaw.[2] Although he had not been found guilty of heresy or treason, his outlawry carried its own penalties, including the forfeiture of his lands and possessions.

But although King Henry V could be brutally decisive when he judged it necessary, he was not a vindictive man. He had issued a general pardon to all but a handful of conspirators, and now that the rising had been firmly suppressed, there was no great purge of all the Lollards.

That September Thomas Brooke and a colleague of his were brought before the court on charges of stirring up rebellion and holding heretical opinions. It is by no means clear that they were innocent, but the jury were not willing to convict them. They pleaded not guilty, were acquitted of all the charges, and Thomas walked out of the Tower of London a free man.

Even if this was not what he had intended, the king continued to be magnanimous. He granted to Brooke and to one Richard Clitheroe (who might have been Sir John's son in law) the custody of all the possessions that Sir John had held in the right of, or conjointly with, his wife.[3] So Joan did not lose Cooling, or her other estates: she was supported by Brooke and other friends and relations in picking up the pieces of her old life.

The family did not even lose Oldfield's lands in Herefordshire. Apparently Joan was regarded as the joint proprietor of them, so they were included in the lands that were returned to her. (However, she did lose her Burnham Norton estates, and perhaps some others; for years afterwards she was petitioning to have them restored to her.)

Herefordshire is a very long way from Kent. Joan presumably continued to live at Cooling, travelling from time to time to her other estates in East Anglia and the Midlands, and perhaps to see her daughter in the West Country. It seems less likely that

she spent time at Almeley, even after she regained the estate. Perhaps Thomas Brooke and his family helped to ensure that these distant lands were supervised.

As time passed, and the botched-up strengthening of the walls crumbled, daily life at Cooling would have fallen back into much its old rhythm. The stewards and bailiffs, the lawyers and merchants who did business with the Cobham estate were probably glad that some semblance of normal service had been resumed. Perhaps many of them too would have liked to see the Church reformed, and the taxation system as well, but they were not fanatics, and they were not willing to risk their lives in that cause.

It is not easy to evade the king's officers of justice. The difficulties presented to someone trying to do so in 1414 were not the same as fugitives face today, but they were formidable none the less. England was a small society, and a notorious knight could not readily remake himself within it, even if he had wished to do so, which quite likely Sir John Oldcastle did not. It seems, rather, that he was seduced by his own legend, reluctant to give up his grand dreams, and (possibly in any case seeing few alternatives open to him) determined to set about the long slow task of remaking his plans and trying again.

He did not escape abroad, conceivable though that might have been. It would probably have been impossible for him to reinvent himself as a merchant or craftsman: those men lived in tight-drawn coteries, much of their work regulated by guilds, and most decently paid jobs other than that of man at arms required skills that Sir John would not have had. He was not the man to resign himself to a peasant life, hiring himself out to a farmer at a country fair. The Robin Hood dream of a merry life as an outlaw in the royal forests was never a truly credible one, albeit some men eked out a bare kind of survival in this way. His only real option was to entrust himself to the network of Lollard sympathizers, live off them, rant to them and try to inspire them, and work with them to rebuild his shattered network and his plans for revolution.

This would have been easier if he had had sources of income other than the charity of his colleagues, and most likely he did. The income on the Almeley estates was drawn by a man called John ap Harry, who had been a comrade of Oldcastle's and had fought

Stained glass from
St Mary's Church,
Saxlingham Nethergate,
Norfolk

with him against the Welsh. Joan seems to have made no attempt to claim it, and quite likely that was because it had been made known to her that the money that passed to ap Harry was passed directly on to Sir John. Why not? He had to live, or at least from her perspective that would have been preferable to the alternatives.

In time, the crisis mode faded too from the king's officers of justice. They knew that Sir John was still at large, and they knew that there was a great reward on offer. But more recent, more immediately pressing, concerns probably occupied their time. And some of them were among the great commons of England that had wanted – still wanted – reform. Sir John had plenty of supporters still, men who did not know he had planned to kill the king, or did not care, or believed it was all a trumped-up story and his real intentions had been to do exactly as they wished he had managed to do. If word came to some such men that Sir John was in their territory, they might have thought on the reward, and then thought on the danger and difficulty of confronting the legendary outlaw (and the supporters who still travelled with him), and decided that pretending they had not heard that word was a much more practicable way forward.

K ing Henry was making serious preparations now for a great military campaign against the French. England was as close to peace as it ever was, and although he had always to be wary of plots against his rule, the risk of a Lollard rebellion in his absence did probably not figure large in his calculations. At the Christmas of 1414 friends of Oldcastle – friends who had clearly learned they risked little by admitting to that status – asked the king if he would consider including Sir John in the pardons he had issued. Joan might have been among them, or if she was not, she was perhaps in contact with them as they prepared their pleas. It must have seemed a large demand. Many of the men who had joined in the plot had already been executed, and this was not a man peripheral to it, it was the most wanted man in England, one whom everyone believed to have been the instigator and the prime mover of the planned revolt. Few kings would have granted him a pardon. But this was no average king, and he listened. Then he let it be known that if Sir John Oldcastle were to come out of hiding and submit himself to the king, his misdeeds would all be excused.

Sir John did not come. Those who had worked hard to get that offer must have been dispirited by that. The king must have been dispirited too. Yet again he had done far more for Sir John than could reasonably have been asked of him, and yet again he had had poor return for his generosity.

The king set out letters patent, and gave them to men who, it was believed, would be able to get them passed to Sir John, to make sure his silence was not because he had never learned of the proposal. Perhaps the letters reached Sir John, but he still did not emerge from hiding.

Why? Those still close to him perhaps knew the

Brass of an unknown woman from Holy Trinity
Church, Chrishall, Essex

answer, though it is obscure to us today. Perhaps he feared he would be walking into a trap, that the pardon would become something else once he was safely in chains. Perhaps he thought the better, the only tolerable, way forward was to continue to work to raise a revolt and bring the king down. His pardon was conditional on his surrender, since the king could scarcely pardon a man who was still plotting against him, so because he had not surrendered, the price remained upon his head.

Perhaps he had gone mad.

Then he was heard from, reliably heard from. He had heard that the king was assembling an army to invade France, and apparently believing that it had already set sail – which it had not – he sent a threatening letter to one Lord Abergavenny. He believed he had suffered injuries at the man's hands, and even at this risk to his security, he was determined to get revenge. In this, he made his usual error of hopelessly underestimating his adversary. Abergavenny put together a force of men. The chroniclers claimed there were nearly five thousand of them, an incredible number to set off in pursuit of a lone fugitive. But perhaps they sensed that Sir John was not alone, had never been alone. Even now, he had followers.

This army in waiting – it would next go to France – set off from Worcestershire, Lord Abergavenny's home, to Malvern, from where Sir John's letter had apparently come.

They nearly caught him. They caught several of his comrades, but Sir John had slithered away into the countryside. So they tortured the comrades for what they could tell, and learned that Sir John had a secret hiding place where he had been piling up arms, money, and Lollard-inspired banners for an army to carry.

But the arms, the money, the banners: all was lost now. When King Henry, at Portsmouth waiting to sail, announced that he had uncovered a plot against his throne, and followed it up with trials and executions, some men might have whispered the word 'Lollard', and believed that Sir John had been behind it. Almost certainly though, he was not.

With the money and banners and arms all gone, and quite a few of his associates too, Sir John went back to lying low. And his wife kept her own counsel, it seems – although perhaps she, at least, managed to thank King Henry for his offer of a pardon – and continued to live her own life, supported by her son in law.

Church of St Peter Hungate, Norwich

36 The loss of a nose

On the morrow, when all was ready, the king asked what time it was of the day, and they said, 'Prime'. Then said the king, 'Now is a good time, for all England prayeth for us, and therefore be of good cheer, and let us go to our journey.' And anon every English man knelt down, and put a little portion of earth in his mouth. And then said the king with a big voice, 'In the name of Almighty God, and of Saint George, Avaunt banner! and Saint George this day thee help!'

Davies' Chronicle[1]

In a different world, Sir John Oldcastle would have sailed with his king to France, and taken part in the battle of Agincourt, one of the greatest victories the English ever achieved. He would have served with distinction, like many other commanders, in the English army that won King Henry the promise of the throne of France. He would have achieved lasting renown, earned a fortune, and come back to England a hero.

But in the world he had helped to engineer, Sir John remained somewhere in the Welsh Marches, a fugitive still dreaming of changing it for a better one.

Henry was a justly popular king, but he sat on his English throne only a little more

From a brass in St Mary
Magdalene's Church,
Cobham, Kent

securely than his father had done (and he was never to sit on the French one he had been promised at all). There were people throughout his realm who fomented rebellion, not least because they resented the hard line he continued to take against heretics. The king might have offered mercy to his old friend, but he had not continued a general amnesty to all rebels. In 1416 the law caught up with William Fisher, the parchment maker who had sheltered Sir John after he escaped from the Tower. Fisher denied all the charges against him, but he was found guilty even so, and went to the gallows as a result.

One of Sir John's former chaplains – whether it was John Lay, or another of them, is not recorded – was seized and accused of heresy. Understandably enough he chose to recant his heretical beliefs, and he was released.

Months passed, years passed, and Sir John remained at liberty. Meanwhile his wife must have remained living without a husband, turning to her estimable (though perhaps, on the evidence, not quite so charming and likeable) son in law when she needed help – and increasingly perhaps to her daughter too.

Joan junior had not inherited her mother's bad luck with her children. She was to give Thomas as many as fourteen sons and daughters. Their first was a son, Edward, born in about 1411, and Reginald, Hugh, Thomas, John, Robert, Margaret and the rest followed in steady succession. Perhaps as the years passed Lady Joan came to spend more time with the Brooke family in Somerset, and she must have taken great pleasure in the knowledge

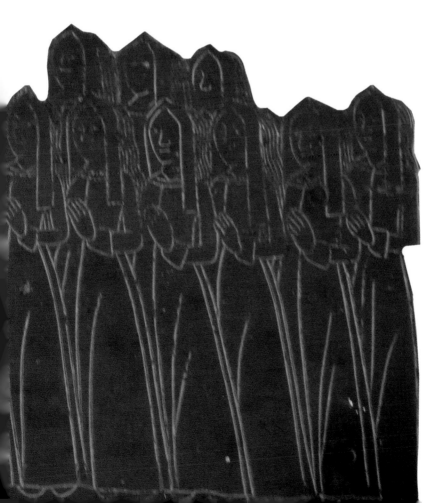

that through her daughter, her family would descend securely through the generations to follow.

From there, and through Thomas, perhaps from time to time she was still in contact with Sir John. She showed no disloyalty to him, at least in public.

Thomas Brooke must at times have seemed to his mother in law to be all that her errant husband was not. He was not touched with brilliance, perhaps, but he made up for it in steadiness. He seems to have shared the Cobhams' Lollard faith, and at times it – or perhaps rather, his connection with Sir John – brought him close to disaster. But he did not have Sir John's fanaticism, or his fatal inability to compromise. Although the king and his officers evidently suspected him of supporting Sir John, they were never able to prove a case against him.

His own good sense, and perhaps his mother in law, seemed to help when he did come closest to trouble. On 13 July 1417 Brooke and his half-brother, Richard Cheddar, a combative kind of man who had almost lost his nose in a fight a few years earlier, were forced by the king's council to give a pledge of £1,000 for their good behaviour. They promised that neither would make or lead unlawful assemblies, adhere to Oldcastle against the Church or secretly maintain him in his heresies. The Cobham estates, the Oldcastle estates, and Sir Thomas's own lands must have enabled them to make this huge payment. And if Sir Thomas was suspected by the king's agents at Westminster, he remained popular with his colleagues in Somerset. In 1417 both he and Cheddar were appointed to Parliament as the representatives for Somerset.

This was to prove a difficult appointment, because it was during the Parliament that Sir John Oldcastle was finally captured.

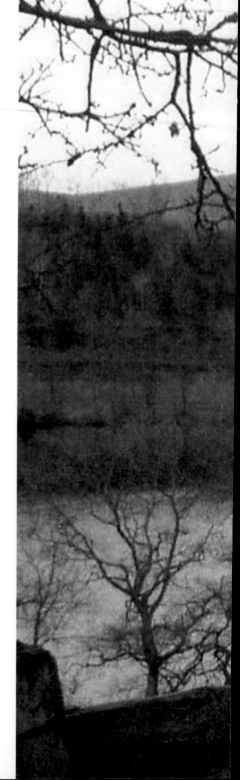

Llyn Du. The stile is at the foot of Broniarth Hill; the road down to Meifod is on the far shore. Photo courtesy of Mark Lange.

37 Taxes for Welshpool

And anon after, he brucke out off the seide Toure and wente into Wales, and their kepte hym long tyme. And atte the laste the Lorde Powis mette with hym and toke hym, ut he stode ate grete defense longe tyme and wasse sore wounded or he wolde be take.

From *An English Chronicle 1377–1461*[1]

Perhaps at one point Sir John Oldcastle was in hiding in a villein's house in St Albans, where the abbot's servants – hoping to claim that famous reward – managed to capture some men who might have been his companions, and discover a cache of blasphemous books, including standard works of devotion from which someone had scrubbed out every mention of the Virgin Mary and the saints.[2] Or perhaps that was just a rumour, because every mention of a heretic, every hint of unrest, in the four years and more that Sir John remained a fugitive drew a whisper of his name.

Some of those rumours were probably true. The man who had declined to surrender himself under King Henry's assurances was certainly plotting, even if his plots were increasingly unrealistic.

The Tower of London

Some of the other men who claimed they had come close to capturing him might genuinely only just have failed to grab him by the tail, though other claims might have been no more than tall stories. And with all the tall tales, the rumours, the sense of invincibility that surrounded the most wanted man in England, two sons of Sir Griffith Vaughan, a Marcher knight who lived near Welshpool, perhaps did not really believe it when his father heard what he reckoned was reliable information that the famous Sir John was holed up in a farmhouse nearby at Broniarth. But their father told them to saddle up, round up some men to take with them – a few of their servants and friends, not the five thousand that Lord Abergavenny had thought appropriate – and go to investigate on his behalf.

This is hilly country, but not mountainous; country fit for farming, hence the farmhouse, where it seems Sir John had indeed been staying. The Vaughan brothers and their men must have approached with care, but they were perhaps still surprised to find the notorious rebel actually there.

Maybe they found him in the fields, maybe in the farmhouse itself; and maybe not all

of its residents had been happy to harbour a traitor, because one account has a woman (who would hardly be one of the Vaughan boys' troops) setting upon Sir John with a stool, and breaking his leg.[3] But even if this happened, and hampered him, he got as far as a nearby field, which is still known as Cae'r Barwn, the baron's field.

Sir John had always been good at a fight, and years as a fugitive must have honed his skills. He had men with him – Sir John had always had men with him – and they fought too. It was quite a skirmish, and according to some tales, several men lay dead on the field before Sir John collapsed, too severely wounded to fight any longer.

The Vaughan brothers, who doubtless knew of the reward on his head, had no intention of letting Sir John die. They managed to lug him to Welshpool (also known as Powis) Castle, where the lord of Powis sent word to London. Word came back from Prince John, the duke of Bedford, who was regent in England while King Henry was campaigning in France, that he must be brought immediately to London, and kept alive so that he might be put on trial. To make sure he survived, he had the indignity of being carried all across England in a horse litter. It must have been securely guarded, but many people would have come out to the road, hoping to catch a glimpse of the famous Sir John Oldcastle on his last long journey, and have a tale they could tell their children. Mind, the Vaughan boys' tale would have been a better one.

Lady Cobham must have visted many people in the Tower of London during her lifetime, but always she had been escorted out again after her visit. After her husband's arrest, she was escorted in – not to his cell, but to a different one – and the door clanged shut behind the guard.

She must have known much loneliness in the years that Sir John had been a fugitive, but there can be nothing more lonely than to stand in an empty room in the Tower of London, where those awaiting execution had chiselled their names into the stone in their last empty days, and wait to learn what was to happen to her, and what to her husband.

She must have had some visitors: some of them the king's men, coming to question her and find out what she knew, and some her own friends and relations, coming to offer what little comfort they could. This was an untrodden road: so much had been astonishing about Sir John's story that few would have dared to be confident of his fate, and none could have been sure what would happen to his wife. She certainly cannot have been sure herself.

King Henry was not in the country, so neither she nor Sir John was visited by him. And without the king – even perhaps with the king – many would have feared to offer either of them kindness, so probably they were not permitted to see each other. But someone would have told her, eventually, that Sir John was to appear before parliament. Perhaps that someone was Sir Thomas Brooke, a member of that parliament for Somerset, and one of those who passed a resolution condemning the traitor. Sir Thomas was not among those who judged him, though: Sir John was a lord, and he was judged not by the Commons but, as was customary, by his peers. Some would have told her, later, what Sir John had said when he was brought before the parliament. He rambled, apparently, to such a degree that he had to be asked to come to the point. Perhaps by then there was no point; there had long since ceased to be any point to his wanderings and plottings. And he was an injured man, in pain, with broken limbs. He claimed that King Henry was not the king, that Richard II was still alive. He asked for mercy, then he changed his mind, and said it mattered little whether he was condemned by human agency – since, it must be supposed, he was placing himself under the protection of God.

He did not see Archbishop Arundel, because that scourge of heretics had not lived to see his nemesis recaptured; he had died the previous February.

A condemned man is customarily given a last chance to confess his sins, a mass and absolution. But Sir John would not have been willing to receive the last rites from a Catholic priest, and no Lollard preacher would have been found for him, so he probably went to his death unshriven. He was a man who believed his path to God was best left unmediated, so it is doubtful whether this omission troubled him. Perhaps a priest – not a Lollard priest – visited his wife in her own cell, and told her what was to happen to her husband. Perhaps she prayed: for him, for herself, for the country.

There was no forty days' grace this time. The day after sentence was passed he was hauled, in the same horse litter, to St Giles Fields, where he had last sat on his horse with Sir Roger Acton, waiting for the hundred thousand men they believed would join them, and where the scaffolds that had been set up three years earlier were still standing. He had been found guilty of both treason and heresy, so his sentence was to be both hanged and burned. A strong chain was set on the gallows, and they hauled his broken body up to it. His last words, spoken after he had been hanged, and perhaps his entrails drawn out, were to the elderly soldier Sir Thomas Erpingham, who was among many who had come to witness his end. He prophesied that he would rise again on the third day. Then the flames rose up, and consumed body, gallows and all.

St Giles Fields is some distance from the Tower, so Joan would have heard little more than the shouts from the crowd when he was escorted out of his prison. Then someone, later, probably came to tell her it was over.

Lord Powis claimed the reward. And in fairness he should have passed a good chunk of it on to the Vaughan boys and the survivors among their men, and to the widows of those who had died in capturing Sir John. But when he died himself three years later, it had not yet been paid to him.

As far as is known, the district of Welshpool was also not rewarded, and has continued to pay the usual taxes.

38 Cold moats

Allas! That thou that were a manly knight,
And shoon full cleer in famous worthynesse
Standynge in the favour of euery wight,
Haast lost the style of cristenlye prowesse
Among all hem that stande in the cleernesse
Of good byleeue …

Thomas Hoccleve,
'To Sir John Oldcastle'
(1415)

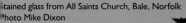

Sir John's end was not one that would have prompted Lady Cobham to embark immediately on another marriage, even if she had been at liberty to do so.

She was not kept in prison for long, however. Once the three days were up, and Sir John, as far as could be ascertained on Earth, had failed to rise from the dead, she was permitted to leave the Tower, on the security of three friends – the same Sir Thomas Erpingham who had heard her husband's last words was one of them – that she would appear before the king's council if she was summoned.[1] But there can have seemed little reason to summon her. The parliament had not been one to petition for the disendowment of the Church; even the Commons had called for Sir John to be convicted. Whatever Joan and others had believed and hoped for in the past, there would be no new resurgence of Lollardy. Even in Bohemia, the cause seemed lost: that same year their great reformer Jan Hus was also executed.

Joan presumably went back to Cooling. Sir John's lands had been forfeit again on his conviction, so there was another legal battle to be fought, to win them back once more. But Joan and her agents must have been familiar with that process by now. In time most at least of the lands that had been her own were restored to her, and in further time (quite a lot further time) Sir John's own heirs were given back the family lands he had inherited, which had also been confiscated.

Every society has its rituals prescribed for the bereaved. If they do not stop the pain of the living, they do at least provide a structure for their lives in a time of change and adjustment. The arrangement of a great funeral; the planning of a tomb; the paying of priests to say masses, the attendance at those masses: all those were part of the ritual for a noble lady who has lost her husband. But if that husband has been convicted of heresy and treason, his body confiscated, his coat of arms expunged from the record, his legacy little more than disgrace, and there is no funeral to arrange, memorial to be ordered or grave to pray at, what then is his widow to do?

Joan's situation as a fugitive's wife had been a strange and unusual one, but to be the widow of a traitor was much less uncommon. Under every English king those conspiring against the regime had been convicted, sentenced, done to death. Many women had endured their husbands making the journey to the scaffold. Many had had to find a path through the wilderness that followed. But even so, there were probably no reliable guides on how they should act in such a situation.

Had she loved him to the end? Or had he tried her patience even worse than he had tried King Henry's, and squandered all that she had given him? Did she weep, or did she walk from the Tower dry-eyed, unmoved at the thought of his last moments at St Giles Field? Whatever she felt inside, there is no indication that she let it escape her. She was a great lady, and she lived in a time when suffering was the lot of every man and woman. She suffered, she endured, she survived.

There were still masses for the souls of the dead – and the living too – being said at Cobham church, albeit they did not mention Sir John Oldcastle. Even though Joan might have shared her late husband's disdain for such expensive rituals, she probably continued to attend them, and to pray at the graves of those she had lost. Perhaps she silently added Sir John's name to the list of those she mourned; and then again, perhaps she did not.

Even before all her lands were restored, there must have been dowered and entailed lands that escaped confiscation: she would never have been poor, as many of the wives of the Lollards executed four years earlier certainly had been. She had no living children by Sir John, to suffer from the disgrace. His adult children were not her problem, they lived on the other side of the country, and she would have seen little or nothing of them. Her daughter and son in law might share Sir John's – her own – beliefs, but they had avoided being martyred for them, and would continue to tread the kind of careful path that her grandfather and her parents had trodden. These were, if not great blessings, at least reasons why things were not as bad as they could possibly have been. Worse had been known.

Cooling was still a remote place, curled in the marshland, with the gulls crying overhead and the water cold in the moats. It would have been quiet now: there was not just no Sir John, there were none of the men who had attended him, none of the men at arms who had served under him, none of the messengers who had brought word from him, and if there were still chaplains, they probably omitted to rant. The months after the death of a husband are a time for quiet and contemplation, whatever the circumstances, and through that winter and spring that was probably the essence of Lady Cobham's life.

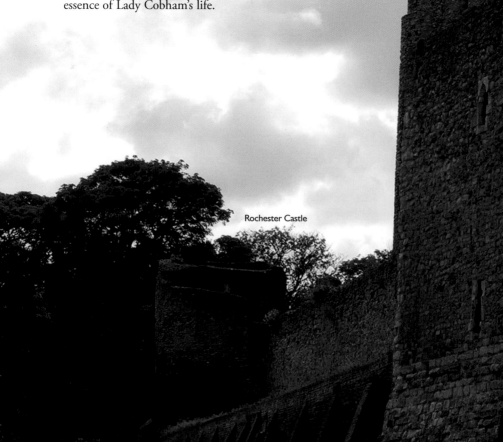

Rochester Castle

39 Of funerals, niggardly and otherwise

'On my faith,' the spectators said, 'they have gallantly performed their first course.'
  Jean Froissart, 'A deed of arms at
    Bordeaux before
  Sir John Harpedon' (1387)[1]

Howwer little we can be certain of regarding Lady Cobham's character, it would
be difficult to deny that she was a doughty survivor.

In time she would have emerged from her mourning, and rejoined the world.
It was a world at war, albeit the war was being fought in France. This was not like the
time of her childhood, when the French had sailed mockingly past the Norfolk coast, and
pirates had threatened places like Cooling. The French now were embattled in their own
country, of which King Henry and his troops were slowly continuing to take command.

There was only one man in Lady Cobham's close family, since she had neither husband
nor sons still living, and that man went with the rest to war. On 21 May 1418 Thomas
Brooke took out royal letters of protection, a standard step for a man at arms about to
serve overseas, and later that year he was knighted by the king. He served with the royal
army at the siege of Rouen, a terrible winter siege in which thousands of the inhabitants
died of hunger. The men stationed in France rarely made the hazardous journey back
across the channel, so quite likely Sir Thomas (as he had now become) remained in
France until February 1421, when King Henry came back to England, and Brooke seems
to have done so too, since he represented Somerset in the parliament that was called by
the king on his return.

King Henry was a king capable of generosity, as Sir John Oldcastle could have attested
if he had been capable of recognizing it. Sir John's widow was probably capable of that
recognition, and of the humility and realism necessary to seek that generosity. The king
was married now, to a French princess, Catherine of Valois, and although his court was
somewhat martial in temperament, it was a court at which ladies such as Joan Cobham

Stained glass from St Agnes's Church, Cawston, Norfolk. Photo Mike Dixon

might find a place. Probably Sir Thomas used Cobham's Inn as his base when he was at Westminster, and perhaps it was at some such time that his mother in law also returned to court, bowed low to the king (though not as low as she had been used to bow to King Richard II), and received his gracious acknowledgement in return.

The martial court did not survive long. King Henry went back to France in the hope of completing his conquest, but instead he sickened and died. His next return to England was as a corpse. He had been a great king, one of England's greatest, and might have become greater still if he had survived for a full span of life. Perhaps, even, he would have reformed the Church, although he doubtless would not have done it in quite the way the Lollards proposed. He was succeeded by his son, a small child, and a long confused period of government during Henry VI's minority, which continued for the rest of Joan's life.

She could have married again now if she wished. And at some point in the years after Sir John's death she did indeed do so. She did not rush to remarry, as she had done each previous time she had lost a husband. But it seems that, varied though her experiences had been, she had concluded that there were more pluses than minuses in going through life in partnership with another person.

She chose, of course, a man who would fit in with her life. She seems to have had no intention of leaving Cooling, or tying herself to someone who would prevent her from making the rounds of places, friends, servants that had been long familiar to her. If she had married a great baron she would have had to make compromises, and it seems she always cared less for the status of her husband than for the ability to keep control of her life.

The man she chose, Sir John Harpedon or Harpenden, was possibly a foreigner, from a family that originated from Poitou in France.[2] As such, he was a little removed from the pattern of English society that would have placed him either in support of, or in opposition to, Sir John Oldcastle. That must surely have seemed an advantage.

Not much more is known about this second Sir John. Indeed not even that is known for sure: at least some of the French Harpedons had changed their name to Belleville, after they gained the manor of Belleville through a useful marriage, and although the French chronicler Froissart records a Sir John Harpedon as having hosted a grand tournament in Bordeaux in 1387, it is not clear whether this was Joan's husband's father, his grandfather, or no relation at all. Joan's Sir John Harpedon was also the lord of Harpsden in Oxfordshire, by its name evidently a place with which his family had been long associated, but that does not mean he was not part of the Poitou family: English settlers had been going to Gascony for generations, and they and the Gascons had often intermarried.

It seems more certain that the Sir John Harpedon whom Joan married was the one who had fought at Agincourt (on the English side) with the well-known English commander Sir John Cornwall, and then from 1417 had served in Normandy, and later in Aquitaine, as part of the English garrisons (or at least, Lancastrian garrisons, for they were more Anglo-French than purely English, and were certainly intended by the king to be so). He had had a distinguished career, although he seems never to have become a household name. But then, that too was perhaps not what Joan would have wanted. Perhaps Sir Thomas Brooke had met this man in France, and when they both retired to England (Sir John presumably as a much older man than Sir Thomas) he introduced him to his mother in law, as the kind of man with whom she would feel comfortable.

Sir John seems to have proved a diligent steward of Joan's estates, but he never took the title of Lord Cobham, and presumably his wife never sought it for him. There was no question of the couple having children of their own: that time in Joan's life was now well behind her. And nor was there any question of Sir John inheriting the Cobham estates should he survive his wife, since they had been firmly settled on her daughter. The couple probably lived a quieter life than Joan had been used to in her earlier marriages. But she was older now, and quite likely that suited her well.

The drama of her life was now all behind her, and there is little to be said (not least because there is little known) about this last phase. She was not ready for Eternity yet: whatever physical weaknesses had sent all but one of her children to an early grave, she was spared them, just as her living daughter was. She lived on for more than sixteen years after Sir John Oldcastle was executed, and as far as can be known, she spent many of them happily with Harpedon. She survived to see her grandchildren grow up, and squabble with their father. Sir Thomas remained an inveterate Lollard, albeit he must have kept his faith circumspectly: when he died (a couple of years after Joan: he did not make old bones) he made a point of specifying a funeral his biographer called 'niggardly', and made his bequests direct to the poor, rather than through the monasteries, which he deliberately omitted from his charitable dispositions. He also referred to the 'evil will' of his children towards his 'true servants', who probably were supporters of his own faith. Sir Thomas's life had been blighted by his association with the Lollards; his eldest son (who became in his turn Lord Cobham) was never to take the same course. What Lady Brooke believed we cannot know.

And of what Joan then believed, how she chose to worship, there is no indication, for her will has not survived. Perhaps she, like her grandfather, had arranged her memorial before her last illness, and perhaps she too opted for a simple funeral and the minimum of requiem masses. She died on a January day in 1433, most likely at her beloved home of Cooling.

She was interred, of course, at Cobham church, alongside her grandfather, two of her husbands – although she shared the vault of neither, she had one of her own – and most, presumably, of her children. Her grave was covered with another life-sized brass, not much different in style from those that had been made for her husbands. It shows her – it is in Cobham church still – simply dressed, with her hands clasped in prayer. At her right side there are images of five sons; at her left, of five daughters. Some have quibbled that this presents her as the mother of a great healthy brood, something that, alas, she never was.[3] But those sons and daughters must have figured large in her life, and larger still in her thoughts. It was as their mother, and the wife of Sir Reginald Braybrooke, that she chose to be presented to later generations.

Her last husband lived on for another four years, and then was interred in Westminster Abbey, in the same chapel as her first husband, although this was probably no more than a coincidence. Let us home some people missed both him and Joan, and prayed at their gravesides.

Acknowledgements and Notes

My grateful thanks are due to all those who helped me in the production of this book. Drafts at different stages were read and commented on by Lis Eastham, Suzie Hanna and Bobby Hanna. My husband Paul Simmonds both read and proofread the text, and my sister Meg Norman also proofread it.

Particular thanks to all those who have given me permission to use their photographs in the book. Mike Dixon has been unfailingly generous with his work for three of my historical biographies. Thanks too to Lloyd Patton (walwyn – professor-moriarty.com) for the Robert Fitzroy glass on page 12; Robert Brown and the Axminster TASK Centre for offering me a choice of photos from their website (the one I chose is on p. 147); and Mark Lange, who sent me a selection of photos of the Broniarth area. I have not succeeded in contacting Malene Thyssen whose bonfire photo I used on page 189; she offered her work copyright free on the web, and I am grateful to her and indeed all others who do so. Where no other photographer is credited, the photos are my own.

Thanks too to all those who were helpful during my researches, including the kind woman who opened up Chrishall Church especially for us, and all those who work to ensure other churches are open to visitors. Ian Edwards obtained a crucial book for me from the UEA Library. Paul Simmonds has accompanied me on many research trips for this and previous books, and I am as always indebted to him.

I owe an immense debt too, of course, to all those who have preceded me in researching this area, and have made documents available. Specific references are given below and in the bibliography that follows.

1 The king's beloved servant

1 The king's description of William de la Pole (Joan's great-great uncle), cited on Harvey (1957) p. 42, from CPR 1338-40, 386.
2 Core specific sources for this chapter are Fryde (1988), Harvey (1957) and Horrox (1983).
3 Harvey (1957) p. 55. Richard's premises were actually in the parish of St Edmund the King. St Michael's is still to be found on Cornhill, although the church Richard de la Pole would have known was destroyed, but for its later tower, in the Great Fire of London (as was St Edmund's). It must have occupied about the same footprint as the present church, and had a cloister on its south side.
4 Harvey (1957) noted that (at least in his time) one copy remained in Hull Guildhall.
5 In February 1330. Harvey (1957), p. 71.
6 Harvey (1957) p. 18.
7 It was not easy to obtain land in those days, there was no kind of established land market, and only a few large estates changed hands through sale, so to some extent it was a question of accepting what became available.
8 The Malsoures were a family prominent later in Milton's history.
9 Harvey (1957) p. 6, citing the Hull Corporation Bench Book, vol. II, 140.
10 Horrox (1983), p. 32.

2 The dead goats

1 From *The Decameron*, trans. F. Winwar (New York: Modern Library, 1955), xxiv. There are many sources for information on the black death: among those I have relied on is Gottfried (1983), in which this is quoted.
2 McFarlane (1973), pp. 169–70.

3 Of murder, witchcraft and a bishop

1 'The moral balade of Chaucer', from *The Works of Geoffrey Chaucer, vol. 1, from the*

text of Professor Skeat, London etc.: Henry Frowde, 1903, p. 304. A rough modern version: The first stock [i.e. man] was father of gentility: any man who claims to be a gentleman must follow his guide, and turn his wits to serve the virtue and flee the vices.

2 Harvey (1957) p. 56, citing Cal. IPM VIII, 430 (no. 596).

3 Horrox (1983), p. 33.

4 https://en.wikipedia.org/wiki/Walter_Langton

5 Calendar of Inquisitions Post Mortem (CIPM), ix, no.180, for which I am indebted to Vaut (n.d.).

6 Horrox (1983), p. 33.

7 Harvey (1957), p. 58.

8 The writer Leland described it then as 'now clene down … and … made a septum for beestes'. Cited at www.british-history.ac.uk/report.aspx?compid=66356 (accessed 22 August 2014).

9 *Victoria County History of Northamptonshire.*

10 Harvey (1957), p. 57, citing the Calendar of Patent Rolls (CPR) 1350–54, 270.

11 Saul (2001), p. 205.

12 Horrox (1983), p. 33; Saul (2001), p. 205.

13 Horrox (1983), p. 34.

4 Of the Cobhams, the Cobhams and the Cobhams

1 This version is from Chaucer (1969), p. 76.

2 Although I have drawn on many sources for the history of the Cobham family, note should be made here of a central and indispensable one, Saul (2001).

3 Hasted (1797).

4 Cobham, Kent should not be confused with another historic town called Cobham in Surrey.

5 Two bars wavy

1 From 'L'envoy de Chaucer', version taken from Chaucer (1969), p. 245. An aventail is a piece of chain mail that protects the neck, throat and shoulders.

2 Nigel Saul argues that John's mother Margaret Peverell was the first of the family to move to Chrishall, but I am not entirely convinced of this.

6 The highest hill in Essex

1 The end of a letter sent by Matilda to Hubert the Chamberlain and other dignitaries commanding them to look after the people of Chrishall. With acknowledgement to a post by Irene Cranwell, Chrishall historian and Fred Davies, Chrishall local history recorder.

2 Saul (2001) is again a major source here: this from p. 206. Information on Chrishall in this chapter comes from *Inventory of the Historical Monuments in Essex* (1916a) and various other sources.

3 Flanders was perhaps on the site of what is now Chiswick Hall.

4 For economic information I am particularly indebted to Bolton (1980).

7 A marriage and two funerals

1 The translation is mine, adapted from those in Waddell (1929, p. 169) and Consolatio (nd).

8 Of oyster beds and salt pans

1 The two translations I have consulted (Power, 1992 and Bayard, 1991 via Portland Community College, nd) are identical.

2 Blomefield (1806b), who is also a major source on Sir Robert. Other information on Burnham Norton is taken from Norfolk Heritage (nd).

9 The new king, the old king

1 Translation from Thompson (1966), p. 171.

10 The bishop wields a two-edged sword

1 Rot. Parl. II, 363–4, cited in Dobson (1970), pp. 104–5.

2 Quoted in Dobson (1970), p. 260.

11 Knoweth your friend from your foe

1 Various sources, but this is adapted (with the spelling modernized) from the version in Dobson (1970), p. 381.

12 The natural

1 www.history.ac.uk/cipm-19-part-ii, no. 155.

2 This too is set down in the CIPM on Sir Robert.

13 Of patience and piety

1 Stow (1598/1956), p. 125.
2 Quoted by Waller (1877), p. 71, to whom I am also indebted for this translation: 'He was worthy, patient, pious and liberal, provident and just, strong in the virtue of manners; he was not an indirect, but a true friend of the kingdom.' He also attributes it to Holinshead's *Chronicle*.

14 The forest of masts and the wooden fort

1 http://www.british-history.ac.uk/no-series/parliament-rolls-medieval/october-1386 (accessed 13 October 2015).
2 https://en.wikipedia.org/wiki/Invasions_of_the_British_Isles (accessed 18 August 2015).
3 Saul (1997), p. 156.
4 According to the Dictionary of National Biography.

15 Leading the knights on silver chains

1 https://british-history.ac.uk/no-series/parliament-rolls-medieval/january-1390 (accessed 14 October 2015).
2 Of the various sources for details of Richard's 1390 tournament, the fullest is in Froissart's *Chronicles*.
3 This was not Fulham Palace, the bishop's historic country residence, but his London residence, which was close to St Paul's Cathedral.

16 Of fraud, collusion and an abbey

1 (in slightly different spelling) Chaucer (1969), pp. 248–9.
2 Blomefield (1806b).
3 CIPM, Inquisition into Sir Robert Hemenhale, Hemenhall 1 May 1405.
4 Victoria County History, original source Feet of F. Div. Co. file 55, no. 195; *Cal. Close*, 1389–92, p. 335.
5 From the entry on Sir Reginald Braybrooke in the History of Parliament.

17 One sparrowhawk or two shillings

1 Hasted (1797).
2 This is what Saul (2001) suggests, although it's not clear what his evidence or reasoning is.

3 *Victoria County History of Kent.*
4 All details from Waller (1877).
5 Waller (1877) p. 74.
6 *Victoria County History of Kent.*
7 In modern language: Know you, all who are and shall be, that I was made to aid the country. In knowledge of which thing, this is charter and witnessing. The plaque still survives.

18 The merlin, the trap

1 The translation is mine.
2 Of the various sources I have used for information on Sir Reginald, the core one is his biography in Roskell et al's *History of Parliament*.

19 Laughing, jangling, weeping

1 Modernized from the version cited in Cummins (1988), p. 6
2 Saul (1997), p. 340.
3 Stow (1598/1956), p. 142.
4 Saul (1997), p. 456.
5 McFarlane (1952/1972), p. 87.
6 McFarlane (1952/1972), pp. 123–4.
7 McFarlane (1952/1972), pp. 130–1.

20 Salcey Forest

1 The translation is by Kirtlan (1912).
2 Saul (1997), p. 473.
3 This account draws heavily on Cummins (1988), especially pp. 64–6.

21 The sun and the clouds

1 Quoted in the commentary to the Parliament Rolls for 1397–8. See the bibliography for the online reference. (Clearly, the chronicler was an uncritical royalist.)
2 Or at least she died, apparently suddenly, at this time, and this is one possible cause of her death.
3 Saul (2001), pp. 100–1, fn 71, referencing BL Harley ch. 54 G. 48.
4 Waller (1877), p. 81.
5 All details are from the Parliament Rolls and the online introduction to them.
6 Arundel had earlier been archbishop of York; in 1396 he moved to Canterbury.
7 Again, from the Parliament Rolls.
8 According to the commentary on the Parliament Rolls, 'both Usk and the St

Albans chronicler report that he expressed regret at this, saying that he had hoped to enjoy eternal life sooner than he now would'.

22 Miserable oppression

1 Quoted in Given-Wilson (1993).
2 This was Lord Latimer. Again, the core source for information on Sir Reginald is his biography in Roskell et al's *History of Parliament.*
3 From the Calendar of Close Rolls, 20 November 1399.
4 Bennett (1999).

23 St Mary and St Lazarus

1 From British History Online, www.british-history.ac.uk/cal-close-rolls/hen4/ (accessed 10 October 2015).

24 Striking fear into minds

1 The text of the statute can be read on www.ric.edu/faculty/rpotter/heretico.html (accessed 1 October 2015).

25 The stone walls of Sluys

1 www.lieder.net/lieder/get_text.html?-TextId=106450 (accessed 18 October 2015). The (loose) translation is mine.
2 Wylie (2013[1884]) p. 102.

26 The Trinity canopy

1 www.poesies.net/poeme0.html (accessed 7 October 2015). Again, the loose translation is mine.

27 To escort a princess

1 My rough rendering, adapted from Kirtlan (1912) and Klein (2007).
2 It is Nigel Saul's repeated suggestion about Joan's marriages that her husbands were found for her by others (e.g. Saul 2001, pp. 27–9: 'Joan's next husband was almost certainly found for her by the king'). But he gives no evidence, and neither is there anything in the record to suggest that Joan was incapable of selecting a husband herself.
3 Hawberk carried 'checky argent and gules, a chief nebulee per fess gules and or'. Sources generally for the little that is

known about him include Saul (2001) and Waller (1877).
4 Waller (1877), p. 90.
5 Saul (2001), citing CPR 1396–9.
6 Hawberk was in fact not yet a knight at that time, he was still a simple esquire. Details of the case are in CPR 1388–92, 319.
7 Waller (1877), p. 92: 'His arms had in both shields been wilfully defaced, as if by the heralds, in officious exercise of their craft. Hawberk by them was evidently not considered entitled to bear them.'

28 The fish in the ring

1 A translation: I was made of earth, and now I am returned as earth to the earth. Quoted in Saul (2001), p. 98.
2 Some sources suggest that Lord Cobham was buried in Greyfriars, London, and only his brass is at Cobham. There were so many Lord Cobhams and John Cobhams that it seems impossible to be sure.
3 Some less affluent families held very large funerals: see Curran (2016).
4 According to Waller, when an old tilting helmet thought to have been Sir Nicholas's still hung in Cobham church, it had a crest of the same design (1877, p. 91). The word *ichthys* means fish in Greek, but the letters are also the initials of five Greek words that mean 'Jesus Christ, Son of God, Savior' (Iesous Christos Theou Yios Soter). And Christ told his disciples in Matthew 4:19, 'Follow me, and I will make you fishers of men.'

29 Fifteen earls and 1,500 knights

1 www.british-history.ac.uk/no-series/parliament-rolls-medieval/january-1410 (accessed 1 October 2015).
2 Waugh (1905a), p. 435. Waugh (1905a, 1905b) is the most extensive of many sources I have used for information on Sir John.
3 They did have some lands in the neighbouring parishes of Kinnersley and Letton, and property in and around Hereford.
4 Waugh (1905a), p. 450.
5 Some say three daughters, the third

being the Joan that others ascribe to Joan
Cobham, although it is unlikely that if she
had borne Oldcastle a daughter, she would
have given her the name of her already
living daughter. Perhaps there was no third
daughter at all.

7 This too is part of Saul's (2001) apparent
conviction that Joan could not have
contracted her own marriages.

8 The original source of this, related in
various secondary sources, is BM
Valenciennes MS 860, fol. 67.

9 Most of the details that follow are from the
online record of this parliament (see note 1
to this chapter).

10 Reproduced in *Selections from English
Wycliffite Writings* , ed. Anne Hudson
(Cambridge, 1978), 135–7; *The St Albans
Chronicle 1406-1420*, ed. V. H. Galbraith
(Oxford, 1937), 52–5; and re-reproduced
in the online presentation of the parliament
roll.

30 The toad and the spider

1 www.biblestudytools.com/wyc/matthew/2.
html (accessed 18 October 2015).

2 This was probably not leprosy, but opinions
vary over what it was.

3 As such, there is a biography of him in the
History of Parliament Online, which is a
source for most of the information on him
in this book.

4 Parliament Rolls fn. f1410int-16.

31 The dunghill

1 Chaucer (1969), p. 168.

2 Waugh (1905a), p. 446.

32 In the king's closet

1 Quoted in Waller (1877), p. 96.

2 Tait (0000).

3 Waugh (1905a), p. 448.

33 The head and tail of the antichrist

1 Trans. from the Latin by Frank Taylor and
John S. Roskell, Oxford: Clarendon Press,
1975, pp. 7–9.

2 Waugh (1905a), p. 454.

3 The dates of this are confused, and some in
the official record are probably wrong, but

all of this happened in October 1413.

4 That night, and perhaps the next, he
probably stayed at Fisher's house, but after
that he moved out of London.

34 The parchment maker and the plot

1 http://www.biblestudytools.com/wyc/reve-
lation/2.htm l (accessed 18 October 2015).

2 Waugh (1905b), p. 1905.

3 Waugh (1905a), p. 644.

35 The accomplices

1 The original is in Latin. From 'Memorials:
1416', *Memorials of London and London
Life: In the 13th, 14th and 15th centuries*
(1868), pp. 624–44. Letter-Book I. fol.
clxxxi. www.british-history.ac.uk/report.
aspx?compid=57753 (accessed 19 March
2013).

2 Waugh(1905b), p.. 651.

3 Waugh p. 651 fn 64; various original
sources.

36 The loss of a nose

1 Davies (1856), my modernization of
spelling.

37 Taxes for Welshpool

1 Marx (0000), p. 49.

2 Waugh (1905a), 654).

3 Tait (n.d.).

38 Cold moats

1 Waugh (1905a), p. 656 fn 90.

39 Of funerals, niggardly and otherwise

1 Froissart (c. 1387).

2 The sources on Harpedon are sparse, and
Saul (2001, e.g. p. 218) is the best of the
secondary ones.

3 Saul suggests this was a stock image, and
the number of sons and daughters shown
is arbitrary. But I can see no real reason
to doubt that it was the actual number of
children she bore.

Sources and select bibliography

Abelard, Peter (c. 1100) 'David's lament for Jonathan'. Consolatio, www.consolatio.com/2005/04/davids_lament_f.html (accessed 13 October 2015).

Alban, J. R. (2014) 'An East Anglian knight's indenture for military service at sea, 1933', *Norfolk Archaeology*, Vol. 47, Part 1, pp. 1–12.

Alban, J. R. and Allmand, C. T. (1976) 'Spies and spying in the fourteenth century', pp. 73–101 in C. T. Allmand (ed.), *War, Literature and Politics in the Late Middle Ages: Essays in Honour of G. W. Coopland*. Liverpool: Liverpool University Press.

Allen, Thomas (1826) *The History and Antiquities of the Parish of Lambeth, and the Archiepiscopal Palace in the County of Surrey*. London: J. Allen (via Google Books, accessed 1 October 2015).

Archer, Rowena E. and Walker, Simon (eds) (1995) *Rulers and Ruled in Late Medieval England*, London: Hambledon Press.

Aziz, Jeffrey, H. (2007) 'Of grace and gross bodies: Falstaff, Oldcastle and the fires of reform', PhD dissertation, University of Pittsburgh (via Google Books, accessed 19 June 2015).

Barber, Richard and Barker, Juliet (1989) *Tournaments: Jousts, Chivalry and Pageants in the Middle Ages,* Woodbridge: Boydell Press.

Bennett, Michael J. (1999) 'Richard II and the wider realm', in A. Goodman and J. L. Gillespie (eds), *Richard II: The Art of Kingship*, Oxford: OUP, pp. 187 ff.

Bevan, Bryan (1994) *Henry IV*. London: Rubicon.

Blomefield, F. (1806a) 'Gallow and Brothercross Hundreds: Burnham Westgate', pp. 32-40 in *An Essay towards a Topographical History of the County of Norfolk*, Vol. 7, www.british-history.ac.uk/report.aspx?compid=78298 (accessed 19 March 2013).

Blomefield, F. (1806b) 'Hundred of Depwade: Hemenhale', pp.181–7 in *An Essay towards a Topographical History of the County of Norfolk*, Vol. 5, www.british-history.ac.uk/topographical-hist-norfolk/vol5/pp181-187 (accessed 2 June 2015).

Bolton, J. L. (1980) *The Medieval English Economy, 1150–1500*. London: Dent.

Boyles Murray, Thomas (1859) *Chronicles of a City Church: Being an account of the parish church of St Dunstan the East in the City of London,* London: Smith, Elder & Co. (via Google Books, accessed 8 June 2015).

British Listed Buildings. 'Hempnalls Hall, Cotton, Suffolk', www.britishlistedbuildings.co.uk/en-281611-hempnalls-hall-cotton-suffolk (accessed 27 August 2014).

Calendars of Close Rolls for the reign of Henry IV, British History Online. www.british-history.ac.uk/cal-close-rolls/hen4/

Calendar of Patent Rolls for the Reign of Richard II, University of Iowa, http://sdrc.lib.uiowa.edu/patentrolls/r2v4/body/Richard2vol4page0319.pdf (accessed 24 September 2015).

Celtic Casimir, 'Joan de la Pole, 4th baroness Cobham,' www.celtic-casimir.com/webtree/18/43220.htm (accessed 19 March 2013).

Chaucer, Geoffrey (c. 1386) *The Canterbury Tales.* http://www.librarius.com/cantales.htm (accessed 19 August 2015).

Chaucer, Geoffrey (c. 1386/1969) *The Canterbury Tales: A selection,* London: Penguin.

Chaucer, Geoffrey (1532/1903) *The Works of Geoffrey Chaucer, vol. 1, from the text of Professor Skeat,* London etc.: Henry Frowde.

Chrimes, S. B. (1959) *An Introduction to the Administrative History of Mediaeval England*. Oxford: Blackwell.

Chrishall, Essex village site: http://www.users.waitrose.com/~waldenrg/ (accessed 5 June 2015) http://en.wikipedia.org/wiki/Chrishall (accessed 5 June 2015).

Coss, Peter (1998) *The Lady in Medieval England, 1000–1500*. Stroud: Sutton.

Coulton, G. G. (1938/1961) *Medieval Panorama, Vol II: The horizons of thought*. Cambridge: Cambridge University Press/London: Fontana.

Creation tips (n.d.) 'Christian fish symbol explained', www.creationtips.com/fish_symbol.html (accessed 25 September 2015).

Cummins, John (1988) *The Hound and the Hawk: The art of medieval hunting*. London: Weidenfeld & Nicolson.

Curran, Susan (2011) *The English Friend: A life of William de la Pole, first duke of Suffolk (1396–1450)*. Norwich: Lasse Press.

Curran, Susan (2016) 'The funeral of John Paston', in N. Groves (ed.), *Of Churches, Toothache and Sheep: Selected Papers from the Norwich Historic Churches Trust Conferences, 2014 and 2015*. Norwich: Lasse Press.

Davies, S. (1856) *An English Chronicle of the Reigns of Richard II, Henry IV, Henry V, and Henry VI, Written Before the Year 1471* (with appendices). London: Camden Society.

De Hæretico Comburendo (1401) Text of statute, www.ric.edu/faculty/rpotter/heretico.html (accessed 1 October 2015).

Dictionary of National Biography, 'Michael de la Pole, first earl of Suffolk'. www.oxforddnb.com/view/article/22452/?back=,22453 (accessed 5 June 2015).

Dobson, R. B. (ed.) (1970) *The Peasants Revolt of 1381* (a collection of original documents). London: Macmillan.

Dockray, Keith (2007) *Warrior King: The life of Henry V*. Stroud: Tempus.

Ecastles. 'Cooling Castle', wwwe.ecastles.co.uk/cooling.html (accessed 22 August 2014).

Froissart, Jean. *Chronicles of England, France, etc.,* tr. Thomas Johnes. London. http://sites.fas.harvard.edu/~chaucer/special/lifemann/tournmt/froistor.html (aqccessed 14 October 2015)

Froissart, Jean (c. 1387) "A deed of arms at Bordeaux before Sir John Harpedon (1387)" ed. S. Muhlberger, http://faculty.nipissingu.ca/muhlberger/froissart/bordeau1.htm (accessed 6 October 2015).

Fryde, E. B. (1988) *William de la Pole, Merchant and King's Banker (d. 1366)*. London: Hambledon Press.

Gatehouse. Cooling Castle. www.gatehouse-gazetteer.info/English%20sites/1910.html (accessed 19 August 2015).

Gatehouse. Weycroft Hall, Axminster. www.gatehouse-gazetteer.info/English%20sites/897.html (accessed 5 October 2015).

Geni.com. 'Joan de la Pole (Cobham).' www.geni.com/people/Joan-de-la-Pole/6000000005953297192 (accessed 19 August 2015).

Geni.com. 'Sir Reginald Braybrooke.' www.geni.com/people/SIr-Reginald-Braybookc-of-Cooling-Castle/6000000006108037860 (accessed 27 August 2014).

Gibson, James M. (n.d.) *Cobham College*, printed for the President and Trustees of the New College of Cobham.

Given-Wilson, C. (1993) *Chronicles of the Revolution: The reign of Richard II*. Manchester: Manchester University Press.

Gottfried, Robert S. (1983) *The Black Death: Natural and human disaster in medieval Europe*. London: Robert Hale.

Graves, D. 'Sir John Oldcastle'. Christianity.com, www.christianity.com/church/church-history/timeline/1201-1500/john-oldcastle-lollard-lord-11629875.html (accessed 19 March 2013).

Harriss, G. L. and Harriss, M. A.(eds) (1972) 'John Benet's Chronicle for the years 1400 to 1462', *Camden Miscellany*, Vol. 24, pp. 151–232.

Harvey, A. S. (1957) *The de la Pole family of Kingston upon Hull*. Hull: East Yorkshire Local History Society.

Hasted, Edward (1797) 'Parishes: Cobham', pp. 404–42 in *The History and Topographical Survey of the County of Kent: Vol. 3* (Canterbury), www.british-history.ac.uk/survey-kent/vol3/pp404-442 (accessed 18 May 2015).

Heritage Gateway, 'Haughley Castle', www.heritagegateway.org.uk/gateway/Results_Single.aspx ?uid=MSF5472&resourceID=1017 (accessed 27 August 2014).

Hicks, M. A. (ed.) (2012) *The Fifteenth Century Inquisitions Post Mortem: A companion.* Woodbridge: Boydell & Brewer.

History of Parliament online. Braybrooke, Sir Gerard I (c.1332–1403), of Colmworth, Beds. and Horsenden, Bucks. Published in *The History of Parliament: the House of Commons 1386-1421*, ed. J. S. Roskell, L. Clark, C. Rawcliffe., 1993. www.historyofparliamentonline.org/volume/1386-1421/member/braybrooke-sir-gerard-i-1332-1403 (accessed 20 August 2015).

History of Parliament online. 'Brooke, Sir Thomas.' www.historyofparliamentonline.org/volume/1386-1421/member/brooke-thomas-1391-1439 (accessed 1 October 2015).

History of Parliament online. 'Cheddar, Richard.' www.historyofparliamentonline.org/volume/1386-1421/member/cheddar-richard-1379-1437 (accessed 6 October 2015).

Holmes, George (1974) *The Later Middle Ages, 1272–1485.* London: Cardinal.

Horrox, Rosemary (1983) *The de la Poles of Hull.* Hull: East Yorkshire Local History Society.

Hunting, Penelope (1981) *Royal Westminster.* London: RICS.

Inquisitions Post Mortem, 'The feudal system.' http://blog.inquisitionspostmortem.ac.uk/contexts/the-feudal-system/ (accessed 10 June 2015).

Inventory of the Historical Monuments in Essex (1916a) 'Chrishall', *Vol. 1, North West*, London, www.british-history.ac.uk/rchme/essex/vol1/pp64-67 [accessed 5 June 2015].

Inventory of the Historical Monuments in Essex (1916b) 'Radwinter', *Vol. 1, North West*, London, www.british-history.ac.uk/rchme/essex/vol1/pp213-218 [accessed 9 June 2015].

Jacob, E. F. (1961) *The Fifteenth Century, 1399–1485.* Oxford: Clarendon Press.

Jones, Terry (with Robert Yeager, Torry Dolan, Alan Fletcher and Juliette Dor) (2003) *Who Killed Geoffrey Chaucer? A medieval mystery.* London: Methuen.

Keen, Maurice (1984) *Chivalry.* New Haven, Conn. and London: Yale University Press.

Kirtland, Ernest J. B. (trans.) (1912) *Sir Gawain and the Green Knight, Rendered Literally into Modern English from the Alliterative Romance-Poem of A.D. 1360, from Cotton MS. Nero A x in British Museum.* London: Charles H. Kelly. http://rpo.library.utoronto.ca/poems/sir-gawain-and-green-knight (accessed 15 October 2015).

Kline, A. S. (2007) Translation of *Sir Gawain and the Green Knight.* www.poetryintranslation.com/PITBR/English/GawainAndTheGreenKnight.htm (accessed 15 October 2015).

Lewis, Samuel (ed.) (1848), 'Radnage – Raithby', pp. 630–3 in *A Topographical Dictionary of England* (London), www.british-history.ac.uk/topographical-dict/england/pp630-633 (accessed 5 June 2015).

Leyser, Henrietta (1995) *Medieval Women: A social history of women in England, 1450–1500.* London: Weidenfeld & Nicolson.

Lydon, J. F. (1963) 'Richard II's Expeditions to Ireland,' *Journal of the Royal Society of Antiquaries of Ireland*, Vol. 93, No. 2, pp. 135–49.

Macfarlane, Alan (1986) *Marriage and Love in England: Modes of reproduction 1300–1840.* Oxford: Blackwell.

Manning, C. J. (1847) 'Notice of an undescribed sepulchral brass', *Architectural Journal*, vol. 4, pp. 338–40, http://archaeologydataservice.ac.uk/archiveDS/archiveDownload?t=arch-1132-1/dissemination/pdf/004/004_338_340.pdf (accessed 22 May 2015).

Marx, William (ed.) *An English Chronicle 1377–1461*, ed. from Aberystwyth, Nat Lib of Wales MS 21068 and Oxford, Bodleian Library Ms Lyell 34., Woodbridge: Boydell.

May, Teresa (1967) 'The Cobham family in the administration of England, 1200–1400', *Archae-ologia Cantiana*, Vol. 82, pp. 1–31. www.kentarchaeology.org.uk/Research/Pub/ArchCant/Vol.082%20-%201967/082-01.pdf (accessed 19 August 2015).

McFarlane, K. B. (1952/1972) *Wycliffe and English Non-Conformity.* London: Penguin.

McFarlane, K. B. (1973) *The Nobility of Later Medieval England.* Oxford: Clarendon Press.

McFarlane, K. B. (1981) *England in the Fifteenth Century.* London: Hambledon.

McKisack, M. (1959) *The Fourteenth Century, 1307–1399*, Vol. V of the Oxford History of England. Oxford: Oxford University Press.

Memorials of London Life in the 13th, 14th and 15th Centuries (1868) London: Longmans, Green, www.british-history.ac.uk/no-series/memorials-london-life/pp178-185 (accessed 23 May 2015).

Napier, Henry Alfred (1858) *Historical Notices of the Parishes of Swyncombe and Ewelme in the County of Oxford.* Oxford: James Wright.

National Archives. Petition no. SC 8/29/1407 http://discovery.nationalarchives.gov.uk/details/r/C9061593 (accessed 1 October 2015).

Neillands, R. (1990) *The Hundred Years War.* London: Routledge.

Norfolk Archaeological Trust. 'Burnham North Friary.' www.norfarchtrust.org.uk/burnhamnorton (accessed 2 June 2015).

Norfolk Heritage. 'Burnham Norton.' www.heritage.norfolk.gov.uk/record-details?TNF188-Parish-Summary-Burnham-Norton-(Parish-Summary) (accessed 2 June 2015).

Oman, Charles (1924/1991) *A History of the Art of War in the Middle Ages, Vol. 2: 1278–1485AD.* London: Greenhill.

Page, William (ed.) (1926) 'Colleges: Cobham', in A History of the County of Kent, Vol. 2, London, pp. 231–2. www.british-history.ac.uk/vch/kent/vol2/pp231-232 (accessed 19 August 2015).

Parliament Rolls of Medieval England. Henry IV, Parliament of January 1410. www.british-history.ac.uk/no-series/parliament-rolls-medieval/january-1410 (accessed 1 October 2015).

Parliament Rolls of Medieval England. Richard II, Parliament of September 1397. www.british-history.ac.uk/no-series/parliament-rolls-medieval/september-1397 (accessed 22 September 2015).

Peerage.com. 'John Cobham, 3rd Lord Cobham (of Kent)', www.thepeerage.com/p1067. htm#i10667 (accessed 22 August 2014).

Pisan, Christine de. *Poesies.* www.poesies.net/poeme0.html (accessed 7 October 2015).

Pisan, Christine de (1891) *Oeuvres poétiques de Christine de Pisan*, ed. M. Roy. Paris: Firmin Didot, p. 237. https://archive.org/details/oeuvrespotiqu01chri (accessed 11 March 2016).

Portland Community College. *Medieval Sourcebook: Selections from The Goodman of Paris, 1392/4* (with text from Tania Bayard's translation, *The Medieval Home Companion: Housekeeping in the Fourteenth Century* (Harper Perennial, 1991). www.pcc.edu/staff/pdf/818/GoodmanofParis.pdf (accessed 13 October 2015).

Pounds, N. J. G. (1994) *The Medieval Castle in England and Wales: a political and social history.* Cambridge: Cambridge University Press.

Power, Eileen (trans.) (1992) *The Goodman of Paris: A treatise on moral and domestic economy by a citizen of Paris, c. 1393.* London: Folio Society.

Pritchett, H. J. (1998/2006) 'St Mary Magdalene, Cobham, Kent: the brasses', leaflet, Cobham and Luddesdowne Chuches.

Pryor, Francis (2006) *Britain in the Middle Ages: An archaeological history.* London: Harper Press.

Radwinter History Society. Website. www.radwinterhistory.org.uk/radwinter/radwinter.html (accessed 9 June 2015).

Rex, Richard (2002) *The Lollards*, Social history in perspective. Basingstoke: Palgrave.

Richardson, Douglas (2011) *Plantagenet Ancestry: A study in colonial and medieval families,* 2nd edn. Salt Lake City, Utah.

Riley, H. T. (ed.) (1868) 'Memorials: 1416', pp. 624–4 in *Memorials of London and London Life: In the 13th, 14th and 15th centuries*, www.british-history.ac.uk/report.aspx?compid=57753 (accessed 19 March 2013).

Salter, Mike (2013) *Medieval Walled Towns.* Malvern: Folly.

Saunders, Frances Stonor (2004) *Hawkwood: Diabolical Englishman*. London: Faber & Faber.

Saul, Nigel (1997) *Richard II*, New Haven, Conn. and London: Yale University Press.

Saul, Nigel (2001) *Death, Art and Memory in Medieval England: The Cobham family and their monuments, 1300–1500*. Oxford: Oxford University Press.

Sherborne, James (1994) *War, Politics and Culture in Fourteenth-Century England*, ed. Anthony Tuck, London: Hambledon Press.

Sir Gawain's World. 'Sir Robert Hemenhale.' http://sirgawainsworld.wordpress.com/tag/sir-robert-hemenhale (accessed 27 August 2014).

South Northamptonshire Council. 'Milton Malsor', www.southnorthants.gov.uk/Milton_Malsor_VDS.pdf (accessed 22 May 2015).

Stow, John (1598/1956) *Stow's Survey of London*, intro. H. B. Wheatley, London: Dent.

Suffolk County Council (2006) 'Archaeological Monitoring Report: Hempnalls Hall, Willow Lane, Cotton.' http://archaeologydataservice.ac.uk/archiveDS/archiveDownload?t=arch-415-1/dissemination/pdf/suffolkc1-15259_1.pdf (27 August 14)

Tait, James. 'Oldcastle, John' in *Dictionary of National Biography, 1885–1900, Vol. 42*. https://en.wikisource.org/wiki/Oldcastle,_John_(DNB00) (accessed 1 October 2015).

Thompson, Peter E. (ed. and trans.) (1966) *Contemporary Chronicles of the Hundred Years War, from the works of Jean le Bel, Jean Froissart and Enguerrand de Monstrelet*. London: Folio Society.

Thomson, John A. F. (1983) *The Transformation of Medieval England, 1370–1529*. London: Longmans.

Thornbury, Walter (1878) 'Smithfield', pp. 339–44 in *Old and New London, Vol. 2*. London. www.british-history.ac.uk/old-new-london/vol2/pp339-344 (accessed 14 October 2015).

Tuchman, B. (1979) *A Distant Mirror: The calamitious 14th century*. London: Macmillan.

Tudor Place. 'The Brooke family.' www.tudorplace.com.ar/BROOKE1.htm#Edward BROOKE (1° B. Cobham) (accessed 6 October 2015).

Vaut, G. 'Ancestors of Alexandra Catlin Vaut, et al.' http://wc.rootsweb.ancestry.com/cgi-bin/igm.cgi?op=GET&db=gregv&id=I7501 (accessed 22 May 2015).

Victoria County History of Kent. ' Cobham, Kent', pp. 404–42 in Vol. 3. www.british-history.ac.uk/survey-kent/vol3/pp404-442 (accessed 22 May 2015).

Victoria County History of Northamptonshire. 'Castle Ashby', pp. 230–6 in Vol. 4. www.british-history.ac.uk/vch/northants/vol4/pp230-236 (accessed 22 May 2015).

Vision of Britain. 'Milton Malsor, Northamptonshire.' www.visionofbritain.org.uk/place/8082 (accessed 22 May 2015).

Vision of Britain. 'Salcey, Northamptonshire.' http://www.visionofbritain.org.uk/place/25263 (accessed 16 October 2015).

Waley, Daniel (1964) 'The troubles of the Roman Church', pp. 116–39 in *Later Medieval Europe: From St Louis to Luther*. London: Longmans.

Webster, B. (1984) 'The community of Kent in the reign of Richard II', *Archaeologia Cantiana*, Vol. 100, pp. 217–29.

Westminster Abbey. 'Sir John Harpedon.' www.westminster-abbey.org/our-history/people/sir-john-harpedon (25 August 2013).

Waller, J. G. (1877) 'The Lords of Cobham, their monuments, and the church' (Part I), *Archaeologia Cantiana*, Vol. 11, pp. 49–112, www.kentarchaeology.org.uk/Research/Pub/ArchCant/Vol.011%20-%201877/011-08.pdf (accessed 23 May 2015).

Waugh, W. T. (1905a) 'Sir John Oldcastle, Part 1', *English Historical Review*, Vol. 20, No. 79, pp. 434–56.

Waugh, W. T. (1905b) 'Sir John Oldcastle, Part 2', *English Historical Review*, Vol. 20, No. 80, pp. 637–58.

Westcott, Brooke Foss. (1095) *A General View of the History of the English Bible*, 3rd edn. London: Macmillan.

Wikipedia. 'The Battle of North Walsham.' http://en.wikipedia.org/wiki/Battle_of_North_Walsham (accessed 5 June 2015).

Wikipedia. 'Chrishall, Essex.' http://en.wikipedia.org/wiki/Chrishall (accessed 23 May 2015).

Wikipedia. 'Cobham, Kent.' http://en.wikipedia.org/wiki/Cobham,_Kent (accessed 22 May 2015).

Wikipedia. 'Crusades of the 14th and 15th centuries.' http://en.wikipedia.org/wiki/Crusades#Crusades_of_the_14th_and_15th_centuries (accessed 27 May 2015).

Wikipedia. 'De_heretico_comburendo.' https://en.wikipedia.org/wiki/De_heretico_comburendo (accessed 1 October 2015).

Wikipedia. 'Haughley Castle.' http://en.wikipedia.org/wiki/Haughley_Castle (accessed 2 June 2015).

Wikipedia. 'Henry de Cobham, 1st Baron Cobham.' http://en.wikipedia.org/wiki/Henry_de_Cobham,_1st_Baron_Cobham (accessed 22 May 2015).

Wikipedia. 'John de Cobham, 2nd Baron Cobham.' http://en.wikipedia.org/wiki/John_de_Cobham,_2nd_Baron_Cobham_(of_Kent) (accessed 22 May 2015).

Wikipedia. 'John de Cobham, 3rd Baron Cobham.' https://en.wikipedia.org/wiki/John_de_Cobham,_3rd_Baron_Cobham (accessed 22 August 2014).

Wikipedia. 'John Wycliffe.' http://en.wikipedia.org/wiki/John_Wycliffe (accessed 7 June 2015).

Wikipedia. 'Maiden Bradley.' http://en.wikipedia.org/wiki/Maiden_Bradley_with_Yarnfield (accessed 8 June 2015).

Wikipedia. 'Mayors of Kingston upon Hull.' http://en.wikipedia.org/wiki/List_of_Mayors_of_Kingston_upon_Hull (accessed 25 May 2015).

Wikipedia. 'Milton Malsor.' http://en.wikipedia.org/wiki/Milton_Malsor (accessed 22 May 2015).

Wikipedia. 'Robert Braybrooke.' http://en.wikipedia.org/wiki/Robert_Braybrooke (accessed 27 August 2014).

Wikipedia. 'St Michael Cornhill.' http://en.wikipedia.org/wiki/St_Michael,_Cornhill (accessed 25 May 2015).

Wikipedia. 'Walter Langton.' https://en.wikipedia.org/wiki/Walter_Langton (accessed 12 October 2015).

Wikitree. 'Sir Reginald Braybrooke.' www.wikitree.com/wiki/Braybrooke-12 (accessed 19 March 2013).

Woodger, L. S. 'Braybrooke, Sir Reynold.' History of Parliament Online, www.historyofparliamentonline.org/volume/1386-1421/member/braybrooke-sir… (accessed 22 August 2014).

Woods, William (1976) *England in the Age of Chaucer*. London: Book Club Associates.

Wycliffe translation of the bible. www.biblestudytools.com/wyc/matthew/2.html (accessed 18 October 2015).

Wylie, James Hamilton (2013[1884]) *History of England under Henry the Fourth,* London: Forgotten Books.

Stained glass from St John the Baptist's Church, Thaxted, Essex

General index

Note: where individual names changed, the person is generally indexed under their final name, with cross-references as necessary. Otherwise, individuals have been indexed under the names by which they are best known. The titles 'Sir' and 'Lady' are omitted. Buildings are indexed under their town location.

Stained glass from All Saints Church, Poringland, Norfolk. Photo by Mike Dixon.

Index of illustrations

Stained glass is in **bold.**

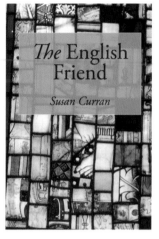

An illustrated biography of William de la Pole, first duke of Suffolk (1394–1450).

Suffolk spent half his life fighting for in France for Henry V and Henry VI, in the later stages of the Hundred Years War. The war cost him his father and his four brothers. Taken prisoner, he lost a fortune paying his ransom – and gained two friends: his captor, the bastard of Orleans, and the bastard's half-brother, the famous French poet Charles of Orleans. Suffolk, also a poet, was to become Orleans' jailer. Rising to head the king's council under Henry VI, he spent the remainder of his life trying to bring about peace between England and France. It made him the most hated man in England.

'rich with illustrations … [a] vivid biography'
– Keiron Pym, *Eastern Daily Press*
'really enjoyable to read'
– Steven Russell, *East Anglian Daily Times*

When Margery Paston announced that she wished to marry her family's land agent, Richard Calle, her mother and her brothers resisted so strongly that they created a public feud which culminated in her being examined in public by the bishop of Norwich in 1469.

John Paston III wrote to his elder brother that Richard Calle 'should never have my goodwill to make my sister sell candles and mustard at Framlingham'. True, Richard's family ran a shop, but he was a well-educated professional man, perfectly capable of keeping a wife in the manner Margery's family might expect. So why were they so determined to prevent the marriage?

The Paston letters are well known as an unique source of knowledge about an English family in the 15th century. They form the main source for this account of Richard and Margery's lives, which also draws on a history of the Calle family and the author's first-hand knowledge of the places the Pastons knew and lived in.

'a colourful and engaging narrative'
– Trevor Heaton, *Eastern Daily Press*

To see the rest of our list, download our catalogue and order direct, visit
www.lassepress.com